MW00846639

Stock Trading Terms

Financial Education Is Your Best Investment

Published February 26, 2020

Revision 2.2

Financial Terms Dictionary

Copyright And Trademark Notices

Limits of Liability and Disclaimer of Warranties

The materials in this book are provided "as is" and without warranties of any kind either express or implied. The Author disclaims all warranties, express or implied, including, but not limited to, implied warranties of merchantability and fitness for a particular purpose.

The Author does not warrant that defects will be corrected, or that that the site or the server that makes this eBook available are free of viruses or other harmful components. The Author does not warrant or make any representations regarding the use or the results of the use of the materials in this book in terms of their correctness, accuracy, reliability, or otherwise. Applicable law may not allow the exclusion of implied warranties, so the above exclusion may not apply to you.

Under no circumstances, including, but not limited to, negligence, shall the Author be liable for any special or consequential damages that result from the use of, or the inability to use this eBook, even if the Author or his authorized representative has been advised of the possibility of such damages.

Applicable law may not allow the limitation or exclusion of liability or incidental or consequential damages, so the above limitation or exclusion may not apply to you. In no event shall the Author's total liability to you for all damages, losses, and causes of action (whether in contract, tort, including but not limited to, negligence or otherwise) exceed the amount paid by you, if any, for this eBook.

Facts and information are believed to be accurate at the time they were placed in this book. All data provided in this book is to be used for information purposes only. The information contained within is not intended to provide specific legal, financial or tax advice, or any other advice whatsoever, for any individual or company and should not be relied upon in that regard. The services described are only offered in jurisdictions where they may be legally offered. Information provided is not all-inclusive and is limited to information that is made available and such information should not be relied upon as all-inclusive or accurate.

You are advised to do your own due diligence when it comes to making business decisions and should use caution and seek the advice of qualified professionals. You should check with your accountant, lawyer, or professional advisor, before acting on this or any information. You may not consider any examples, documents, or other content in this eBook or otherwise provided by the Author to be the equivalent of professional advice.

The Author assumes no responsibility for any losses or damages resulting from your use of any link, information, or opportunity contained in this book or within any other information disclosed by the author in any form whatsoever.

About the Author

Thomas Herold is a successful entrepreneur, mediator, author, and personal development coach. He published over 35 books with over 200,000 copies distributed worldwide and the founder of seven online businesses.

For over ten years Thomas Herold has studied the monetary system and has experienced some profound insights on how money and wealth are related. After three years of successful investing in silver, he released 'Building Wealth with Silver - How to Profit From The Biggest Wealth Transfer in History' in 2012. One of the first books that illustrate in a remarkable, simple way the monetary system and its consequences.

He is the founder and CEO of the 'Financial Terms Dictionary' book series and website, which explains in detail and comprehensive form over 1000 financial terms. In his financial book series, he informs in detail and with practical examples all aspects of the financial sector. His educational materials are designed to help people get started with financial education.

In his 2018 released book 'The Money Deception', Mr. Herold provides the most sophisticated insight and shocking details about the current monetary system. Never before has the massive manipulation of money caused so much economic inequality in the world. In spite of these frightening facts, 'The Money Deception' also provides remarkable and simple solutions to create abundance for all people, and it's a must-read if you want to survive the global monetary transformation that's underway right now.

In 2019 he released an entirely new financial book series explaining in detail and with practical examples over 1000 financial terms. The 'Herold Financial IQ Series' contains currently of 16 titles covering every category of the financial market.

His latest book "High Credit Score Secrets" offers the most effective strategies to boost the average credit score from as low as 450 points to over 810. It teaches the tactics to build excellent credit, repair credit, monitor credit and how to guard that good score for a lifetime. It reached bestseller status in 2020 in three categories.

For more information please visit the author's websites:

High Credit Score Secrets - The Smart Raise & Repair Guide to Excellent Credit
https://highcreditscoresecrets.com

The Money Deception - What Banks & Government Don't Want You to Know
https://www.moneydeception.com

The Herold Financial IQ Series - Financial Education Is Your Best Investment
https://www.financial-dictionary.com

The Online Financial Dictionary - Over 1000 Terms Explained
https://www.financial-dictionary.info

Please Leave Your Review on Amazon

This book and the Financial IQ Series are self-published and the author does not have a contract with one of the five largest publishers, which are able to support the author's work with advertising. If you like this book, please consider leaving a solid 4 or 5-star review on Amazon.

Herold Financial IQ Series on Amazon

Table Of Contents

Algorithmic Trading

Algorithmic trading has many names. Users also know it as black box trading and algo trading. This system of trading works with complicated and highly advanced mathematical formulas. It takes these models and engages in rapid decisions to execute transactions in various financial markets. This type of trading is only possible with super fast computers and programs. It combines these with the algorithms to come up with trading strategies that deliver the maximum returns.

There a variety of trading and investment strategies that can benefit from algorithmic trading. Some of these are inter-market spreads, speculation, market making, and arbitrage. Nowadays this style of trading is able to operate and automate trading and investment strategies by working on electronic platforms. This means that the programs themselves can carryout specific trading instructions. They can be set up to consider special scenarios like volume, price, and timing.

Bigger institutional investors who buy enormous amounts of shares are most likely to use algorithmic trading. These programs help them to gain the optimal price in the market without substantially impacting the price of the stock or making their buying costs higher.

Among the most popular types of algorithmic trading strategies are trading in advance of index fund re-balancing, scalping, arbitrage, and mean reversion. These are complex strategies that mostly require speed of discovery and instantaneous decision making to be effective.

Trading in advance of index fund re-balancing has to do with mutual funds. Pension funds and other retirement accounts are heavily invested in these vehicles. Because the underlying assets held in these funds constantly change, they must purchase or sell index funds to match. This algorithmic trading strategy looks for the points where the mutual funds are ready to re-balance. It then buys or sells first. In reality it makes money for the algorithmic traders at the expense of the mutual fund investors.

Scalpers look to make money on the bid versus ask spreads. If they trade the difference quickly enough repeatedly during the day, it can make them significant amounts of money. For it to work, the movement in the price of the stock has to be less than the spread of the security or stock in question. These kinds of movements happen anywhere from seconds to minutes. Only the quick decision making of the algorithm formulas is sufficient to maximize this strategy.

Arbitrage refers to finding the differences in pricing of two related entities. Global businesses utilize this effectively all the time. They can buy supplies for less or contract labor cheaper by getting it in different nations. It helps them to lower their expenses and boost their profits.

In algorithmic trading, arbitrage strategies work with examples like S&P 500 stocks versus S&P futures. These two markets for the securities or index will often encounter price differences. Stocks on NYSE or NASDAQ could move ahead of or behind the futures market for them. The powerful and fast algorithms are able to both track and trade such differences and profit as a result.

Mean reversion refers to coming up with the average for short term low and high prices on a security. The algorithms are able to compile such an average rapidly. When the price moves towards or away from this average mean, the programs can rapidly trade them as they move back towards it.

There are a few other strategies that algorithms are able to enhance. Some of these pertain to dark pools of capital and reducing their transaction costs. Dark pools are unregulated and off market trades created when institutional investors make their own private exchanges.

Arbitrage

Arbitrage refers to the practice of taking advantage of the price imbalances sometimes arising in two or even more markets. People who work in foreign money exchange run their whole businesses on this model. As an example, they look for tourists who require a rapid exchange of their cash for the local currency. Tourists agree to accept this local money for a lower amount than the actual market rate, and the money changer gets to keep the spread created by the higher rate that he charges them for the local currency. This spread that the different rates create becomes his profit.

Many different scenarios allow for investors or businessmen to become involved in the arbitrage practice. Sometimes, one market is not aware of the existence of the second market, or it simply can not access it. Arbitrageurs, persons who avail themselves of arbitrage, are also able to benefit from the different liquidities present in various markets.

Arbitrage is typically employed to discuss opportunities with investments and money rather than price imbalances for goods. Because of arbitrageurs operating in various markets whenever they spot opportunities, the prices found in the higher market will commonly drop while the prices in the lower market will usually rise so that they meet somewhere around the middle of the price difference. The phrase efficiency of the market then deals with the rate of speed at which these differing prices converge towards each other.

There are people who make arbitrage their livelihood. Working in arbitrage offers the possibilities of lucrative gains and profits. It does not come free of risk though. The greatest danger is that the prices may change rapidly between the varying markets. As an example, the spreads could rapidly fluctuate in only the tiny amount of time that is necessary for the two transactions to take place. In instances where these prices are moving quickly, arbitrageurs may not only find that they missed the chance to realize the profit between the differences in the prices, but that in fact they lost money on the deal.

Examples of arbitrage in the financial markets abound. Convertible arbitrage is working with convertible bonds to realize arbitrage. The bond can be converted into stock of the issuer of the bond. Sometimes, the amounts of shares that the bond will convert to are worth more than the price of the bond. In this case, an arbitrageur will be able to make a profit by purchasing the bond, converting it into the stock shares, and then selling the stock on the exchange to realize the difference.

Relative value arbitrage is using options to acquire the underlying shares of stock. It might be that the option is less expensive relative to the shares of stock that it will purchase. If a stock trades at $200, and the option that permits you to buy a share of the stock for $120 is trading at only $50, then you could buy the option, exercise it for the shares, and sell it for $200. You would only have spent $170 per share on the purchase, and then realize a $30 per share profit.

Asset Allocation

Asset allocation involves diversifying an investor portfolio into a variety of different assets based on the appropriate level of risk. This procedure has investors divide up their investments between varying types of assets. Among these might be stocks, real estate, bonds, and cash.

The goal is to maximize the reward and risk balance using the investors' own goals and scenarios. This has become one of the critical ideas behind money management and financial planning today. There are several different types of asset allocation to consider. These are strategic, tactical, and dynamic.

In strategic asset allocation, the investor sets out target allocations for the desired different classes of assets. When the percentage balance deviates from the original set levels, it will involve the investor rebalancing the overall portfolio. The allocations will be reset to the original ones as they change significantly because of different returns that each class earns.

Strategic asset allocation sets these initial allocations up using a number of different considerations. Among these are the investor objectives, the intended time frame of investing, and the risk tolerance. These allocations can be changed in time as the different variables alter.

A good comparison to this form of allocating is a traditional buy and hold investment strategy. This form of strategic allocating of assets and the tactical allocation approach are both derived from modern portfolio theory. They seek diversification so that they can lower risk and boost the returns on portfolios.

Tactical asset allocating is more active than strategic forms of the discipline. Investors who follow tactical allocating will re-balance the asset percentages in different categories on a more regular basis. They will do this in an effort to benefit from market sectors that are stronger or poised for gains. They might also re-balance in an effort to capture anomalies in market pricing.

Tactical allocating is well suited to professional portfolio managers. They study the markets and look to find extra returns from scenarios that develop. This is still only considered to be a strategy that is moderately active. When the short term gains are attained, these managers go back to the original strategic asset balance of the portfolio.

Investors or managers who look for tactical asset allocators often choose ETF exchange traded funds or index funds for this purpose. The goal of these vehicles concentrates on asset classes rather than individual investments. This reduces the costs of rebalancing. The transaction costs of buying and selling index funds is far less than with many individual stocks or even several mutual funds.

For an individual investor, they allow them to pick a stock index fund, bond index fund, and money market fund. It is also possible to focus on sub-sectors within the bigger funds. There are foreign stocks, large cap stocks, individual sectors, and small cap stock funds or ETFs from which to choose.

When tactical allocating in sectors, investors can pick out those which they believe will perform strongly for either the near term or intermediate time frames. Those that believe health and technology will do well in upcoming months or even a few years might rebalance some of the portfolio into ETFs in those industry segments.

With dynamic asset allocation, investors are focused on re-balancing the portfolio to keep it near its long term goals of asset mix. This means that positions in assets classes that are outperforming have to be reduced. Those that are under-performing must then be increased with the proceeds from the outperforming assets. This restores the portfolio mix to the desired allocation. The reason investors would do this is to keep the original asset mix so that they can capture appropriate returns that meet or beat the target benchmark.

Asset Classes

Asset classes are different groups of securities which demonstrate characteristics in common, are governed by similar regulations and laws, and behave similarly in the markets. There are five principle classes which include equities (stocks), fixed income (bonds), money market instruments (cash equivalent), commodities (like gold and oil), and real estate (including land, houses, and commercial buildings), as well as some other less common alternative classes of assets.

Many times these different classes of assets are intermingled by financial advisors and analysts. They like these different types of investment vehicles to diversify portfolios more effectively and efficiently. Every asset class is anticipated to provide differing levels and types of risks versus returns among its investment characteristics. They also are supposed to perform differently in any given investment climate. Those investors who seek out the highest possible returns typically do this by lowering their overall portfolio risk by performing diversification of asset classes.

Financial professionals typically focus their clients on the different asset classes as a means of steering them into proper and effective diversification of their investment or retirement portfolios. The various classes of assets possess differing amounts and types of risk as well as varying cash flows. By purchasing into several of the competing asset classes, investors make certain they obtain a proper level of diversification in their investment choices. The importance of diversification can not be overstated. This is because all financial professionals in the know understand that it lowers risk while maximizing the opportunities to earn the highest possible return.

There are a variety of different types of investment strategies available to investors today. They might be associated with value, growth, income, or a combination of some or all of these factors. Each of them works to categorize and label the various investment options per a particular grouping of investment criteria.

There are many analysts who prefer to tie traditional valuation metrics like price to earnings ratios (PE ratios) or growth in earnings per share (EPS) to the investment selection criteria. Still different analysts feel like performance is less of a priority while asset type and allocation are more critical. They know that investments which are in the identical class of assets will possess similar cash flows, returns, and risks.

The most liquid of these various asset classes prove to be equities, fixed income securities, cash- like instruments, and commodities. This also makes them the most frequently quoted, traded, and recommended classes of assets available today. Other asset classes are considered to be more alternative such as real estate, stamps, coins, and artwork, all of which are tradable forms of collectibles. There are also investment choices such as venture capital funds, crowd sourcing, hedge funds, and bitcoin, which are considered to be even more alternative and mostly for sophisticated investors. In general, the rule is that the more alternative the investment turns out to be, the less liquidity it actually possesses.

Some of these investments, such as hedge funds, venture capital funds, and crowd sourcing can take years to exit from, if investors are able to withdraw from the investment at all. Lower liquidity does not necessarily correlate to lower return potential though. It only means that it may be a while before holders are able to find a willing buyer to sell the investments to so they can cash out of the investment.

Many of the most alternative types of investments have boasted among the highest returns over the decades, sometimes significantly better returns than the most popular two asset classes of stocks and bonds. In order to get around this lack of liquidity and often enormous investment capital requirement, many investors choose to utilize REITS. Real Estate Investment Trusts provide greater liquidity while still participating in price appreciation of the real estate asset class.

Assets Under Management (AUM)

Assets under management (AUM) refer to the aggregate market value of all assets which an investment management firm or other financial institution (such as a bank) manages for its investor clients. The exact definition of AUM varies from one company to another. Each of them has their own distinctive proprietary formula for figuring up this all important statistic.

There are financial institutions, management companies, hedge funds, and banks that include the client bank deposits, cash, and mutual funds within their calculations. Still others choose to limit this figure to the funds which are under actual discretionary management using the sole choices of the fund manager. In this case, the investor gives over total investment responsibility and control to the management firm and fund manager in question.

Assets under management describe the amount of investment money which such an investment management firm actually controls. These investments are kept within a hedge fund or mutual fund. They are usually actively managed by a brokerage company, venture capital firm, or portfolio manager.

Assets under management express the amount of cash in the fund. It can also reveal the total amount of assets which they manage for their total client base. Alternatively it can be used to refer to the complete amount of assets the company manages for only one particular client. This would include all of the money which the manager is able to utilize in making transactions. As an example, if investors have placed $50,000 within their investment portfolios, the manager of the fund is allowed to purchase and sell whichever shares he so chooses by applying the funds of the investors without having to obtain their consent in advance.

The actual AUM fluctuates daily on every given market trading day. This depends on the investor money flow from one asset fund to another. The performance of assets also changes the Assets under management figure as well. The change in fund value or company investments will therefore alter the total AUM.

Every regulatory regime makes its own rules regarding how large a company must be to be closely regulated. Within the United States, after a given investment management firm possesses in excess of $30 million under management, they are required by law to register their company with the supreme oversight agency the SEC Securities and Exchange Commission. A given investor's AUM total will decide on what level of service they will receive from their brokerage firm or financial advisor. A great number of companies maintain minimum AUM amounts for certain kinds of investments. This has much to do with qualification levels of the investor in question. Some forms of investments also involve minimum purchase agreement requirements.

Figuring up the total Assets under management requires one of several calculations. With superior investment performance, the figure will rise in every case. As new customers join a firm or additional assets are obtained, this will also increase the AUM. The figure will drop as performance of the investments diminishes, with clients leaving the firm, redemptions, withdrawals, and fund closures. Because AUM includes all investor capital, it may also be comprised of the executives' assets with the firm.

The total currency amount of Assets under management matters immensely to a management company because of the management fees which they derive from these figures. It is true that an investment company garners a certain percentage in management fees based upon these assets. They are also able to employ their AUM numbers as a type of marketing tool to bring in still more investors and assets to the fund. Investors get a true feel for the size of the financial management company and its operations compared to the various competitors within the industry when they consider the figure. This still does not reveal full details about the potential of the investment company and its various investment choices and strategies.

Bear Market

Bear markets are periods in which stock markets drop for an extended amount of time. These pullbacks typically run to twenty percent or even greater amounts of the underlying stock values. Bear markets are the direct opposites of bull markets, when prices rise for extended amounts of time.

Bear markets and their accompanying drastic drops in stock share prices are commonly caused by declining corporate profits. They can also result from the correction of a too highly valued stock market, where stock prices prove to be overextended and decline to more historically fair values. Bear markets commonly begin when investors become frightened by lower earnings or too high values for their stocks and begin selling them. When many investors sell their holdings at a single time, the prices drop, sometimes substantially. Declining prices lead still other investors to fear that their money that they have invested in the stock market will be lost too. This motivates them to sell out through fear. In this way, the vicious cycle down progresses.

There have been many instances of bear markets in the United States since the country began over two hundred years ago. Perhaps the greatest example of an extended bear market is that found in the 1970's. During these years, stocks traded down and then sideways for more than a full decade. These kinds of encounters keep potential buyers out of the markets. This only fuels the fire of the bear market and keeps it going, since only a few buyers are purchasing stocks. In this way, the selling continues, as sellers consistently outnumber buyers in the stock exchanges.

For long term investors, bear markets present terrific opportunities. A person who is buying stocks with the plan to keep them for tens of years will find in a bear market the optimal sale price point and time to purchase stocks. Though many individual investors become frenzied and sell their stocks continuously during a bear market, this is exactly the wrong time to sell them.

Bear markets provide savvy investors with the chance to seek out solid companies and fundamentals that should still be strong ten to twenty years in the future. Good companies will still do well in the coming years, even if their share prices fall twenty or forty percent with the overall market. A company like Gillette that makes razors will still have a viable and dependable market going years down the road, even if the stock is unfairly punished by a bear market. Making money in a bear market requires investors to understand that a company's underlying core business has to be distinguished from its short term share price. In the near term, a company's fundamentals and stock prices do not always have much in common.

This means that a discounted price on a good company in a bear market is much like a periodic clearance sale at a person's favorite store. The time to buy the products heavily is while they are greatly discounted. The stock market is much the same. History has demonstrated on a number of different occasions that the stock prices of good companies will rebound to more realistic and fair valuations given some time.

Binary Options

Binary Options are a fairly new means of trading on the financial markets in the United States. They became a legal vehicle within the U.S. only back in 2008. Since then, they have rapidly evolved into what is now one of the quickest and simplest means of trading. These options are different from most other forms of trading since participants do not assume ownership of anything. Instead, they are simply trying to forecast the price direction of the asset that underlies the binary trade.

The most basic form of such binary options involves only two directions to potentially correctly predict. Will the underlying security go up or down is the only question traders must attempt to answer in this scenario. These are "all or nothing" trades without any confusing grey area in the middle. It makes them far easier to understand. Once traders arrive at their final conclusion on the price direction, they can punch in the security and see the percentage return on that given scenario if they are right before actually committing to the trade. It means traders know exactly how much time they have for the trade to work, what the maximum profit point is, and the maximum (total invested) loss amount could be. The simplicity of this idea appeals to countless traders.

Binary options permit trading on any of the significant cross currency pairs, stock market indices, many individual stocks, and commodities like gold and silver. This means that all of these various instruments, ranging from the British Pound Sterling currency versus the U.S. Dollar, to Apple stock, to gold futures can all be speculated on from a single unified and cohesive platform. It eliminates the need to switch back and forth between laptops or computer screens while trading internationally without having to switch from one broker to the next. This is especially true since a great number of the top binary options brokers have a wide range of stock market indices and individual stocks from the U.S., Europe, and Asia. This permits international traders to utilize their platforms without difficulties or hindrances. It makes these brokers a one-stop shop for binary options trades.

It is important to remember with these forms of option trades that every trade will entail a specific time line that the trader must pay careful attention to in order to profit. They may be set for shorter or longer time periods depending on the markets and the individual instrument involved. For those who resent having their funds committed for long, there are 5 minute options and even 60 second time frame trades available. Those who prefer to have more time for the trade to pan out are able to enter into trades with several hours and even days. These expirations can be changed as often as the trader wishes until the trade is executed. At this point, the time restriction becomes immutably set. Most binary options do not permit the traders to sell out early either at a partial profit or loss. Instead, they have to wait till the option expiration to realize their total gain or loss.

Three different kinds of binary options are available. These are the ones described above, as a basic straight call or put. Will the price be up or down at time of expiration? The second type is known as the one touch trade. In this binary option, traders select a target price before executing and committing to the trade. Should the underlying asset "touch" that price or surpass it at any point in the trade's life time, even just one time, then the investment is considered to be a profitable one. The final type is called a boundary trade. In this scenario trade, the broker supplies a range of prices to the traders. The traders have to decide if the price will fall within or without the provided range at expiration.

There are also several creative variations on these three kinds of trades along with a few exotic versions that feature higher payoffs of even 300 percent. Some of these are one touch trades with far-away target prices. While the odds of the underlying asset achieving such a price are considerably lower than with a closer target, the potential returns can be hundreds of percent if the traders are in fact correct in their prediction by expiration time.

Bitcoin Cash

Bitcoin Cash refers to the first split from the legendary crypto-currency market leading Bitcoin block chain. On August 1st the splinter group created its new crypto-currency Bitcoin Cash. The developer of this rival to the original behemoth is Calin Culianu. He explains that there are two principle noteworthy changes to the new bitcoin. These are an increase in the size of the block chain to eight megabytes and a removal of the SegWit code change that could activate on the bitcoin block chain by the end of August.

There are many detractors from this first Bitcoin splinter group who refer to the new Bitcoin Cash as merely an "altcoin." This refers to a software fork which leads to a newer crypto-currency that has its own independent market. The splinter Bitcoin has already taken a severe beating on the crypto-currency markets by trading at only $461 to the real Bitcoin's hefty price tag of $2,568. This represents approximately an only 18 percent valuation against the original on the futures market. It reveals the still limited level of confidence in and support for this altcoin which it boasts from current Bitcoin backers.

What gives the Bitcoin Cash crypto-currency some legitimacy is that it will maintain the same transaction history as the real Bitcoin does all the way up to the point of the split. This means that current users of bitcoin would have it on the two block chains. The newer project will also allow for multiple implementations of the new software. The first software that has implemented the Bitcoin Cash protocol is Bitcoin ABC. The splinter group's ultimate goal is for many more such implementations in the future. In fact, developer Culianu is already working on Bitcoin Classic and Bitcoin Unlimited as future implementations which will boost the block size of the BTC. Their goal is to ensure that they are compatible with the original implementation of Bitcoin Cash.

While there are a few supporters who are eager to embrace the changes, the majority of Bitcoin mining pools, mining companies, developers, and users are uninterested. The leading firm that has enthusiastically embraced the new code is the Chinese-based mining company ViaBTC. They control a nearly four percent of all Bitcoin computing power today. ViaBTC even operates its own BTC exchange. It is the first one to list the new crypto-currency format and even has plans set to launch its own mining pool which is entirely dedicated to the new Bitcoin Cash.

Certainly the Bitcoin Cash has garnered much-needed support from those users who long to see an increase in the size of the block chain. This includes the developers from the new rivals Bitcoin Unlimited and Bitcoin Classic.

Many former supporters of the new rivals such as Bitmain and Bitcoin.com are hesitant to actually back the new breakaway efforts now that they have formally split off. They are still committed to the Segwit2x scaling proposal which is set to be implemented on the main Bitcoin by end of August.

In fact it was Bitmain that came up with the inspiration for Bitcoin Cash. Despite this, they announced that they will only switch over to the rivals if the conditions are right. They have left the door open to support both Segwit2x main BTC as well as the newer varieties going forward.

Meanwhile, Bitcoin.com has announced that it will permit its miners in the pool to decide if they want to mine the newer Bitcoin Cash tokens which go under the acronym of BCC. It will mine the traditional Bitcoin and its revised Segwit2x chain itself. Yet it threatened that it will support the rival forthwith should the block size increase planned by SegWit not materialize as scheduled.

Bitcoin Crash

The Bitcoin Crash refers to one of five different incidents when the decade old crypto-currency saw its prices plunge off a cliff, sometimes by more than 50 percent in only two trading days. The most recent crash in the BTC has happened in 2017. In this spectacular crisis of the world's greatest and leading crypto-currency, the BTC price plunged from $2,800 per coin to $1,800 apiece in under 48 hours. This represented a steep and eye-watering 35 percent drop. By any measure of the percentage decline this qualifies as a crash in the ultimate crypto-currency. It is because of an apparent imminent split in the crypto-currency that this occurred.

Some analysts have claimed that the Bitcoin crash of 2017 was actually a bullish event from a certain point of view. The charts demonstrated along the rising trend lines that the BTC price can decline all the way to between $700 and $1,100 and still be considered to be in an intact and longer term bull market. The 2013 peak trend line shows that the price of $1,100 will hold. Analysts have pointed to the three trend lines of bitcoin to argue that the BTC price will hover somewhere above $1,200 to $1,300. So long as this remains the case and this area holds, then it can be easily argued that the 2017 Bitcoin crash is actually a bullish occurrence.

This means that the speculators are withdrawing from the crypto-currency. The Bitcoin holders are rotating out as the weak hands changed out for the stronger hands, or the investors and consumers who choose to keep holding them.

The prior Bitcoin crash occurred in 2015. At this time, the currency dropped by over a quarter in only two days. This kicked off fears that the crypto-currency was experiencing its fourth major crash. At the time, BTC traded as low as $195. This was an overall drop of over 80 percent from the November 2013 prior record high price of $1,150.

The two Bitcoin crashes before this one in 2015 happened in the spring of 2013 and the summer of 2011. These both resulted from the popping of straight up speculative bubbles in the price. The 2015 crash represented more of a consistent decline that actually transpired gradually starting back in June of 2014. After a number of months of consistent price stability in the neighborhood of $600 per bitcoin, the price began to fall.

Part of the underlying causes for these various every other year crashes in the leading crypto-currency have to do with the ways that it is created. The network of Bitcoin powers on the processing and uncovering efforts of the various miners. These are massive computer arrays which are assigned the tasks of solving highly complex algorithmic puzzles. The reward for these equations solving are bitcoin. Firms have ploughed many millions of dollars into creating specialized servers that now dominate the process of bitcoin mining. They attempt to recoup their considerable startup costs using their share of the bitcoin rewards.

The problem has come in as these firms borrowed real millions of dollars in order to begin their operations. Some of their loans were called in early as the prices of the underlying Bitcoin crashed and burned. This forced the companies who were mining to sell off some of their reward BTC which they had hoped to keep until the price of the underlying BTC crypto-currency recovered.

Two events have helped to contribute to the continuing bitcoin crashes. One of these was a hacking attack on Bitstamp in January of 2015. Around $5.6 million in BTC were stolen by the successful hackers. This was a minor hack attack though compared to the one that destroyed the long-time leading Bitcoin exchange Mt. Gox back in 2013/2014.

Bitcoin Currency (BTC)

Bitcoin is the name of a new electronic currency. An unknown individual who called himself Satoshi Nakamoto created this currency in 2009. This world's first widespread virtual currency appeals to many individuals because there are no banks or governments involved in issuing, trading, spending, or processing the transactions. There are also no transaction fees involved. Owners do not have to provide their actual identity to use them.

Bitcoin users like that they are able to purchase goods and services completely anonymously. They also enjoy the inexpensive and simple to use international payment system. This exists because this currency is not heavily regulated nor tied to any single bank or nation. Small businesses tend to like Bitcoin since they do not have to pay any credit card usage fees.

Many speculators have purchased Bitcoins for investment. Booms and busts in this currency are all too common. Those who bought in to the crypto currency early made spectacular returns as the value skyrocketed with growing demand. Others lost fortunes as the price of the Bitcoins subsequently crashed in value.

There are several ways to obtain these Bitcoins. Users buy them on open marketplaces known as Bitcoin exchanges. Those who wish to have them can buy and sell it with a variety of different currencies. Mt. Gox was the largest Bitcoin marketplace until it spectacularly collapsed and went bankrupt. Many clients who held their Bitcoins at Mt. Gox lost most of their money there at the time.

Individuals also buy and sell Bitcoins by transferring them to each other and by paying with them. They can do this with their computers or mobile apps. This is much like sending cash with a digital service like PayPal.

A last way to obtain Bitcoins is by mining them. Mining is the way that individuals create new Bitcoins. They do this by utilizing computers to solve complicated math problems or puzzles. When such a puzzle is solved, 25 Bitcoins are awarded to the group which solves them.

Owners keep their Bitcoins in a digital wallet. This can be stored on a personal computer or in the cloud. A virtual wallet is much like an electronic bank account which permits owners to receive or send Bitcoins, to save their money, or to pay for their goods and services. These wallets do not receive the protection of FDIC insurance as do traditional bank accounts.

To users, Bitcoins are simply computer programs or mobile apps which give the owners the Bitcoin wallet. The payment system is easier to utilize than is a credit card or debit card purchase. An individual does not require a merchant account in order to receive the currency. All an individual has to do to make a payment is to put the payment amount and address of the recipient then click send.

An important fact about Bitcoin is that no one owns the actual network. Bitcoin users control the Bitcoin currency. Various developers work on the software to improve it. Users are able to decide which version or software they use it on, which prohibits developers from forcefully changing the operation. For the software to work properly, all Bitcoin users have to work with programs that abide by the same rules.

As with most new currencies Bitcoin is not without problems. When digital wallets are left in the cloud, some servers have been hacked and coins stolen. Bitcoin exchanges like Mt. Gox have failed. Other companies have disappeared with their clients' Bitcoins. When the wallets stay on a person's computer, they can be destroyed by viruses or accidentally deleted.

Increasing government regulation appears to be in the future of Bitcoin and other crypto currencies. Because of the anonymous nature of the currency, they have evolved into the preferred payment method for illegal activities such as drugs and smuggling. Governments are concerned about being able to trace these types of activities back to the users. They are also worried about not being able to tax transactions made in Bitcoin currency.

Black Monday

Black Monday refers to three separate stock market crashes that coincidentally happened on Mondays. These were the crashes of October 19 in 1987, the one on October 28 in 1929, and the stock market correction crash of August 24 in 2015.

The Black Monday in 1987 proves to be the most common reference for the phrase. It was the biggest single day percentage drop in the markets in the history of the stock market. This dark day saw the Dow Jones Industrial Average plunge 22.61% on October 19, 1987 when the market cratered 508 points down to 1738.74. At the same time, the S&P 500 plummeted 57.64 points down to 225.06 for a 20.4% loss. The Dow did not recover this single day loss for two years.

The background to this crash started with a five year long bull market. The Dow Jones had run up 43% in just 1987. This brought it to a peak o 2,747.65 in the trading session of August 25, 1987. A little bit lower range held over a month until October 2. At this point, the markets began to decline precipitously. They declined 15% over the two weeks that led to Black Monday.

Various studies were done to determine what caused this nearly 37% drop in the markets in two weeks. The SEC Securities and Exchange Commission analysis decided that traders' nervousness about anti takeover legislation being reviewed in the House Ways and Means Committee led to it.

On Tuesday, October 13 they introduced this bill, and it passed October 15th. In only three days, stocks tumbled over 10%. This represented the biggest three day decline in markets in 50 years. The securities which declined the most steeply proved to be the corporations which would have suffered most from the legislation's impacts.

The bill had proposed to do away with a tax deduction on corporate takeover loans. Congress was attempting to better regulate the markets. Wall Street reacted with Black Monday. The upsetting tax deduction proposition was removed from the bill before it passed into law after the damage in the stock markets had already occurred.

More factors than this aggravated the crash. Stock trading programs were already computerized at this point. They caused the sell off to be worse than it should have. These programs were set up with sell stop loss orders that entered sell orders as the markets declined by a specific percentage. As the programs all began to react at the same time, the New York Stock Exchange dealers became overwhelmed. There simply were not enough buyers available on some of the stocks. This forced them to halt trading on the exchange.

Besides this, an October 16th announcement from then Treasury Secretary James Baker unsettled the markets. He stated the U.S. could permit the dollar's value to fall. This would have created lower stock prices for foreign investors. A great number of them decided to sell then to buy back in after the dollar declined. Baker was only attempting to lower the worrisome increase in the U.S. trade deficit.

Numerous investors, economists, and observers feared that the devastating crash would lead to recession. The Federal Reserve managed to hold it off by forcing money into banks. This stabilized the markets and led to a partial recovery. At the conclusion of October, the Dow was back up by 15%. The rest of the year saw the Dow confined to a narrower trading range. It stayed between 1,776 and 2,014 until 1988. Though there was no direct recession resulting from Black Monday, it did serve as a precursor to the Savings and Loan Crisis of 1989 and the recession of 1990-1991.

Black Thursday

Black Thursday began the stock market crash of 1929. That Thursday saw the markets decline steeply by 11%. The following Black Monday of 1929 a few days later proved to be worse. Stocks crashed another 13% that Monday, October 28th. The following day became known as Black Tuesday as all of the remaining gains for the whole year were wiped out in that continuing stock market rout. This comprised the worst markets crash in American history. Black Thursday and the subsequent few days of crashes eventually led to the Great Depression.

The day before Black Thursday, investors had already taken significant losses and were feeling nervous. That prior Wednesday the markets declined by a steep 4.6%. The Washington Post made matters worse with their Thursday morning headline that roared, "Huge Selling Wave Creates Near Panic as Stocks Collapse." The market opened at 305.85 on Thursday morning and proceeded to drop 11% throughout the day. The losses of this first crash day proved to be greater than a typically lengthy stock market correction.

Wall Street bankers became worried as they observed that stocks had already retraced almost 20% from the record close of September 3, 1929 at 381.2. The Black Thursday volume turned out to be three times as high as the daily average at 12.9 million shares. This made matters worse. After the three stock market crashes of Black Thursday, Black Monday, and Black Tuesday, the three foremost banks attempted to restore market confidence by purchasing stocks. This intervention seemed to work for a time, but it proved to have only a temporary effect.

These crashes alone did not begin the Great Depression of 1929. They did set the scene in destroying business investing confidence. Next individuals understood that the banks had taken their savings and invested them in stocks on Wall Street. They raced to be the first to withdraw their deposits. Banks closed down for the weekend then only disbursed ten cents for every dollar.

A great number of individuals who had never participated in the stock markets similarly lost all of their life time savings. The banks that no longer had deposits were forced into bankruptcy. This meant that businesses could no longer access loans and individuals were unable to purchase houses.

Wall Street sought safety in gold and pushed up the prices of the precious metal. At the time the dollar was on the gold standard. People traded in their dollars in exchange for gold which dangerously reduced gold reserves. This forced the Federal Reserve to increase interest rates to safeguard the dollar's threatened value. It was this contractionary monetary policy that severely worsened the self destructive economic down spiral.

The irrational exuberance of the Roaring Twenties led to the black week of 1929. Stock market investing grew to become a national hobby. Stock market values roared up by 218% in the years from 1922 up to just before the crash. These returns amounted to more than 20% per year.

The financial situation became aggravated as people with no cash to invest could simply buy stocks on margin from their stock brokers with as little as 10% or 20% down. Banks began investing their depositor's money without letting them know.

The resulting misappropriation of funds caused the run on the banks that came to characterize the Great Depression. Because of these all too common events, President Roosevelt came up with the Federal Deposit Insurance Corporation as part of his New Deal in order to restore confidence in the banks and to safeguard future depositors' money.

Black Wednesday

Black Wednesday refers to September 16, 1992. This proved to be the day that Britain was forced to withdraw from the European Exchange Rate Mechanism system of currency band pegs. The same day it had to allow the pound to be devalued by 15%. The catastrophe for the Bank of England and British government occurred only two years after British sterling had become a member of the long running EU ERM in 1990.

From the beginning of becoming a member of the Exchange Rate Mechanism, British Prime Minister John Major had struggled to keep the pound within its designated floating band. The weekend following Wednesday September 16 was to be a French referendum on the Maastricht Treaty. Polls showed 58% of the French were against closer economic and political union with the rest of the EU. This had put markets on edge and increased the pressure on the pound, considered to be the weakest member of the fledgling monetary union.

The European ERM system mandated that governments keep their participating currencies within a band pegged to other currencies in the system. In order to hold these values steady compared to each other, countries with the more valuable currencies were supposed to sell their own currency and purchase the weakest ones.

In September of 1992, the British pound turned out to be the weakest in its band while the German Deutschmark remained the most powerful currency. In fact it was not only the British pound struggling ahead of the French referendum. The Spanish peseta and Italian lira were also falling under intense pressure. The pound had the misfortune of getting the most media attention.

The antagonist in the day's bloodbath turned out to be currency hedge fund speculator George Soros. He and his Quantum Fund took on the Bank of England directly in the currency markets. He accomplished this by borrowing UK gilts bonds and selling them. He then purchased them back moments later for lower prices. Soros and other speculators following his lead were able to repeat this action every couple of minutes and turn a profit with every trade. Soros later explained how he had earned £1 billion

(British pounds) by selling the pound sterling he never even owned.

The pressure grew throughout the day as the Bank of England kept purchasing British pounds in an effort to support their price within the band. At middle of the morning, Bank of England officials had to purchase £2 billion every hour in order to defend against the global speculators' selling pressure.

They also pushed interest rates up to 12% in an effort to support the pound. Prime Minister Major refused to accept defeat easily and later that day raised British interest rates higher to 15%. By the time currency markets closed in London, the pound still remained outside of its required currency band.

At 7:40 pm that night, the government announced Britain had suspended membership in the ERM. It was never to re-enter it. The entire European Exchange Rate Mechanism came close to the edge of collapse over the shock announcement and sudden withdrawal.

The EC monetary committee entered crisis talks to keep the system together. It later emerged that the German Bundesbank had failed to keep up its end of the ERM agreement by selling marks and buying pounds on the critical day. Britain had spent nearly £10 billion, roughly a quarter of their reserves, in efforts to defeat the currency speculators.

Thirteen years after Black Wednesday, the Treasury released papers that proved the Bank of England lost £3.3 billion in the day from the continuously declining value of their own currency they kept purchasing.

Blockchain

Blockchain refers to a technology that serves as a means of structuring and storing data. As such it is the ultimate foundation of the revolutionary crypto-currencies such as Bitcoin and Ether. The true breakthrough in coding capability permits participants to share digital ledgers back and forth over a computer network. Its genius and appeal lies in the fact that it does not require a central authority to run or oversee it. Since there is no meddling central authority like a central bank or boss to the system, no one party can interfere with the financial records.

In other words, the straight math makes sure that all the parties who participate are honest with each other. Blockchain is made up of concatenated transactions blocks. Nowadays, the technology has become so important and offers so many future possibilities for real world applications that over forty of the world's biggest and most important financial firms are experimenting with uses for it.

Blockchains are also public record ledgers of all transactions in a crypto-currency which have ever taken place. For this reason, the chain is always expanding as every new record adds additional completed blocks to it. These become a part of the blockchain via a chronological and linear fashioned order. Every participating node receives a copy of this blockchain as it is updated. Nodes are computers which share a Bitcoin network connection that utilizes the system to validate and relay such transactions which were performed in it. The chain comes as an auto download once a computer network joins up to the Bitcoin network. This chain maintains full information on all balances and appropriate addresses from the very first transaction ever all the way to the latest one which has been performed utilizing the block.

In the end, it is this blockchain that represents the primary technological advance offered by Bitcoin. It amounts to the proof and record of every transaction performed using the network. The blocks represent the current record in the chain that will ultimately record all or at least some of the recent transaction. After it is finished, this block will join the chain as part and parcel of the current and permanent database. Once a block is spoken for, a new block will become generated. Myriads of such blocks exist in the chain. They are linked one to another, much like a physical chain, in their correct chronological and linear order. Each block contains the hash of the prior block in it.

It is always helpful to consider a real world example to better understand a somewhat complex concept like this one. Traditional banking is a solid analogy. This blockchain is much like a complete history of banking records and transactions. Bitcoin transactions must be chronologically entered in the blockchain as real world banking transactions are at financial institutions. Such blocks are something like the statements recording individual bank accounts and banking transactions.

The protocol of Bitcoin is based upon all nodes in the system sharing the blockchain's database. A complete and unaltered copy of the chain will include records of all the transactions in Bitcoin which have ever been executed. This delivers useful insights into the quantity of value that a specific address owned at any time in the past.

The problem with the ever growing nature of the chain is that it has become so very large with over a decade of increasing size that synchronization and storage have become serious issues. These days, the average time of a new block appearing on the chain amounts to only ten minutes. Mining, the process of unlocking new BTC, is adding the majority of new blocks to the chain these days.

Bond Market

A bond market is a financial market where investors buy and sell bonds. In practice this is mostly handled electronically over computers nowadays. There are two principal types of bond markets. These are primary markets where companies are able to sell new debt and secondary markets where investors are able to purchase and resell these debt securities. Companies generally issues such debt as bonds. These markets also trade bills, notes, and commercial paper.

The goal of the bond markets is to help private companies and public entities obtain funding of a long term nature. This market has generally been the domain of the United States that dominates it. The U.S. comprises as much as 44% of this bond market on a global basis.

There are five primary bond markets according to SIFMA the Securities Industry and Financial Markets Association. These include the municipal, corporate, mortgage or asset backed, funding, and government or agency markets. The government bond market comprises a significant component of this market thanks to its massive liquidity and enormous size. Because of the stability of U.S. and some international government bonds, other bonds are often contrasted with them to help determine the amount of credit risk.

This is because government bond yields from countries with little risk like the U.S., Britain, or Germany are traditionally considered to be free of default risk. Other bonds denominated in these various currencies provide greater yields as the borrowers are more likely to default than these central governments.

Bond markets often serve a useful secondary function to reveal interest rate changes. This is because the values of bonds are inversely related to the interest rates which they pay. This helps investors to measure what the true cost of obtaining funding really is. Companies which are perceived to be riskier will have to pay higher interest rates on their bonds than companies believed to have strong and stable credit and repayment abilities. When companies or government entities are unable to make a partial or full payment on their bonds, this becomes a default.

When a company or a government needs to raise money and does not want to issue stock, it can sell bonds. These are contracts the issuers who are the borrowers make with investors who function as lenders. When investors purchase such instruments, they lend money to the issuing organization (company or government). The issuer of the bond promises to repay the original investment back along with interest in the future.

Bonds traded on these markets have many elements in common, whichever type of market they represent. All bonds have a face value. This is the amount of money which a bond would be valued at when it matures and the amount on which interest payments are based. They also have coupon rates that represent the interest rate which the issuer of the bond pays in its interest payments.

The coupon dates turn out to be the times when the issuer will pay its interest payments. Issue prices are the amounts for which the issuer sells the bond in the first place. The maturity date proves to be the exact date when the bond would be repaid. At this time, the issuer of the bond would pay the bond's face value to the bond holder.

Though a holder of a bond might keep it until maturity, this is often not the case. Many investors buy and sell them on the bond markets as their needs dictate. It is possible to sell a bond at a premium when the market value becomes greater than the original face value. Investors could also sell them at a discount to their original face value as the market price declines.

Bonds

Bonds are also known as debt instruments, fixed income securities, and credit securities. A bond is actually an IOU contract where the terms of the bond, interest rate, and date of repayment are all particularly defined in a legal document. If you buy a bond at original issue, then you are literally loaning the issuer money that will be repaid to you at a certain time, along with periodic interest payments.

Bonds are all classified under one of three categories in the United States. The first of these are the highest rated, safest category of Federal Government debt and its associated agencies. Treasury bills and treasury bonds fall under this first category. The second types of bonds are bonds deemed to be safe that are issued by companies, states, and cities. These first two categories of bonds are referred to as investment grade. The third category of bonds involves riskier types of bonds that are offered by companies, states, and cities. Such below investment grade bonds are commonly referred to as simply junk bonds.

Bonds' values rise and fall in directly opposite correlation to the movement of interest rates. As interest rates fall, bonds rise. When interest rates are rising, bonds prices fall. These swings up and down in interest rates and bond prices are not important to you if you buy a bond and hold it until the pay back, or maturity, date. If you choose to sell a bond before maturity, the price that it realizes will be mostly dependent on what the interest rates prove to be like at the time.

Bonds' investment statuses are rated by the credit rating agencies. These are Standard & Poor's, Moody's, and Fitch Ratings. All bond debt issues are awarded easy to understand grades, such as A+ or B. In the last few years of the financial crisis, these credit rating agencies were reprimanded for having awarded some companies bonds' too high grades considering the risks that the companies undertook. This was especially the case with the bonds of banks, investment companies, and some insurance outfits.

Understanding the bond markets is a function of comprehending the yield curves. Yield curves turn out to be pictorial representations of a bond's interest rate and the date that it reaches maturity, rendered on a graph.

Learning to understand and read these curves, and to figure out the spread between such curves, will allow you to make educated comparisons between various issues of bonds.

Some bonds are tax free. These are those bonds that are offered by states and cities. Such municipal bonds, also known as munis, help to raise funds that are utilized to pay for roads, schools, dams, and various other projects. Interest payments made on these municipal bonds are not subject to Federal taxes. This makes them attractive to some investors.

Brokers

Brokers are professional intermediaries that work on behalf of both a seller and a buyer. When brokers function as agents on behalf of only a buyer or seller, they become representatives and principal parties in any deal. Brokers should not be confused with agents, who instead work on the behalf of a single principal. In the financial world, there are stock brokers, commodity brokers, and option brokers.

Stock brokers are highly regulated broker professionals that sell and buy stock shares and related securities. They work on the part of investors who purchase and sell such securities. Stock brokers transact through either Agency Only Firms or market makers in a given security. These types of brokers are commonly employees of brokerage firms, such as Morgan Stanley, Prudential, or UBS.

Stock brokers are essential in stock transactions, since these exchanges of stocks can only occur between two individuals who are actual members of the exchange in question. A regular investor can not simply enter a stock exchange like the NASDAQ and ask to buy or sell a stock. This is the role that brokers fulfill.

Within the stock broker realm, three different kinds of broker services exist. One of these is advisory dealing, in which a broker makes recommendations to the client of what types of shares to purchase and sell, yet allows the investor to enact the ultimate decision. A second type is an execution only broker, who will simply transact the customer's specific buying and selling instructions. Finally, discretionary dealing involves brokers who learn all about the customer's goals in investing then carry out trades for the customer based on his or her interests.

These same functions are carried out by other financial market brokers as well. Commodities brokers deal in commodities contracts for clients in commodities such as gold, silver, wheat, and oil. Commodities contracts are comprised of options, futures, and financial derivatives. These commodities brokers act as middle men to an investor to transact buy and sell orders on such commodities exchanges as the New York Mercantile Exchange, Commodities Mercantile Exchange, and New York Board of

Trade.

Options brokers deal in options on stocks, commodities, or currencies, depending on what their area of specialty proves to be. They specialize in providing research, trading, and education on options to individual investor clients. Besides handling the main options that include straddles, option spreads, and covered calls, a number of options brokers facilitate trade in related fields that include ETF's, stocks, bonds, and mutual funds.

Brokers in the financial world are typically regulated by one oversight group or another. Stock brokers, for example, are licensed and overseen by the Securities Exchange Commission. They must pass an exam called the Series 7 in order to practice their trade as a stock broker. Commodities brokers, on the other hand, must obtain a Series 3 license from the Financial Industry Regulatory Authority. They are closely monitored by the Commodities Futures Trading Commission. Options brokers are monitored by the regulatory agency associated with the area of options that they trade.

Capital Flows

Capital Flows relate to the general movements of money and investments so that they can be invested in securities, business, or trade production. This also takes into consideration flows of such capital that occur naturally within a multinational corporation. This might result from capital spending in other divisions, investment capital allocation, acquisitions of rival companies, or R&D research and development spending.

Governments can also engage in capital flow direction by steering money they collect in tax levies into particular policies and programs as well as with their trade policies and financial policies on currency management and bilateral trade with other countries. Even individual investors can be involved in capital flow through their saving and investing personal capital into mutual funds, bonds, and stocks as well as other types of financial securities.

The United States corporate, not for profit, and government organizations direct capital flows as a result of legislation, regulation, and analysis. Economists within the U.S. and other developed nations like to study these various categories of capital inflows and outflows. This includes specific types like mutual fund flows, venture capital, asset class balancing and reallocation, federal budgets, and capital spending budgets of corporations.

In fact there are many different categories of capital flow. Within the movements in asset classes, these can be sufficiently measured as they move back and forth between stocks, cash, bonds, mutual funds, and other forms of financial securities. Venture capital can measure the shifts of investments moving around startup businesses and industries. Mutual funds will actively track the net withdrawals and additional cash deposits from and to a wide range of fund classes. With capital spending budgets, these can be studied on a companywide level. This way firms can monitor their various growth plans. Governments utilize their capital flow studies to match their budgets appropriately up with government spending plans.

Another insight that such capital flow studies provide pertains to the capital markets. They can prove the weaknesses or strengths of the various markets as economists examine the direction and pace of capital inflows and outflows. This is particularly useful for investors who can know the growth rates in specific capital flows which provide them with ideas of trends and possible opportunities. Capital spending flows will help them to know which industries and specific corporations are on the move and might be good investment opportunities. Venture capital flows reveal risks involved with venture financing of different startup industries and even specific startup operations.

Real Estate is another investment arena where capital flow direction can be most illuminating for investors. For example, during the devastating global financial crisis of 2007-2009, the capital inflows to Real Estate markets drastically slowed down. Sales did not again reach the pre-crash levels until the year 2013. By 2015, such capital flows grew as much as 45 percent compared to the levels in 2014 with regards to commercial property investment inflows.

The study of capital flows can also reveal big pictures for emerging market economies as well. As these more volatile economies often undergo rapid growth spurts and sharp contractions, the capital flow can correspondingly rise and fall steeply. Higher capital inflows often create credit booms. This leads to hot money asset price inflation. Sometimes it is offset by currency depreciation losses as exchange rates shift or equities' prices drop.

India is a classic example to consider among the developing nations of the world. The huge nation has experienced significant fluctuation periods which started back in the decade of the 1990s. Capital inflows occurred throughout the 1990s to the first years of the 2000s. This coincided with steady and positive growth. From the first years of the 2000s through 2007, capital inflows shifted into overdrive. The rapidly accompanying growth stalled out suddenly because of the peak of the global financial crisis in 2008/2009. Capital outflows became highly volatile during these several years.

Capital Inflow

Capital Inflow refers to money (in the form of investments) moving into a certain benefitting nation. The country which is the recipient of the inflow is best known as the host country. The source countries are the ones sending or investing the initial funds. Host nations often have a range of causes for attracting such capital inflows.

Direct foreign investment occurs when multinational corporations purchase literal tangible assets in the host country. This could come in the form of purchasing a local company outright or building a manufacturing plant locally. There could also be portfolio investment in the host nation's financial securities. This might include bonds and stocks which may be bought by international banks, foreign residents, insurance companies, pension funds, hedge funds, or other cross-border groups.

A third way that this occurs is when host governments are forced to borrow money off of international governments or foreign banks in order to pay their deficit on the balance of payments. It also occurs when domestic corporations or citizens elect to borrow from foreign banks. Finally inter-company transfers can finance investment and consumption in this category of capital inflow.

A last form of capital inflow happens when the host country has higher interest rates than the source nations' own corresponding rates. In this scenario, shorter term deposits will often flock to the banks' and money market instruments of the host nation. This could be straight up investment or speculation that the host national exchange rate will increase and so lead to a capital gain. This is the opposite of capital outflows. Outflows occur as funds move out of the host nation into other competing countries for the same reasons detailed above.

There are many beneficial effects to a country which receives capital inflows. As money comes into the host country via a business or stock purchase on the nation's stock market exchange, the recipient firm will deploy the funds either for startup purposes or to expand their existing business products and lines. This is really good for the companies which receive the funds. Such expansion of the companies in question then leads both job creation and employment growth in the host nation. Businesses will finally realize profits utilizing the original capital investment and the projects they subsequently fund with it. With these profits, the company is able to pay for additional expansion or investment in other projects and/or financial investments.

In the last few decades, foreigners have invested literally hundreds of billions worth of foreign capital into the United States economy. This has massively advantaged the American economy and workers (besides just creating countless jobs) as it boosted the international value of the dollar, lowered interest rates for American individuals and businesses, and grew the capital supply for loans which banks could make to residents and companies alike. With the onset of the catastrophic Global Financial Crisis from 2007-2009, the capital inflows to the United States dropped considerably. The subsequent Sovereign Debt Crisis in Europe dramatically decreased the capital inflow to Europe as well.

Years later by 2012, China finally surpassed the U.S. to capture the spot as the globe's greatest host of direct foreign investment . At the conclusion of 2012, the United States managed to recapture this coveted top spot. China had several reasons to steal the American thunder this way. The Chinese economy grew quicker than the United States as well as the other developed nations. Besides this, China has finally matured into a country that does not appear to be a high risk investment any longer. This has helped to draw in direct foreign investment by the hundreds of billions over the decades.

Capital Outflow

Capital Outflow is a phenomenon where financial assets and money move away from a given nation. All countries of the world consider this to be a negative action. It typically occurs as a result of economic and/or political instability or at least the perception of it. Such asset flight results from domestically and especially foreign-based investors choosing to sell their stakes within a certain nation. They do this as they see potential weakness in the economy or political establishment of a country. They begin to feel that greater and safer opportunities for investment lie overseas.

When such Capital Outflows become too fast and great, it is a serious indicator that economic and political turmoil is present and a primary cause of the asset and capital flight. Many governments will begin to set limitations for capital choosing to exit. The connotation of such actions tends to warn still other investors who have not left that the condition of the host nation and economy is rapidly deteriorating.

Abnormal capital outflow creates increasingly severe pressure on the macroeconomics of a country and its economy. It tends to dissuade domestic and foreign investors alike from investing in the state and its companies. There are a range of valid explanations for why such capital flight actually occurs. Among them are unnaturally low national interest rates and growing political unrest.

It often helps to look at a real world example to better understand a difficult concept. Japan chose to decrease its interest rates to actual negative levels back in 2016. This applied to all government bonds and securities. They simultaneously began unprecedented aggressive stimulatory measures to boost the growth of the GDP Gross Domestic Product at the same time. The economic problems in Japan started after massive capital outflows from the island nation throughout the decade of the 1990s kicked off two long decades of sub-par stagnated growth in the country which formerly boasted the position of second greatest economy in the world.

Often times, governments impose severe restrictions on capital flight in a valiant effort to stop the fleeing money and financial assets. This is in an endeavor to shore up the capital markets and especially domestic banking institutions and system which can fail if all the money is simultaneously withdrawn. Too few bank deposits often cause banks to crater into insolvency when a great number of assets depart all at once. Subsequently, many banks find it difficult if not outright impossible to call back in existing issued loans in order to make good on customer withdrawal demands.

Consider the sad case study of Greece. Back in 2015, the government of the world's first democracy had no other choice than to instate a week long bank holiday. Wire transfers became restricted only to those recipients with Greek bank accounts. When such events occur in developing (or sometimes third world) countries, the weakness it institutes can create a vicious downward spiral that leads to domestic public panic and foreign investment fear and resistance.

There are also dramatic effects on exchange rates. The supply of a given country's currency rises dramatically as investors cash out of the state. Investors in China have periodically sold off the Yuan in order to obtain American dollars. This drives down the value of the Chinese Yuan, which has the additional side benefit of reducing the costs of Chinese exports while simultaneously boosting the costs to import foreign goods. It unfortunately also leads to inflation since import demand will fall while exported goods demand increases. During the second half of the year 2015, Chinese assets to the tune of $550 billion departed China looking for a higher ROI return on investment. This caused not only Chinese government fears but ensuing worldwide government worries.

Similarly Argentina suffered from sudden, unexpected, and runaway capital outflows back in the decade of the 1990s following a dramatic currency realignment. Their new fixed exchange rate created a resulting recession. The nation has now become the popular example and poster country for fledgling economies and the difficulties they all too often encounter in boosting their economic development.

CBOE Volatility Index (VIX)

The CBOE Volatility Index (VIX) refers to the VIX ticker symbol on the CBOE Chicago Board Options Exchange. This is the famed volatility index that displays the expectations of the market for future volatility in the markets over the coming 30 days. This number comes from utilizing the implied volatilities from a huge selection of the index options on the S&P 500. The volatility measurement is intended to be looking forward, comes from the results of volatilities on both puts and calls, and has become the most popular measure for assessing market risk. This is why investors often refer to it as the gold standard of "investor fear gauge."

This crucial measurement of market participants' expectations for shorter-term volatility is revealed by the stock index options prices set for the S&P 500. It was unveiled back in 1993 and has since grown into the leading bell weather for market volatility and investors' sentiment in the globe. Since a number of larger and important investors wanted to have tradable instruments based on the market expectation for future volatility, VX based futures arose in 2004. In 2006, the exchange introduced the VIX options.

Originally, the Chicago Board of Options Exchange created the CBOE Volatility Index (VIX) to develop a range of volatility based products. After the CBOE led the way in innovation, a few other measures of volatility indices were also created. The VXN tracks volatility on the NASDAQ 100 while the VXD tracks volatility on the DJIA Dow Jones Industrial Average.

Yet it is the CBOE Volatility Index (VIX) that remains the original attempt at developing and instituting a form of volatility index. Originally this was intended as a weighted measure for the implied volatility for eight S&P 100 calls and puts with strike prices that were then at the money. After ten years of wild success in 2004, the options expanded to a broader index the S&P 500 that permits a more representative portrayal of the expectations of investors for future market volatility.

When the CBOE Volatility Index (VIX) values rise to over 30, then huge amounts of volatility are on display because of the uncertainty and fear of investors. Values under 20 reveal a complacent and less stressed epoch in the stock markets. For much of 2017, these levels at been at record lows below 12.

Computers actually figure up the VIX as they compile the S&P 500 index. It is different in that it is not based upon underlying stock prices. Rather it relies on the options prices from the S&P 500 to estimate the volatility levels of such options and how they will change from that date to the expiration date of the underlying options. The CBOE then compiles the prices of multiple options to derive their number of aggregate volatility that the index actually tracks.

Thanks to the options based upon the VIX, investors are able to trade them. The CBOE also offers another 24 volatility based ETP exchange traded products that bring the VIX indices up to a total 25.

Actual movements in the CBOE Volatility Index (VIX) mostly come down to the market reactions. Consider an example to better grasp this somewhat challenging concept. On June 13th of 2016, the VIX itself roared higher by over 23 percent. It reached a daily high of 20.97, its best level in more than three months. This spike occurred as a result of a worldwide U.S. equities hard sell off.

Global investors feared the uncertainty in the markets and opted to cash out of all gains and to realize some losses. This led to a greater supply of equities. According to the well-proven law of greater supply and decreasing demand, this led to higher market volatility and a greater VIX number as a direct result.

Chicago Board of Options Exchange (CBOE)

CBOE is the acronym for the Chicago Board of Options Exchange. The exchange arose in 1973. Since then it has grown to become the biggest options' market on the planet. As a market leader in technological innovation and creative financial products that are new and ground breaking, it has pushed the envelope on electronic forms of trading over the years. The Chicago Board concentrates its efforts on options contracts pertaining to indices, single stock equities, and interest rates. This exchange has such a broad and deep reach in options that it can claim to host a majority of the options traded around the globe. Industry insiders refer to this largest option exchange in the world as the "See-bo."

The CBOE has come an enormous distance since its very first trading day back in 1973. On that first day, the exchange offered 16 individual stocks and actually traded 911 contracts. The daily average volume nowadays is well in excess of a million contracts every market day. They trade these massive numbers of options primarily on single equity options, indices options, and options on ETF exchange traded funds and ETN exchange traded notes.

The market is the home for the volatility index options, which trade on this index investors affectionately call the VIX. This VIX is universally held to be the leading equity market volatility barometer in the globe. Besides this index, investors can also trade options on such internationally known and popular indices as the SPX S&P 500, the DJX Dow Jones 30 Industrials, the London FTSE, the MSCI, the NDX NASDAQ 100, and the RUT Russell 200 Index.

The exchange has counted itself a global leader and even pioneer in the purveying of stock indices options which are cash settled. Investors are able to take advantage of these tools in order to hedge their portfolio exposure and manage their risk. They can also gather regular premium income to help increase or stabilize the returns on their various portfolios. Every single trading day, literally billions of dollars in value of options transact through these ranges of popular and beloved indices.

The CBOE boasts creating the single stock options market all by itself, as well as the universe of ETF and ETN options. Investors throughout the world can utilize these exchange traded product and single stock options to hedge the positions they have in the stocks, manage their risk, and create additional income through writing covered calls.

Today's exchange provides the vast range of literally thousands of different publically exchange traded stocks, ETNs and ETFs with option tradability. By selling cash secured puts and covered calls, investors are able to boost their portfolio income and hedge their various literal stock positions. It is important to keep in mind that these particular financial products come with physical settlement when expiration occurs. This means that any options on single stock securities still held at expiration would be delivered. With the options on the various indices, the expiration settlement is cash-based.

CBOE worked to ensure that investors of all sizes could participate in these contracts. To that effect, they pioneered the concept of mini options. The exchange's website offers a full range of product details and contract specifications on the various mini options contracts, such as the ever popular Mini S&P 500 contract.

In other ground breaking product firsts, CBOE led the world with such innovative options ideas as weekly options that offer end of week expiration for precisely targeted strategies, quarterly and end of month options on the S&P 500, FLEX Options that permit investors to customize their options contract terms (including styles of exercise, exercise prices and dates), strategy benchmark indices like the PUT and BXM indices, and social media indices. With the Social Media Indexes, the Chicago Board of Options Exchange is partnering up with SMA Social Market Analytics to create a range of interesting indices based on such SMA data which allows for the CBOE-SMA Index Suite of products based on social media.

Clearing House

A Clearing House refers to a financial intermediary that exists between sellers and buyers of financial instruments such as stocks, bonds, futures, options, and mutual funds. At the same time, it is also an agency which operates in tandem with a futures exchange. In this capacity, they handle clearing trades, settling trading accounts, collecting and maintaining monies for margin accounts, reporting trades, and regulating delivery of the relevant financial instruments. These clearing houses serve as third parties for all options and futures contracts. They are also simultaneously buyers for each seller who is a clearing member and sellers for every buyer who is a clearing member.

Another way of looking at this is that the clearing houses take on the opposite side of every trade transacted. As two investors consent to a financial transaction and its terms, the clearing house will work in the critical capacity as middle man for the two participating third parties. This involves selling and buying securities. The ultimate reason of existence for clearing houses lies in boosting the efficiency of markets and increasing the financial stability of the relevant markets.

Futures markets are most closely connected to clearing houses. The reason for this is that their financial instruments prove to be exceedingly complex. They must therefore have a stable financial intermediary backing them up. Every futures exchange maintains its own proprietary clearing house. This forces every exchange member to clear its trades via the clearing house by no later than the end of every trading session. They will have to deposit a given amount of margin money with the clearing house based on the maintained margin requirements so that they can cover any deficit member balance.

It always helps to consider a real world clear example to illuminate a challenging concept such as this one. If Godfrey's Futures, a member broker, alerts the clearing house of the commodity and futures exchange at trading day end that it net bought 30,000 bushels of May soybeans for its customer accounts, then it will subsequently be required to deposit the margin cover of six cents or each individual net bushel position. This would amount to $1,800 in total deposit to be on hand with the clearing house in question. Since every member will have to clear out all trades via the house and so has to keep enough funds to cover their debit balances, it is ultimately the clearing house that carries the responsibility to all member broker dealers to fulfill the contracts according to the appropriate terms.

Within the United States today, there exist two separate most important clearing houses. These are the NASDAQ and the NYSE New York Stock Exchange. At the NYSE, they facilitate all mutual funds, bonds, exchange traded funds, stocks, and derivatives trading and contracts. They serve as the middle man on every side of an auction trade which allows for investors and brokers to purchase and sell off securities to other third parties and customers. They do this by matching up the highest bid price with the lowest ask price.

The NYSE actually maintains an expansive physical trading floor in pursuit of this important mission and purpose. On the other hand, the NASDAQ also has to do the same functions, yet it does not have the advantage of a physical trading floor on which to do it. All NASDAQ trades they match up entirely electronically for their various broker dealers and investor customers.

Closed End Funds

Closed end funds refer to those investment companies which are publicly traded and regulated by the SEC Securities and Exchange Commission. They are similar to mutual funds in some ways. Both represent investment funds which are pooled and overseen by a portfolio manager. The closed end varieties raise fixed amounts of capital. They do this in IPO initial public offerings. Such funds will then be established and structured, listed on a stock exchange, and finally then traded, bought, and sold as a stock is on one of the exchanges.

Other names for these closed end funds are closed end mutual funds or closed end investments. These funds have things in common with the open end funds as well as characteristics which are unique to them and which set them apart from such ETF exchange traded funds and mutual funds.

Closed end funds are only able to raise their capital in a single instance by utilizing an IPO and issuing a set quantity of shares. Investors in this closed end operation will then buy the shares like stock. They do have an important difference from typical stocks. Their shares are actually a certain interest within a given portfolio of securities that an investment advisor will actively manage. Usually they focus on a chosen and particular sector, geographic area and market, or industry.

Stock prices of these closed end funds vary with the market supply and demand forces. They also fluctuate based on the changes in the values of the underlying assets or securities which the fund contains. While there are many of these particular closed end funds, among the biggest in the fund universe is the Eaton Vance Tax-Managed Global Diversified Equity Income Fund.

There are a number of important characteristics which the closed end and open end funds share in common. Management teams run their investment portfolios in the two cases. The two types similarly assess and collect their annual expense ratio. They also may both provide capital gains and income distributions to their stakeholders.

The differences between the two types of funds in this universe are important. While open ended funds have their own particulars of trading, the closed end funds will trade exactly like stocks on their respective exchanges. The open ended variants receive a value and pricing only one time per day at the end of trading. The closed end variety will be both priced and traded repeatedly all through the market trading days. The closed end funds need a broker service to sell or buy them. In marked contrast to this, investors in the open ended funds many times may buy and sell their relevant shares directly with the provider of the fund.

A closed end fund also has some unique characteristics in the ways that its shares become priced. There is a difference between the funds NAV net asset value and the trading price. The NAV will be figured up at regular intervals throughout the day by computers. The actual price for which they trade on exchanges becomes set only by demand and supply forces interacting on the exchange. The end-result of this unique set of features is that the closed end fund might actually trade at a discount or premium to the net asset value.

This might occur for several different reasons. Those funds which are closed ended might be concentrating on a sector in the markets which happens to be more popular, such as biotechnology or alternative energy sources and technology. This would allow sufficient interest from investors to bid up the price of the fund to a premium over its actual NAV. When such funds are run by a stock picker with a successful track record, they can trade for a premium. At the same time, when investor interest is insufficient or there is a negative profile of risk and return perceived on the fund, it will often trade for a discount to net asset value.

CME Group

The CME Group is the Chicago Mercantile Exchange group of futures market companies. It calls itself the most diverse and global leading marketplace for futures and derivatives. The group itself is made up of four different DCM Designated Contract Markets. These include the Chicago Mercantile Exchange (CME), Chicago Board of Trade (CBOT), New York Mercantile Exchange (NYMEX), and the Commodity Exchange (COMEX). All four exchanges have their own commodities which they trade as well as different historical beginnings.

The world comes to the CME Group to manage its risk. The group provides the greatest variety of worldwide benchmark products in every significant class of assets. Through these offerings they assist businesses around the globe in compensating for the many risks they face in the uncertain global economy of today. Chicago Mercantile Exchange received the honors of Exchange of the Year and Risk Awards Winner for 2016.

Beyond their various trading products they offer an educational Futures Institute with a Futures Challenge competition to try to help potential investors learn how to trade these markets. This program takes six days and allows participants to learn interactively and simulate their own trading while they compete against others for cash awards. First place offers $1,000, second place $500, and third place a $250 reward. In order to compete, participants must complete six training modules, lay out their trade plan, and pass a quiz. This gives them a good understanding of the basic operations of futures trading.

The Chicago Mercantile Exchange represents the largest futures and options on futures exchange in the United States and the second largest one in the world. The commodities available to trade on this exchange center on currencies, interest rates, stock indices, equities, and a few agricultural products. CME was established in 1898 as a non profit company. In its early days investors knew the exchange as the Chicago Butter and Egg Board all the way till 1919. CME proved to be the first financial exchange in the U.S. to demutualize so that it could become a company owned by stockholders in November of 2000.

The CBOT's roots go back to 1848. In its initial days it allowed for trading of agricultural products like soybeans, corn, and wheat. Today it offers trading in agricultural as well as financial contracts. Futures contracts and options today are available on a number of additional products such as energy, U.S. Treasury bonds, gold, and silver.

For many decades the exchange functioned solely as an open auction market. Traders would get together in a trading pit and utilize hand signals to buy and sell. Now the CBOT also offers futures contracts that are electronically traded. The entity became a for profit company via an IPO on the New York Stock Exchange in October of 2005.

NYMEX is the largest futures exchange for physical commodities in the world. The trading done here occurs through the two divisions of NYMEX and COMEX. On NYMEX, traders can participate with platinum, palladium, and energy markets. In COMEX they are able to trade precious and industrial metals such as silver, gold, and copper. COMEX also offers index options on the FTSE 100 exchange in London.

During the day, NYMEX and COMEX utilize a system of open outcry on the floor. After regular trading hours, all trading is done on an electronic trading system. Dairy merchants originally founded the NYMEX as the Butter and Cheese Exchange of New York. NYMEX and COMEX merged together in 1994. Today the exchanges specialize in precious metals and energy products.

Commodities

Commodities turn out to be items that are taken from the earth, such as orange juice, cattle, wheat, oil, and gold. Companies buy commodities to turn them into usable products like bread, gasoline, and jewelry to sell to other businesses and consumers. Individual investors purchase and sell them for the purposes of speculation, in an attempt to make a profit.

Commodities are traded through commodities brokers on one of several different commodities exchanges, such as COMEX, or the Commodities Mercantile Exchange, NYMEX, or the New York Mercantile Exchange, and NYBOT, or the New York Board of Trade, among others.

Commodities are traded with contracts using a great amount of leverage. This means that with a small amount of money, a great quantity of the commodity in question can be controlled and traded. For example, with only a few thousand dollars, you as an investor are able to control a contract of one thousand barrels of heating oil or one hundred ounces of gold.

As a result of this high leverage that you obtain, the amounts of money made or lost can be significant with only relatively small moves in the price of the underlying commodity. This leverage results from the fact that commodities are nearly always traded using margin accounts that lead to significant risks for the capital invested. For example, with gold contracts, each ten cent minimum price move represents a $10 per contract gain or loss.

Commodity trading strategies center around speculation on factors that will affect the production of a commodity. These could be related to weather, natural disasters, strikes, or other events. If you believed that severe hurricanes would damage a great portion of the Latin American coffee crop, then you would call your commodity broker and instruct them to buy as many coffee contracts as they had money in the account to cover.

If the hurricanes took place and coffee did see significant damage in the region, then the prices of coffee would rise dramatically as a result of the negative weather, causing the coffee harvest to be more valuable. Your coffee contracts would similarly rise in value, probably significantly.

A variety of commodities can be traded on the commodities exchanges. These include grains, metals, energy, livestock, and softs. Grains consistently prove to be among the most popular of commodities available to trade. Grain commodities are usually most active in the spring and summer. Grains include soybeans, corn, oats, wheat, and rough rice.

Metals commodities offer you the opportunity to take positions on precious metals such as gold and silver. Changes in the underlying prices of base metals may also be traded in this category. Metals include copper, silver, and gold.

Energy commodities that you can trade are those used for heating homes and fueling vehicles for the nation. With the energy complex you can trade on supply disruptions around the world or higher gas prices that you anticipate. Energy commodities available to you are crude oil, unleaded gas, heating oil, and natural gas.

Livestock includes animals that provide pork and beef. Because these are staple foods in most American diets, they provide among the more reliable pattern trends for trading. Pork bellies, lean hogs, and live cattle are all examples of tradable livestock commodities.

Softs are comprised of both food and fiber types of commodities. Many of these are deemed to be exotic since they are grown in other countries and parts of the earth. Among the soft markets that you can trade are sugar, coffee, cocoa, cotton, orange juice, and lumber.

Commodities Futures Trading Commission (CFTC)

The CFTC is the regulatory agency whose acronym stands for the Commodities Futures Trading Commission. This group arose as a direct result of the Congressionally enacted Commodity Futures Trading Commission Act of 1974. Since that time, the group has carried the responsibility of regulating both the commodity options and futures markets. Their goals range from protecting investors from manipulative endeavors of firms to promoting fair, efficient, and competitive futures markets to stopping fraud and other abusive trading practices.

This regulatory group with vast powers is a fully independent agency under the umbrella of the United States' government. Besides their core objectives listed above, they seek to use their considerable powers to safeguard against systemic risk and to encourage transparent and financially viable markets. Following the Global Financial Crisis of 2007-2009 they have been working towards greater transparency and more stringent regulation of the swaps market, a multiple trillion dollar enterprise. The Dodd Frank Wall Street Reform and Consumer Protection Act of 2010 gives them this authority and ability to transition into this additional role as safe guardian of the swaps markets.

Five different committees comprise the CFTC. Each of these governing groups reports to a commissioner. The President of the United States appoints these commissioners directly which the Senate must then approve. The areas of concentration for the five committees include global markets, technology, agriculture, energy and environmental markets, and cooperation with the SEC Securities Exchange Commission. Each committee is made up of people with backgrounds in and connections to various industries and their interests. This includes the commodities exchanges, the futures exchanges, traders, the environment, and consumers.

The history of regulation of these futures and commodities markets stretches back nearly a century. While these contracts have been trading in the United States for longer than 150 years, they have only been Federally regulated from the 1920s. The original Congressional act that gave the government the authority to regulate and monitor these high stakes and leveraged markets was the Grain Futures Act of 1922. This authority was expanded by the Commodity Exchange Act of 1936.

With the advent of technological advances in the 1970s, the futures and commodity contracts trading has rapidly grown well beyond the original agricultural and other physical types of commodities. It now spans a dizzying range of financial instruments. Among these are the securities of foreign (and American) governments, foreign currencies, and foreign and American stock indices, and even individual company shares. Because of this rapid and spiraling expansion into countless other arenas, Congress decided to act to ensure that the oversight functions of these markets were adequate to handle the vast array of new activity.

They passed the Commodity Futures Trading Commission Act of 1974 in order to establish the CFTC. This new agency took the place of the U.S. Department of Agriculture and its Commodity Exchange Authority with regards to regulating both commodity futures and options exchanges and markets throughout the U.S. This new Act enabled vast changes to the old simple powers which the Commodity Exchange Act of 1936 had granted.

When their original mandate expired around the year 2000, Congress updated it with the Commodity Futures Modernization Act of 2000. This act mandated that the CFTC and the SEC begin to establish a combined regulatory authority for the relatively new single stock futures. These financial instruments had started trading in November of 2002. By 2003, such swaps had massively and exponentially expanded from the time when they had been originally introduced in the latter years of the 1970s.

As with the SEC, the CFTC does not exercise direct regulatory control for individual companies in the commodity and futures markets and their corporate financial soundness. The exception to this general rule pertains to huge swap participants and the now-regulated swap dealers. For these organizations, the CFTC actually sets the minimum capital standards as mandated by the Dodd-Frank Act.

Since 2014, the Commodities Futures Trading Commission has also gained oversight over the DCM designated contract markets. This includes the derivatives clearing organizations, swap execution facilities, swap dealers, swap data repository, commodity pool operators, and futures commission merchants, as well as other intermediary groups. This regulatory body also coordinates its efforts with major international counterparts, such as the British regulatory group the Financial Conduct Authority that oversees the London Metal Exchange.

Commodity Broker

A commodity broker commonly is an individual who makes commodity trades for his or her customers. The term also refers to the brokerage company that manages the trades for whom this broker works. This is an oversimplification as there are several different kinds of brokers. Where the CFTC Commodities and Futures Trading Commission is concerned, there are FCM Futures Commission Merchants, IB Introducing Brokers, and AP Associated Persons who are the individuals at the various commodity broker firms.

Commodity brokers do interesting jobs. They are involved in facilitating trades done in the commodity markets on behalf of the typical investor. The main other way to place such trades is by having one's own seat on the commodities exchange or by trading in the open outcry commodity pits. For the majority of people interested in trading these markets, they will be required to utilize the broker in some fashion to place their trades.

The commodity brokers themselves have one of two ways they can route their clients' trades through to the exchanges. They may have their company's floor traders who can place the trade literally on the exchange floor. Otherwise they will possess a special direct link trading platform that will allow them to place and then execute the trades via the electronic system on the various exchanges.

The commodity exchanges depend on these commodity brokers to gather in the business and clients for them. This is because they are unable to do so directly thanks to the governing rules on the way brokers carry out their business. The exchanges find it much simpler to carry out trade with only several dozens of brokerage firms than they do with literally hundreds of thousands of different customers trying to place their particular trades at the exchange directly.

Besides this valuable introducing service which the commodity broker provides, a great number of individual investors and traders need the brokers to offer them both recommendations and general position trading advice. This is because the commodities markets are often hard to comprehend in the beginning. Without the services and assistance of a good commodity broker, many investors would simply never engage in commodities trading ultimately.

Until the 1990s, the realm of commodities trading was limited to only the commodity pits at the various exchanges. The majority of the different orders came in from what was called a full-service commodity broker. The customers would first call their introducing brokers to make them aware of a trade they wished to enter. Next this broker would write up the order and place a timestamp on it. They immediately called their FCM clearing firm which takes their orders. The broker would articulate the exact trade from the ticket which their customer had phoned in to them.

The clearing firm was receiving calls at a special phone bank directly on the floor of the relevant exchange. A clerk would be taking down the order. The clerk would then write up a ticket to hand off to one of the floor brokers. These individuals stood in the trading pits and physically filled the order. The floor broker would then hand back the ticket to a runner who would run it back to the clerk. Finally the clerk would phone the introducing broker back and provide the trade confirmation and fill price. After the broker received his confirmation information, he would contact the original client back to provide the fill price and other information.

This form of manual trading via the telephone has all but disappeared in the past two decades. Now clients simply log on to the trading platform which their broker provided. They enter the trade information and hit buy or sell using their mouse. Such orders instantly route and match up at the relevant exchange's trading platform so that the confirmation on a market order is no more than one to two seconds away. This has made the trading process far more efficient, less expensive, and faster. Other traders insist on working with the full-service broker model still so they have a professional with whom they can talk about the various trading strategies and possibilities.

Commodity Exchange (COMEX)

The COMEX Commodity Exchange is the wholly owned subsidiary of the Chicago Mercantile Group that is responsible for both precious metals and base metals futures and options on futures trading. This once independent exchange is where the speculators, hedging companies, and traders all come to participate in trading FTSE 100 London exchange index options, along with precious metals silver and gold futures and options on futures, and industrial metals futures such as copper, aluminum, lead, and zinc futures.

For the first more than half a century of its existence, the Commodity Exchange proved to be an individually owned and run commodities futures exchange. COMEX arose in New York back in 1933 in the depths of the Great Depression. Through ups and downs in the markets, this exchange endured.

On December 31st of 1974, the Commodity Exchange launched its gold futures contract. This was the date when Americans regained the right to own gold again after a more than 40 year hiatus. This made it the biggest and most important center around the globe for gold futures and options. COMEX next launched options trading based on their gold futures in 1982 to cement their place in the world futures market and history. Silver has also been traded on the exchange since the 1970s.

COMEX merged with rival exchange NYMEX in 1994 to form the two still separately run exchanges under the listing of NYMEX Holdings, Inc. They did not obtain their publicly traded listing on the New York Stock Exchange until November 17th of 2006 when it began to trade under the ticker symbol of NMX. This new entity did not maintain its independence for long.

By March of 2008 the Chicago Mercantile Exchange Group of Chicago had conclusively committed to an agreement to purchase all of NYMEX holdings at a combined stock and cash offering that totaled $11.2 billion. The deal successfully completed in August of 2008.

From this point forward, the once independent and then jointly held NYMEX and COMEX exchanges continued their existence as Designated Contract

Markets of the CME Group. As such, they joined the two sister exchanges of the organization, the Chicago Mercantile Exchange and the Chicago Board of Trade. All four of these exchanges together make up the DCMs of the CME Group.

COMEX still maintains its separate identity under the CME Group. The precious metals trade is what it is best known for today. This precious metals complex volume that it transacts both monthly and annually is so large that it is greater than the volume of all competing futures exchanges in the world combined.

Commodities Exchange brings in participation from around the globe. A substantial number of the traders from East Asia, Europe, and the Middle East remain at their offices until the daily closure of COMEX.

This fact provides the Commodities Exchange with unparalleled liquidity almost around the clock. This more or less explains why it has been so very successful for the past near century despite intense competition in a constantly changing global trading environment. The hours that it trades continue to reflect the global participation. This is why the Commodities Exchange has opened ever earlier in order to meet the needs of the Asian, Middle Eastern, and European overseas trading clientele base.

Electronic trading on COMEX starts from the night previously from 4pm until the following morning at 7am. The regular trading session occurs from 8:20am through to 2:30pm. This means that COMEX is open for 21 hours per trading day from Monday to Thursday. Sunday electronic hours begin from 7pm EST. The group publishes both exchange open interest and volume every trading day.

Commodity Futures Modernization Act (CFMA)

In the year 2000, the U.S. Government passed the Commodity Futures Modernization Act. The act did several things. First it reaffirmed the regulatory authority of the Commodity Futures Trading Commission over all American futures markets. This authority became extended for a period of five years with this act.

A second and more significant result of the act came about as the government allowed Single Stock Futures to be traded for the first time in the United States. Other countries already allowed their investors to trade these particular types of futures when Congress passed this act. In America up to this point where the CFMA passed, it was illegal for investors to participate. Yet investors were eager to gain the leverage that these futures delivered.

Single Stock Futures are popular precisely because they do allow significant exposure to equity markets. A single stock future is a special kind of futures contract. The instrument allows a buyer to trade a certain number of shares in a single company at a price that they agree on now for a particular date in the future. The price is known as the strike price or futures price. The future date that the two parties set is the delivery date.

Buyers of these contracts are long the future in the stock. Sellers of the contract are short the stock in question. The buyer makes money if the price of the underlying stock increases, while the seller makes money if the value of the underlying stock declines. There is no cost to open the contract besides commissions and fees.

Single Stock Futures trade typically in contracts of 100 shares. Buying the contract does not cause any dividend or voting rights to transfer from the seller to the buyer. Futures trade using margin and provide tremendous leverage. There are no short selling rules applied to them as there are to stocks themselves.

Other countries adopted the Single Stock Futures trading ahead of the United States. The American market was not allowed to trade them before the passage of the Commodity Futures Modernization Act of 2000. This was because there was conflict between the two regulatory agencies the U.S. Securities and Exchange Commission and the Commodity Futures Trading Commission. The two could not work out which agency would regulate these new Single Stock Futures products and trading.

When the government passed the CFMA of 2000 into law, they agreed to a compromise. Both of these agencies decided to share the jurisdiction under a plan that allowed the Single Stock Futures to finally start trading on November 8 of 2002. This allowed the United States based traders to catch up with other countries who were already trading these instruments.

The Commodity Futures Modernization Act brought the United States into a global market of the Single Stock Futures that included Great Britain, Spain, South Africa, India, and other countries. The South African market has traditionally been the largest of the single stock futures marketplaces. Their average numbers of contracts amount to 700,000 each day.

Though the CFMA allowed single stock futures to be traded, this did not establish a marketplace for them on which they could be traded in the U.S. Two different companies began trading them initially. One of these closed. The remaining company trading these types of futures in the U.S. is now known as the One Chicago. This is a joint venture of the main Chicago commodities and futures exchanges the Chicago Mercantile Exchange, the Chicago Board Options Exchange, and the Chicago Board of Trade.

Commodity Markets

Commodity Markets refer to exchanges where individuals and businesses can trade, buy, or sell primary inputs and raw materials either in person or virtually (over the Internet or phones). These days there exist around 50 important commodities markets around the globe. Each of these works in some way to make trade and investment possible in around 100 different main commodities.

Commodities can be subdivided into two principal types. These are soft and hard commodities which entities trade on the commodities markets. Soft commodities refer to livestock and agricultural produce. This includes wheat, corn, sugar, coffee, cattle, pork bellies, and soybeans. Hard commodities are generally the kinds of natural resources which have to be extracted or mined. This includes such famous commodities as silver, gold, oil, and rubber.

A wide range of means exist for investing in such commodities. Investors have the ability to buy stocks in companies whose enterprises are based upon commodities prices. They might also buy them indirectly through ETF exchange traded funds, index funds, or mutual funds which specialize in them. There is a much more direct way to invest in these commodities though. This is through purchasing futures contracts on the commodities themselves from the commodity markets on one of the various commodities exchanges. Such a contract will contractually obligate the owner of the instrument to sell or buy the commodity for a preset price level on a future delivery date.

There are two cities in the United States which host the most important commodities markets and exchanges domestically. These are New York City and Chicago. A few less important exchanges are based in other cities of America. The biggest of them by far is the CME Chicago Mercantile Exchange which became so wealthy and powerful (as the CME Group) that it bought out a host of other rival exchanges. On the CME, investors and traders can buy, sell, and trade such well-known commodities as pork bellies and lean hogs, lumber, cattle, feeder cattle, butter, and milk.

Another exchange is the CBOT Chicago Board of Trade, which dates back to 1848 in Chicago. On this exchange, contracts include gold, ethanol, rice, oats, wheat, corn and soybeans.

On the NYBOT New York Board of Trade, there are a wide range of commodities. Chief among these are the standards of the commodities world orange juice, sugar, cocoa, ethanol, and coffee. On the NYMEX New York Mercantile Exchange investors can trade such commodities as gold, oil, copper, silver, platinum, palladium, aluminum, propane, heating oil, and even electricity.

There are also a few regional American commodity markets. These include the MGE Minneapolis Grain Exchange and the KCBT Kansas City Board of Trade. Both mostly concentrate their commodities offerings on agriculture. Among the biggest and most important international commodity markets are the LME London Metals Exchange and the Tokyo Commodity Exchange.

Nowadays, these commodity markets mostly trade on cutting-edged and state of the art electronic systems. There are a few of the United States' exchanges which still utilize the in-person, open outcry method. Commodities' trading which takes place outside the operating hours and locations of the exchanges is called the OTC over the counter market.

Commodity markets are highly regulated in the United States. It is the responsibility of the CFTC Commodity Futures Trading Commission to regulate the options and futures on commodities markets. Their primary goal is to ensure efficient, competitive, and transparent marketplaces which assist consumers by protecting the clients from manipulation, fraud, and unethical practices.

Once upon a time, the regular investors could not invest at all in commodity markets. This was because it took major amounts of money, time, and know-how to do it successfully. Thanks to the various numerous routes to the different commodities markets today, even those traders who are not professionals can take part in the excitement and opportunity that are the commodity markets.

Commodity Trading Adviser

Commodity Trading Adviser refers to either a firm or alternatively an individual that delivers personalized advice on the purchasing and selling of futures contracts, foreign exchange contracts, or options on futures. For individuals to be commodity trading advisers, they will have to have a CTA registration which is required by the NFA National Futures Association regulatory organization with oversight on the futures industry. The NFA proves to be the self-regulating organization of the commodities trading industry.

These CTAs work and receive their compensation based on commissions in exchange for their advice on the prospects and value of futures trading on options on futures, futures contracts, swaps, and off exchange retail Forex contracts.

Such Commodity Trading Advisers function much as do their stock market counterparts the financial advisors. The difference of course pertains to the delivering advice relevant to commodities trading, hence the CTA designation. Getting this CTA registration means that the applicant must pass proficiency exams such as the Series 3 National Commodity Futures Exam. There are other proofs of proficiency besides this particular exam as well.

One of these is registration with the National Futures Association. The CTA designation would not be required in cases where the adviser is providing advice to no more than 15 individuals in the last 12 months. Of course the individual or company would not be able to herald itself in front of the public as a CTA if they were not actually registered as such.

Such firms and individuals might be involved in many different industries or professions covered by the CEA Commodity Exchange Act or be otherwise registered. So long as this given advice on commodities investing proves to be only incidental to the main business of the firm or professional, then it is generally alright. This also applies if the advice they are dispensing does not require knowledge or is not specifically targeted to the commodity account of the customer in question.

As far as requirements go, the Commodity Trading Adviser designation will always be required for the principals involved in the commodity trading company along with all employees who receive the order from or provide the advice to the clients. This CTA will need to be registered in order to provide advice on all types of commodity investments. This includes everything from futures contracts, to options on futures, to swaps, to forwards, to Forex off-exchange contracts.

Such investments made in commodities typically require that a high degree of leverage be deployed. This argues for a greater level of expertise in order to safely trade such instruments and simultaneously avoid the possibility of taking major losses. It was in the late 1970s when the regulations surrounding commodity trading advisors began to arise as retail investors suddenly gained access to commodity market investing. It was then that the CFTC Commodity Futures Trading Commission began to expand its powers as well as the regulations it maintained surrounding being CTA registered little by little.

CTA funds should not be confused with simple CTA registration. These funds are usually hedge funds which employ futures contracts in order to attain their investing objectives. These CTA funds utilize a range of different trading strategies in order to attain said objectives. These might include such things as trend following and systematic trading. The best fund managers will actively manage the investments relying on a raft of strategies including fundamental and technical analyses, discretionary strategies, and trend following plus systematic trading together.

Common Stock

Common stocks are shares in an underlying company that represent equity ownership in the corporation. They are also known as ordinary shares. These are securities in which individuals invest their capital. Common stock is the opposite of preferred stock.

While common stock and preferred stock both represent ownership in the company, there are many important differences between the two. Should a company go bankrupt, common stock holders are only given their money after preferred stock owners, bond owners, and creditors. Yet, common stock performs well, typically seeing greater levels of price appreciation than does preferred stock.

Common stock typically comes with voting rights, another feature that preferred stock does not have. These votes are used in electing the board of directors at the company's annual meeting, as well as in determining such things as company strategy, stock splits, policies, mergers and acquisitions, and the sale of the company. Preemptive rights in common stocks refer to owners with these rights being allowed to keep the same proportion of ownership in the company' stock, even if it issues additional stock.

Common stocks do not always pay dividends to share holders, as preferred stocks typically do. The dividends of common stocks are not pre-set or fixed. This means that the dividend returns are not completely predictable. Instead, they are based on a company's reinvestment policies, earnings results, and practices of the market in the valuing of the stock shares themselves.

Common shares have various other benefits. They are typically less expensive than are preferred stock shares. They are more heavily traded and readily available as well. The spreads between the buying and selling prices on them tend to be tighter as a result. Common stocks generally provide capital appreciation as the price of the shares rises over time, assuming that the company continues to do well and meet or exceed expectations. Dividends are often paid to common share holders when these things prove to be the case.

Common stocks can be purchased in any denominated amount. Round lots of common stocks are sold by even one hundred share amounts. This means that five hundred shares of common stock would be considered to be five lots of common stock.

Common stocks represent principally capital gains types of investments, as an investor is looking to buy them low and sell them at a higher price. This leads to a capital gain when the stock is sold at this greater level. The capital gain is the difference between the selling price and the purchasing price. Common stocks can also be cash flow types of investments when they pay a reliable stream of dividends every quarter. These income amounts are typically smaller than the one time amounts realized in capital gains, though they are obtained four times per year on a quarterly basis, or occasionally more often on a monthly basis.

Contango

Contango refers to an unusual situation in which a given commodity's future price rises to a higher amount than the anticipated future spot price. As such, it also means that the commodity in question has a future date spot price that is lower than the present price. It relates that investors will pay a greater price for a commodity in the future than the price for the commodity which economists and analysts expect the commodity to fetch. There could be a variety of reasons for this. It could be that individuals would prefer to offer a higher premium over the spot in order to hold the future date of the commodity instead of having to pay for storage costs and/or any carrying costs for purchasing the commodity physically now.

There are other ways of looking at such markets that exist in contango. It is at once a scenario where the price for delivery of the futures contract under discussion must adjust to the downside in order to level off with the futures price. Similarly markets that are in this state show a futures curve (or forward curve) that is sloping upward. The prices must converge closer to each other quickly. If they do not in fact do this, then savvy investors will rapidly recognize that they can begin to set up trades to profit from the unnatural situation by utilizing arbitrage trading. These scenarios are actually not only unnatural, but they are expensive for investors who maintain positions which are net long. This is because the prices for the futures are declining while they are long the positions.

It is helpful to look at a clear example to demystify the concept. Consider than an investor might take a long position using a futures contract at the price of $100. In one year, the contract becomes due. Should the anticipated spot price in the future sit at $70, then the market is in contango. This means that the futures price has to come down (or the spot price for the future must rise). They will have to converge together in some way or another at one point in the near future.

Contango should never be confused with Backwardation. In fact this is the opposite of backwardation. Such a backwardation state is viewed as the typical and natural position of the commodities markets. These markets are in this state as futures prices sit lower than the anticipated spot price in the future in a given commodity. Such a view point means that the futures curve or forward curve slopes downward. This is most optimal for those investors who carry long positions because they hope for the price of the futures contract to increase.

Consider this particular example. The Brent Crude oil trades for $45 per barrel while the contract futures price in a year from now is $55. This means that the commodity is in a state of backwardation since the futures price must increase to converge along with the spot price that is anticipated in the future.

Those investors who have long net positions in commodities which suffer from this state of contango naturally lose when it is time for futures settlement or expiration to occur. The only way that such investors will find it tolerable to remain long in such commodities will be to purchase the contracts at greater prices. This would lead to a negative roll yield though.

As an example, consider Frank the investor who is holding a long futures gasoline contract. It will expire in 9 months. Assume that gasoline is in this state with a $19 price level while the commodity itself trades for only $13. Nine months later, the futures contract has fallen to $16 while the spot has risen to $15. In order for Frank to remain long, he will need to roll his futures contract. He might do this by buying one futures contract at a higher price of $22 that will expire three months from then. The downside would be that he will continue to suffer losses as he rolls such futures contracts over into the future month for a higher price.

Contrarian Investing

Contrarian Investing refers to a well-known style of investing which invests against the main going and popular market trends of the day. It does so through purchasing those assets which are performing poorly to later resell them when they outperform. An individual who proves to be a contrarian investor is of the opinion that those analysts who argue the market will rise are only doing this because they have fully invested their own funds and therefore have no additional purchasing power remaining to them. This would then be the market's peak. Similarly at that point when the analysts and so-called gurus argue a downturn is overdue they have already sold out their own holdings.

Another factor of contrarian investing has to do with those securities which have fallen from favor and therefore possess lower price to earnings ratios. This strategy involves selling and buying in the opposite direction of what the mainstream investors are doing at that given moment in time. They would then choose to wade into the market as other investors feel negative on it and that the value is cheaper than its true intrinsic value.

Overwhelming pessimistic sentiment on any given stock means that the price could be unfairly punished. Contrarians feel that the risks and downsides on the issue have already been blown out of proportion. The trick lies in determining which distressed stocks they should purchase or sell as the company makes a recovery and the stock price recovers accordingly as well. It often times means that the associated stocks will regain value at a far quicker pace than is normal for mid to large cap stocks. At the same time, having an over optimistic opinion on stocks which are over hyped can cause the opposite impact.

The character trait that many different contrarians share is their eternal view of an oncoming bear market. This is called the perm bear syndrome. They may not feel the market will be negative, yet they remain cautiously skeptical on the way that the mainstream investors view the stock markets. They realize that valuations which rise too high will finally end in inevitable declines as the growing expectations of investors do not pan out in the end. Such contrarian principles may be utilized effectively not only with entire markets, but a given industry or even individual company stocks.

This also means that contrarian investing shows many of the hallmarks of classical value investing. The two types of investors are seeking out price discrepancies which would mean that a given asset class is not fairly or fully valued in the given market conditions. There are countless value investors who believe that only a fine line exists between contrarian and value investing since they are both seeking out profits on undervalued securities.

One critical difference between the two disciplines lies in the relative importance of the Price to Earnings ratio, which is centerpiece of value investing. Contrarian investors will naturally consider it but more importantly attempt to ascertain the qualitative mood on the overall market. This means that they place priority emphasis on trading volume, analyst forecasts, and the tone and substance of media commentary.

The contrarian investors also put a lot of value on the basic principles of behavioral finance. They believe that investors act as a large collective and interact with trends as such. When stocks perform badly, this means that they will remain in this trend for a while. Similarly, stronger performing stocks will stay buoyant for many market sessions until something comes along to upset this powerful market moving trend.

Convertible Bond

A convertible bond is like a hybrid between a stock and a bond. Corporations issue these bonds which the bondholders may choose to convert into shares of the underlying company stock whenever they decide. Such a bond usually pays better yields than do shares of common stocks. Their yields are also typically less than regular corporate bonds pay.

Convertible bonds provide income to their investors just as traditional corporate bonds do. These convertibles also possess the unique ability to gain in price if the stock of the issuing company does well. The reasoning behind this is straightforward. Because the bond has the ability to be directly converted into stock shares, the security's value will only gain as the stock shares themselves actually rise on the market.

When the stock performs poorly, the investors do not have the ability to convert the convertible bond into shares. They only gain the yield as a return on the investment in this case. The advantage these bonds have over the company stock in these deteriorating conditions is significant.

The value of the convertible instrument will only drop to its par value as long as the company that issues it does not go bankrupt. This is because on the specified maturity date, investors will obtain back their original principal. It is quite correct to say that these types of bonds typically have far less downside potential than do shares of common stocks.

There are disadvantages as well as advantages to these convertible bonds. Should the issuer of the bond file for bankruptcy, investors in these kinds of bonds possess a lower priority claim on the assets of the corporation than do those who invested in debt which was not convertible. Should the issuer default or not make an interest or principal payment according to schedule, the convertibles will likely suffer more than a regular corporate bond would. This is the flip side to the higher potential to appreciate which convertibles famously possess. It is a good reason that individuals who choose to invest in single convertible securities should engage in significant and extended research on the issuer's credit.

It is also important to note that the majority of these convertible bonds can be called. This gives the issuer the right to call away the bonds at a set share price. It limits the maximum gain an investor can realize even if the stock significantly outperforms. This means that a convertible security will rarely offer the identical unlimited gain possibilities which common stocks can.

If investors are determined to do the necessary research on an individual company, they can purchase a convertible bond from a broker. For better convertible diversification, there are numerous mutual funds which invest in only convertible securities. These funds are provided by a variety of major mutual fund companies.

Some of the biggest are Franklin Convertible Securities, Vanguard Convertible Securities, Fidelity Convertible Securities, and Calamos Convertible A. Several ETF exchange traded funds provide a similar convertible diversification with lower service charges. Among these are the SPDR Barclays Capital Convertible Bond ETF and the PowerShares Convertible Securities Portfolio.

It is important to know that the bigger convertible securities portfolios such as the ETFs track have a tendency to match the performance of the stock market quite closely in time. This makes them similar to a high dividend equity fund. Such investments do offer possible upside and diversification when measured against typical holdings of bonds. They do not really offer much in the way of diversification for individuals who already keep most of their investment dollars in stocks.

Core Holding

A Core Holding refers to a longer term investment which forms the basis of an investor's portfolio or a corporation's assets and operations. Where investments are concerned, one popular strategy for these common cores is to mostly own investments which follow the overall market like the S&P 500. It is through S&P 500 Index Funds that investors are able to participate in this otherwise difficult to acquire and maintain baskets of 500 individual stocks.

Investors might secondarily focus their investment efforts on those holdings which do not show the same results as the market as a whole, like with individual stock holdings. A satellite holding is the name for such secondary types of investments. When investors own a good core holding, they attain the ability to take risks on more volatile holdings in the remainder of their portfolio.

When core portfolio and satellite portfolio holdings are well-constructed, they will generally outperform the results of those rival portfolios based only on a collection of individual stocks. The reason for this is that the majorities of investors are not adept at properly assembling a well- and truly diversified portfolio by only relying on individual stocks. With core and satellite strategies, investors end up owning portfolios which are simple to rebalance and to oversee since they only possess a few different investments overall. Such a strategy is designed to reduce volatility and minimize the negative effects of commissions, fees, and taxes on overall portfolio returns.

Other investors will seek to only have core holdings in their portfolios. These must then be reliable investments which deliver steady and stable returns every year. They would be the key foundation for the remainder of most investors' portfolios. Noncore holdings would be those that are not central to the overall strategy. They could instead concentrate on a single sector like technology stocks, or on a single overseas region like Europe. Such more specifically focused investments can boost portfolio returns, yet they also likely increase the volatility of the overall portfolio.

The entire U.S. stock markets are completely dominated by a relatively small handful of mega multinational corporations. These huge corporations make up approximately three quarters of the entire stock market valuation. This is why for most investors, their core holdings will have to focus on these same overly dominant stock giants. Large capitalization blend funds are a good place for most investors to start. They own huge companies that boast mid-range stock prices. These companies rarely lead the outperformers list, yet they also do not typically head the underperformers list either.

More conservative investors might prefer a conservatively based large value fund. Such funds plow their investors' money into the large and extremely established firms whose stocks remain cheaper than their large cap peers. They also commonly concentrate on those firms whose stocks pay generous, consistent, and increasing dividend payouts. These prove to be the lowest risk ranked funds of all the categories which Morningstar follows.

Smart investors will not simply put all of their investment eggs in the proverbial United States' markets basket. Foreign equity funds are therefore another good core holding choice for most investors because of this critical diversification idea. Such funds will concentrate on the developed markets of the world, as with the MSCI World fund. They will buy the shares of the world's leading international firms, such as BP Oil, HSBC Bank, Nestle, UniLever, Royal Dutch Shell, Glaxo Smith Kline, Vodafone, Diageo, and Astra Zeneca.

A last recommendation for core holdings centers on solid bond funds. These should be ones that focus on high quality bond issues. Intermediate term bonds are the best ones, since they possess shorter maturities and are not as volatile with regards to interest rate swings as the longer term holdings would be.

Crypto Currency

A crypto currency turns out to be a virtual currency. These alternative currencies deploy cryptography as a means of security. It makes them extremely hard to counterfeit since this security feature is complex. An element that consistently defines the various crypto currencies and simultaneously endears them to users is their independent nature. They cannot be issued nor controlled by any of the global central banks or world monetary authorities. The theory is that this makes it difficult (if not outright impossible) for governments to manipulate or control such currencies.

Unfortunately for the governments of the world, this somewhat anonymous characteristic of the global crypto currencies also makes them an ideal vehicle for illegal and otherwise unethical activities. Among these are drug dealing, tax evading, and money laundering carried on around the world.

The world's original (and still leading) crypto currency proved to be Bitcoin. This was the first of the alternative currencies that caught on with the general and investing public. A mysterious individual or group of individuals who go only by the pseudonym of Satoshi Nakamoto created and launched Bitcoin back in 2009. These BTC (as they are abbreviated) must be mined in a tedious process which involves solving complex computer algorithmic problems. There is a maximum limit of 21 million to the total number of BTC which may be created. As of September of 2015, already 14.6 million of these Bitcoins had been mined and were circulating. The success of Bitcoin has been so vast that other competing crypto currencies have been spawned over the years.

The greatest and most successful of these is Ethereum, or Ether tokens. Others that have appeared include Litecoin, PPCoin, and Namecoin. These descendants of Bitcoin are often referred to as altcoins. This name is a derivative of the phrase bitcoin alternative. All of these crypto currencies have at least one thing in common. They all rely on a decentralized control. This stands out in direct contrast to the centralized banking systems of the mainstream traditional currencies.

There are a number of advantages and also some disadvantages to the major crypto currencies and this ground breaking technology. On the positive side, the crypto currencies enable simpler, cheaper, faster transfers of funds between one party and another in a commercial transaction. The transfers of funds occur utilizing both private and public keys to provide greater security.

The transfers happen with the lowest of possible processing and transaction costs. This has disrupted traditional banking and finance significantly. Individuals who transact in a crypto currency are able to side step the hefty middle man fee of financial institutions such as banks with their wire transfer costs, or with money transfer services like Western Union and Money Gram. These last two services charge upwards of ten percent transfer fees.

The great brilliance of Bitcoin and the other major crypto currencies lies in their block chain technology which acts as storage for the transaction ledger online. In fact all transactions in the BTC technology and currency which have ever happened are maintained in the block chain ledger database. Major banks like JP Morgan Chase have already invested heavily in initiatives to reduce the transaction costs of payment processing and transfers utilizing especially the up and coming Ethereum crypto currency.

This does not mean that there are not downsides to the crypto currencies. As they lack a central offline repository, the balance of an online wallet can be completely wiped out by either the invasion of hackers who steal it or the advent of a single computer crash if owners do not backup their holdings with data copies. There is also the negative of the wildly gyrating volatility in the currencies, which can easily swing up or down by even ten or twenty percent in a single trading session or week. There have also been more than 40 instances of online hacking theft of the various Bitcoin exchanges and companies in the short decade of Bitcoin history.

Currency Pairs

Currency pairs are two currencies expressed in terms of each other. They are price quoted in the forex market. One currency's value is always expressed against another currency, such as with GBP/USD. This creates the values of currency comparisons against other currencies. In a currency pair, the first one listed is referred to as the base currency. Forex market brokers call the second currency in the pair the quote currency. The pairing explains the numbers of units of the quote currency investors need to buy a base currency unit.

Forex trades always concern two of these pairs. When investors purchase a currency in the forex market they are buying the one and selling another at the same time. This does not change the fact that the currency pair is still one unit whether the trader buys it or sell it. When they buy the pair, they are actually purchasing the base currency by selling the quote currency. When they sell the pair, they are instead selling the base currency by buying the quote currency.

Currency pair values are expressed by bid and ask prices. The bid is how much it will cost to buy a single unit of base currency in quote currency. The ask price is the selling price to obtain a single unit of the quote currency in terms of the base currency.

As an example, consider the EUR/USD. When this pair is quoted as EUR/USD = 1.12, a buyer who purchases it receives one euro for $1.12 US. A seller of this pair would be trading 1 euro to obtain $1.12 US. These pairs can be quoted in reverse as well, as in USD/EUR. For example in this configuration the pair might list for .8975. Buying a single dollar would cost .8975 Euros with this example. Generally the more expensive currency is listed as the base currency for the pairs in forex markets.

In fact the most commonly traded of the pairs is the EUR/USD. This pairing receives not only interest from people who wish to change dollars for Euros and vice versa. There is additional interest generated by other Euro cross pairs, such as with EUR/CHF against the Swiss Franc, EUR/GBP against the British Pound, and EUR/JPY against the Japanese Yen.

The interest in these pairs is typically opposite the direction of the U.S. dollar. This means that when the market is negative on the U.S. dollar, the Euro will receive bids because of the general selling of USD. The other pairs against the dollar which are less liquid as in USD/CHF also are sold using the more liquid pairings. This would also create bids for Euros in the EUR/USD pair and market.

The second most active pair of forex currencies is the USD/JPY. This pair has a history of having the greatest correlation to political relations between the U.S. and Japan. Many U.S. administrations have employed this currency pair in an attempt to influence trade with Japan. The Chinese have taken over the top trade tension place for the U.S. in Asia. USD/JPY still functions in its role as Chinese regional currency proxy.

There are other major currency pairs that occupy the majority of trades in the Forex markets. The pairs that are considered among the major are the ones that trade against the other majors. Besides the Euro, the U.S. Dollar, and the Japanese Yen, these majors include the British pound, the Canadian Dollar, the Swiss Franc, the New Zealand Dollar, and the Australian Dollar.

Currency Standards

Currency standards are the typical means for fixing a currency at a set rate nowadays. A Currency Standard means that the value of a currency is pegged to a stronger, more internationally recognized currency, like the Euro or the Dollar. These Currency Standards are similarly known as reserve currency standards.

Within the world reserve currency system, single national currencies actually assume the important standard, or role, that gold always carried for hundreds of years in the gold standard. Another way of putting this is that a nation would fix the rate of its proprietary currency to so many units against another country's currency. As an example, Great Britain might choose to fix its British Pound Sterling currency to the Euro at a real exchange rate of one pound equals one point twenty-five Euros. In order to keep this fixed rate of exchange, Britain's central bank, the Bank of England, would have to always be prepared to offer Euros for Pounds, or Pounds for Euros, upon demand for this set rate of exchange. The principal way that the Bank of England would affect this would be to keep Euros in its reserves against a day when a greater demand existed for Euros to be exchanged for Pounds on the world FOREX markets.

These currency standards stand in contrast to the gold standard. Under the long held, incredibly stable period of the gold standard, central banks instead held gold to back up and exchange against their own currency. Using the reserve currency standard, the same central banks instead keep a stockpile of the chosen reserve currency on hand. In whichever case, the reserve currency will be the one to which a given nation fixes its own currency.

The majority of nations that decide to fix their exchange rates will peg to one of two types of currencies. You might see them choose one of the main currencies utilized in international transactions for settlement. Alternatively, they could elect to fix their currencies to that of one of their major trading partners, which would also make sense for settlement purposes.

Because of this, you see many countries around the world peg their national exchange rate to the United States dollar, since it still proves to be the currency that is most widely held and traded around the world. As another fixing choice, the Euro is increasingly utilized for pegs. Fourteen different African countries which had all been French colonies in the past had set up the CFA, or colonies of French Africa, Franc zone. When they did this, they fixed their new CFA Franc to the French Franc.

After the French abandoned their Franc in favor of the newer continent wide Euro in 1999, the CFA Franc became pegged to the Euro. Another example is the Common Monetary Area of South Africa. Participating in this are Namibia, Swaziland, and Lesotho. These nations fix their currency against the South African Rand, the powerhouse currency of the South African continent, and their biggest trading partner by far.

Currency Trading

Currency trading is speculating on the largest financial market on earth. Despite the fact that this is the world's largest, most liquid, and most impressive market, many individual traders do not know much about it. This is mostly because until Internet trading became popular, access to these markets was limited.

Only the large banks, multinational businesses, and shadowy hedge funds were able to trade them. Today the currency markets trade 24 hours per day, 6 days per week. This several trillion dollar market trades on every continent. Trillions of dollars per day change hands in the foreign exchange marketplace. All of this combines to make currency trading markets the most easily accessed on earth.

This speculative currency trading is not the main reason that the Forex, or Foreign Exchange, markets exist. They were set up to help big international companies change currencies from one kind to another. Many of these corporations need to trade currency constantly to pay for such costs as international goods and services payments, payroll, and acquisitions overseas.

Despite the origins of these currency markets, only around 20% of the total market volume comes from these company trades. An incredible 80% of the daily trades in the currency markets are from speculative currency trading hedge funds, large banks, and individual investors who want to take a position on one of the major currency pairs.

Currency traders are able to engage in these markets without many of the constraints that plague the stock markets. If individuals believe that the GBP/USD pair will drop dramatically, they are able to short sell as much of the currency pair as they desire. There are no uptick rules with currency trading. There are similarly no position size limits in currency trading.

Traders could buy tens of billions of any currency pair if they had the money to cover the trade. There are also no rules on insider trading with this type of currency trading. It does not exist. Economic data in Europe is routinely leaked several days ahead of the official release date.

Another way that currency markets are different from stock markets is that there are no commissions in foreign exchange markets. All currency companies are dealers. These dealers take on the counterparty currency in any trade. They earn their money with the spreads between the bid, the cost to buy the currency pair, and the ask, the cost to sell it.

Currency trading is always done in pairs. When a trader enters such a trade, the person is long one currency in the pair and short the other currency. Selling 100,000 GBP/USD means that the trader has sold the British Pounds and bought the U.S. dollars. This means that the trader is long dollars and short pounds.

Currency valuations are expressed in pips, or percentages in point. These pips prove to be the littlest trade increment in the foreign exchange pairs. This makes one pip equal to one-one hundredth of a percent. In all pairs except the Japanese Yen, these prices are quoted out to the fourth decimal point. This means that EUR/USD would be quoted in terms of 1.1595.

There are many different minor currency pairs on the market. The majority of foreign exchange dealers only allow individuals to trade the most seven widely traded and liquid pairs. These include the four major pairs of Euro/Dollar, British Pound/Dollar, Dollar/Swiss Franc, and Dollar Japanese Yen. The other three pairs allowed are the three commodity currency pairs of New Zealand Dollar/Dollar, Australian Dollar/Dollar, and Dollar/Canadian Dollar.

Currency trading is typically done in margin type accounts. The leverage is typically 100:1 on most of the major currency pairs. This means that currency traders are able to control 100,000 of a currency pair with only $1,000 of the base unit currency.

Day Trading

Day Trading is the stock market strategy of purchasing and selling a given stock all in the say day. This form of trading is completely different from long term investing or even momentum or swing trading, which involves time frames of several days to several weeks. Day traders often try to make money on small movements in the stock price. In these cases they are attempting to leverage bigger amounts of investment capital to capture these lesser price movements in indexes or stocks that are extremely liquid.

Day trading can provide profits that allow individuals to make a living at it. It also can be an easy way for traders to lose money if they do not stick to a carefully designed strategy or if they have no experience in it. There are a variety of strategies that these day traders follow. These include selection, entry, and exit policies.

Entry strategies are critical for day traders. These traders first have to find a stock which works well for the day trading concept. Stocks with both liquidity and volatility are the best candidates. When a stock has liquidity, it is easy to get in and get out of the stock with small spreads and little slippage. Spreads represent the distance between a stock's bid and ask price. Slippage is the variance between a stock's actual trading price and the anticipated trading price.

Volatility proves to be the best way to measure the range of the daily price movements. It is in this daily volatility range that day traders work. For day traders, greater volatility can mean the chance to make higher profits or lose more money.

After day traders pick out the right kind of stock, they have to learn the best ways to find good entry points into the stock. Three tools that they utilize in this task are Level II quotes, daily candlestick charts, and actual time news services. Level II quotes show the orders as they occur. Daily candlestick charts give traders price action analysis. Actual time news service is critical since these companies release it directly as the news happens. This kind of news makes stocks move.

Daily and intraday candlestick charts provide a variety of useful information to day traders. They are able to see the volume of the stock and whether it is decreasing or increasing in picture form. The candlesticks can also form patterns like dojis and engulfing patterns that provide insight to these traders. Candlestick patterns may also provide useful elements of technical analysis such as triangle shapes and trend lines of a stock.

The entry strategies that day traders utilize are based on the identical tools that longer term traders employ. A key difference surrounds the proper time to exit the trade. Day traders are looking for the point where the interest in the stock in question decreases. They see this using their Level II volume tools.

Exit strategies are the other main component of a day trading policy. Traders using leverage trade on margin. Margin is borrowed money from the stock broker that multiplies potential gains and losses. Using margin means that a trader has a greater vulnerability to dramatic price movements in the stock than would a longer term trader not using margin. This is why day traders must use stop losses. These exit orders allow traders to sell out of a stock position and limit the losses.

The two different types of stop losses that day traders employ are physical and mental. Physical stop losses are more precise and disciplined. Traders program them to sell the stock at a particular price level that fits the loss the trader is prepared to take.

Mental stop losses are those points where the trader feels his or her reasons for entering have been invalidated. The trader would simply give a sell order at market price to close out of the position immediately. The problem with mental stop losses is that it is too easy for emotions to get involved and for the trader to continue to hold on to the position hoping that it will turn around. This can magnify losses when traders fall into this trap. Day traders should never risk more in a single than they can afford to lose both mentally and financially.

Debenture

A Debenture refers to a form of debt instrument. The differentiating factor of such instruments is that they do not have the physical backing of either collateral or assets securing them. Instead, they are only guaranteed by the overall reputation and creditworthiness of the issuing corporation or municipality. Governments and corporations alike commonly issue such bonds in order to obtain much needed fresh capital. As with other forms of bonds, these are recorded in indentures.

Since such Debentures come without any collateral, the buyers of bonds purchase them on the hopes that the issuer will not default on interest and principal repayments. Government examples of these kinds of bonds abound in the marketplace. T-bills and T-bonds are both classic debentures. They have always been deemed to be completely risk free as the government can always raise taxes to pay its debt obligations or resort to printing money in order to cover them.

Corporations most often resort to issuing Debentures as their longer term loan vehicles. They typically come with a maturity date that is fixed at an interest level that is similarly fixed. Corporations will most often make such interest payments ahead of giving any dividends to the stock shareholders, as with other types of senior debt obligations. This makes debentures beneficial with their lower interest rate and farther away repayment date as compared to other forms of debt bonds and loans corporations and governments can take out.

Two forms of Debentures exist. These are either non-convertible or convertible ones. The convertible ones represent bonds that the holders can convert into stock shares from the issuer once a pre-set time period has elapsed. Investors like these kinds of bonds more than others since they gain the ability to convert to more lucrative and price appreciative stock. Issuers appreciate them best since they come with the lowest of interest rates.

Alternatively, the non-convertible types are more regular Debentures which cannot be exchanged for stock in the issuer. The compensation for this lack of flexibility in the instrument is that they come with a higher interest rate than their non-convertible debenture cousins.

Every debenture on the market comes with particular characteristics. The trust indenture must be drafted. This agreement is set up between the managing trust and the issuing corporation. The coupon rate must subsequently be determined, as it is the critical interest rate which the firm will pay the investors and debt holders. While the rate is often fixed, it may also be floating. This comes down to how high the firm's credit rating or the credit rating of the bond issue itself proves to be.

With non-convertible debentures, the maturity date turns out to be among the key features of the issue. Maturity date is the point when the issuer has to return the principal to the investors. Yet the firms possess several options for how they will repay this money. It is most common for companies to do a redemption from their capital. This means that the issuers will simply offer a lump sum one-time payment on the maturity date. The second choice is known as the debenture redemption reserve. In this form, the issuer is allowed to transfer a set quantity of funds every year up to the point where the debenture has been fully repaid into the fund by the maturity date.

With either way, the company or government agency still repays all funds due on the maturity or repayment date. The only difference lies in whether they set aside the funds in part ever year or have to front them all entirely in the year they are due to be repaid.

Debt Fund

A Debt Fund refers to an investment pool. This might be either an exchange traded fund or a mutual fund. In it the core assets will be various types of fixed income investments. They could choose to invest in longer term bonds or shorter term ones, money market instruments, securitized products, or even floating rate debt. The debt funds feature lower fee ratios on average than do the comparable equity funds. This is in part because the total management costs prove to be significantly lower for the debt funds than for the equity funds.

The primary objectives for investing in a debt fund will commonly be the generation of income as well as preservation of the original capital. They often consider their performance against a comparable major benchmark as a means of measuring success and judging absolute returns with these debt funds. As such, they will invest in as many promising opportunities as they can find. This might include MIP's monthly income plans, liquid funds, STP's short term plans, Gilt funds, and FMP's fixed maturity plans.

In general, these debt funds will be preferred by those investors who do not want to experience scary high volatility which investing in the stock market easily often can present. It means that such a debt fund will deliver low but steady income as compared to equity funds. Yet the volatility is minor by comparison. Debt funds like these provide a number of advantages.

The tax rules have changed to favor them. Investors will have to stay invested for minimally three years in order to enjoy the advantage of lower taxed longer term capital gains. Those which are redeemed in under three years will be treated as ordinary income for taxable purposes. Debt funds thus become far more tax efficient than even fixed deposits when investors hold them for at least three years. Debt funds will only be taxed at the rate of 20 percent once they are indexed, which is often considerably lower than many investors' otherwise earned income tax rate.

There is also no tax deduction for debt funds at the source, known as TDS on any and all gains which they realize. The returns also are linked to the market performance though they do not offer corresponding returns. When interest rates rise, they can lose, though it is a remote chance of them losing. The maturity of the various holdings defines the actual volatility of the debt fund. Those funds which mostly hold shorter term bonds will not demonstrate much volatility and will still provide returns that are approximately equal to the prevailing interest rates.

Debt funds also allow individuals to invest in SIP's. These are the smartest ways to purchase equity or debt funds. With large sums, they can be sunk into a debt fund that will make systematic transfers into the plan or any fund for which an individual opts. Each month, a fixed and predetermined sum will move from the debt fund over to the other funds that the investors selected.

There will also be an exit load on debt funds. This is the tradeoff for vastly greater liquidity than with many competing investments. Individuals are able to withdraw at any point with only a day's notice. Some of the funds do assess a penalty for leaving in under a preset minimum period. Exit loads range from a reasonable .5 percent on up to a steeper two percent penalty. The minimum holding period is often anywhere from six months on out to as long as two years.

Digital Currency

A digital currency refers to an asset which possesses numerous interesting and groundbreaking characteristics. On the one hand, they are much like traditional forms of money that people spend and keep, such as cash and coins. On the other hand, such currencies are not physical. This means that they do not have literal physical representations or the associated physical limitations. This currency is kept in a digital wallet, which can have physical characteristics if it is a cold storage type of digital wallet.

Digital currency in particular and electronic money in general is gradually becoming more significant as the world continuously evolves into a society that is more and more cashless. The amount of money supply which is expressed in digital format is constantly growing. Thanks to the rising popularity of such crypto-currencies as especially Bitcoin, there now exists the distinct possibility of migrating entirely away from traditional paper bills and coins at some point in the future.

Such digital currency only can exist and function when secure transactions are guaranteed online. This makes these currencies both an occupant and hostage of digital environments. They are generally represented and depicted in the form of information. Bitcoin has become so popular that numerous companies currently accept this form of digital currency. PayPal even allows for the utilization of Bitcoin now.

It is interesting to note that Bitcoin is not the only digital currency option available to individuals and businesses for transactions. A range of such currencies exist which can be used to pay for transactions. The next five most important after Bitcoin are Litecoin, Darkcoin, Peercoin, Dogecoin, and Primecoin. They have many advantages over traditional money.

The first of these is the instant transfer ability. Individuals are no longer required to wait on a central clearinghouse somewhere to handle the transaction. The days of from one to five business days waits for transfers are long gone thanks to these digital currencies. Crypto-currencies are so popular precisely because the effect of such a transfer is instantaneous.

The majority of these digital currencies also come with no fees. Whatever something costs in Bitcoin or another such digital currency, people simply pay with it at transaction cost and no hidden fees are applied. This is a stark difference from many credit card or even PayPal transactions.

Individuals and businesses especially love the fact that these digital currencies come completely without borders. This means that a seller or buyer does not have to be concerned with exchange rates or foreign transaction fees (which are often exorbitant). Cross border transactions are simple and effective to put through, though people must still watch the exchange rate at which they are offered in the local currency into which they are paying.

For the majority of applications and scenarios, these crypto-currencies also prove to be extremely secure. It is the digital wallet where the danger lies. The money is not being stored in a bank vault or even on a bank computer. The wallet must be backed up on a daily basis to prevent it from being lost. In order to ensure that it is secure, the only way to guarantee this is by utilizing cold storage.

Cold storage takes the digital wallet completely offline and off network. It means that the "pin code" like authorization element will be stored on a small device that resembles a USB miniature drive device. The nature of these devices is that they do not accept software. This means that Trojan Horses and viruses which steal information can not be imprinted on them. They also are never online long enough to be hacked, as users only connect them to a computer long enough to digitally sign the transaction.

These digital currencies have convincingly changed the rules of the financial transaction game. Their limits are two fold. The first is that a business must be willing to accept Bitcoin or rival currencies in order for a consumer to pay with it. The second is that digital currency regulation is inevitable. Central banks are jealous animals. They are already suspicious of their monopolized currency-printing functions being assumed in a non-regulated and more difficult to track environment by a non-centralized form of money.

Dividend Stocks

Dividend Stocks refer to stocks that pay especially generous and predictable shares of the corporate earnings out to their share holders. They are especially important for those investors who require dependable continuous streams of income off of their investment portfolios, such as retirees. This is why the optimal stock portfolio for those who are officially retired includes a strong and diverse mixture of industry-leading corporations which provide consistent, generous dividend yields.

These Dividend Stocks are famous for paying out significant stock dividends as a distribution on their earnings. They may pay this in the form of additional shares or as cash, depending on the wishes of the share holder in question. Sometimes the company will declare a stock dividend instead of a cash dividend, removing the ability of the shareholder to choose the form in which the dividend actually pays. When dividends become payable strictly as more stock, they are also known as stock splits.

For the companies that declare regular cash dividends of these Dividend Stocks, with each share stake holders have, they receive a set portion of the earnings from the corporation. This is literally being paid for simply owning the stock shares.

Consider a real world example to better understand how these Dividend Stocks work out in practice. Gillette, the world famous market leader in the shaving razors industry, may pay a dividend of $4 on an annual basis. Typically these dividends will be paid practically on a quarterly basis. This means four times each year Gillette would provide a $1 payout for each share of stock which the stake holders possess. If an investor owned 100 shares, he or she would receive four checks per year of $100 each check at approximately the conclusion of each quarter.

Most dividends from these Dividend Stocks come out in cash. Investors have the option to have them reinvested into additional company stock shares. Sometimes the corporation will provide a more advantageous reinvestment price than the current market prices to encourage such reinvesting of dividends in the company stock. These plans are called DRIPS (Dividend Re Investment Plans).

There are also occasional special dividends offered on an only one-time basis. They could be provided if the company wins a large and lucrative lawsuit, liquidates its share of an investment and receives a windfall payout, or sells part of the business to another firm for cash. These dividends can be made in cash, property, or stock share dividends.

There are several important dates with which Dividend Stocks' investors need to be familiar. These are declaration date, date of record, ex-dividend date, and payment date. Declaration date is the calendar day when the company's Board of Directors announces a dividend payout. This is the point where the firm adds a liability for the dividend payout to its company books. This means that it owes money (or shares) to the stake holders. This date will be the one when they announce both the date of record as well as the dividend payment date.

The date of record is the one where the corporation will review the appropriate records to determine who is holding the shares and is thus eligible for the dividends. Only holders of record will receive the dividend payment. The ex-dividend date is the day after which any investors who wish to receive dividends must own the shares. Only stake holders who possess shares on the day before the ex-dividend date get paid. Finally dividends are literally doled out on the payment date.

While most stock companies will pay out dividends on either a quarterly or half yearly basis, real estate investment trusts are structured differently. They pay out their dividends on an every-month basis as they receive monthly income from their various commercial, industrial, and/or residential properties.

Dotcom Bubble

The dotcom bubble inflated during the wild Internet and computer software heyday of the mid to late 1990s. It was epitomized by the dramatic and fast paced rise of equity markets which were powered by Internet-based firms and startup investments. In the midst of this bubble, the values and capitalizations of the stock markets rocketed up astronomically.

The technology-heavy NASDAQ (the so-called "stock market for the 90s and beyond") index roared from a mere 1,000 level to over 5,000 in the years from only 1995 to 2000. Incredible fortunes were then made and lost in the span of half a decade as the bubble violently exploded in a matter of months.

It all began with the stocks of software firms which turned in excellent performances during the 1990s decade. As enthusiasm for this software industry was running at an all time high, many young just out of college and tech-savvy entrepreneurs decided to create their own tiny software startup outfits. Employees of these wiry college students and graduates were mostly paid in pizza and soft drinks, with a promise of stock share wealth to follow if they succeeded. Nearly all software startups of the day aspired to expand into the next Microsoft company.

It made sense that finally a number of these ambitious startup companies would gain the coveted interest of the venture capital firms and funds that were eager to finance the new startups of the brave new frontier of the Internet. They hoped to and actually succeeded in taking a great number of them public before the crash, reaping eye-watering profits in the process. Startups saw the writing on the wall and started to pay their employees with company stock shares instead of money.

The overwhelming majority of such software startup companies of the time arose in San Francisco area Silicon Valley. This became one of the great technology Meccas of the West. By the late 1990s decade, the NASDAQ technology index was running at a torrid pace, turning many investors concentrating on technology into overnight millionaires and billionaires.

Investors continued to recklessly throw their money into these startups believing that they could not fail based solely on the strength of their prescient ideas. All thoughts to traditional measures of a company such as track record, balance sheets, profitability, and revenues versus expenses went out the proverbial window. Investors only cared for the chances of a company involved in technology possibly one day becoming profitable. The overwhelming majority of both venture capitalists and investors abandoned the traditional and time tested approach of analyzing companies out of a fear that they might miss out on the rapidly expanding omnipresence of the Internet and software.

In retrospect, this radical increase in stock prices that defied logic could not simply go on forever. The nation had never before dreamed of such an impressive and rapid growth of capital as it was experiencing by the late 1990s. High technology solid companies such as Microsoft, Cisco, Intel, and Oracle all generated substantial sales, products, and profits and fueled the real growth which was occurring in the technology arena.

The upstart miniscule dotcom bubble companies were the ones powering on the stock market surge from 1995 to 2000 though. Cheap money and the resulting easy to obtain capital provided by the Federal Reserve's historically low interest rates also added proverbial fuel to the fire. This drove overconfidence in the markets and radical speculation pure and simple.

Venture capitalists would throw money by the fistfuls at companies simply because they possessed a .com following their name. The values were based on profits and earnings that did not exist yet and never would unless the future business model actually performed according to optimistic scenario projections. Investors turned blind eyes to the traditional fundamentals and complete lack of track records. Firms which had never earned any revenues, turned any profits, or even produced an on-the-market product were taken public in IPOs which witnessed the never before seen tripling and quadrupling of their stock prices in a single frenzied market trading day.

The dotcom bubble violently erupted after peaking on March 10, 2000 at 5,048. This lofty peak represented a doubling of the previous year's point. It was actually the market leading giants in the high technology sector, including Cisco and Dell, which engaged in enormous sell orders on their own company shares at the market's peak that caused the investor-driven panic selling to commence. Once this began in earnest, it needed only a few short weeks for the market to lose 10 percent of its entire value.

Dotcom companies suddenly found their supply of financial blood rapidly drying up. Those whose market caps had run to hundred of millions of dollars were suddenly worthless in only months. By the close of 2001, the majority of publically-traded dotcom bubble firms had gone bankrupt. Literally trillions worth of investment capital had vanished with the popping of the greatest bubble the world had ever seen to this point.

Dow Jones

Dow Jones is an international and American news company based in the United States. Wall Street Journal co-editor Charles Dow and Edward Jones co-founded the company with fellow reporter Charles Bergstresser back in 1882. The independent history of Dow Jones & Company continued under the Bancroft Family from the 1920s all the way until 2007. At this point, an extensive takeover struggle ensued. In the end, News Corp. took over the company which it has owned and run as a subsidiary since 2007.

The company had been most famous for its continuous publication of stock market indices such as the Dow Jones Industrial Average and the Dow Jones Transportation Average. Besides this, it publishes a number of important financial publications such as its flagship product The Wall Street Journal along with Market Watch, Barron's, Financial News, and Factiva. It has run the Dow Jones Newswire service for decades. This is one of the biggest and most prestigious newswire services in the world.

The Wall Street Journal continues to be a leading daily newspaper that the company publishes in both print and online editions. It covers financial, business, international, and national news and topics throughout the world. They started publishing this gold standard of newspapers on July 8th, 1889.

Today there are 12 different versions of it they produce in nine separate languages. These include English, Japanese, Chinese, Spanish, German, Portuguese, Turkish, Korean, and Bahasa. The Journal has won 35 Pulitzer Prizes for its excellent and world leading journalism.

In 2010, News Corp. sold off the Dow Jones Indexes subsidiary. The CME Group bought it and continues running it. Since then, the company has concentrated its efforts on its publications of financial news and on delivering information and financial news and tools to companies involved in finance.

The company continues its efforts in the arena of publishing and data provision today. It calls itself the ultimate source for business data and news. The company boasts journalism that continues to be award winning, cutting edged technology, and sophisticated data capabilities. They combine these in order to provide news and financial tools and insights that move the world financial markets. Their efforts also help key players to make crucial decisions and major companies and individuals to run their businesses.

The company has expanded from its humble roots as niche news agency provider in a basement on Wall Street to become the global powerhouse of information and news that it is now. It claims that the reason for its success and long lasting appeal comes from a combination of factors. These include their constant commitment to accuracy, innovation and depth, and years of experience. It helps them to keep their efforts firmly focused on their future endeavors.

Dow Jones today calls itself the modern day portal to intelligence. They have state of the art data and information feeds. Their research is performed by experts in the field. The firm utilizes leading and creative technologies and solutions that are fully integrated. Their staff reporters practice journalism that consistently wins awards.

The company's delivery systems and apps can be fully customized to work on a variety of platforms. This helps them to get the important financial and news information gathered, written, and published. Thanks to their leading technologies, they can get it to their customers wherever they are and whenever they require it.

The Dow indices continue to be benchmarks for the overall stock market as a whole. The DJIA includes the thirty leading companies that represent the major U.S. based enterprises. These are no longer primarily industrial in nature as they were when Charles Dow and Edward Jones put their names on them.

Dow Jones Industrial Average (DJIA)

The Dow Jones Industrial Average, commonly referred to by its acronym DJIA, is also many times called the Dow 30, the Dow Jones, the Dow, or even just the Industrial Average. It proves to be the second oldest stock market index in the Untied States after the Dow Jones Transportation Average. The Dow Jones Industrial Average came into being when Charles Dow, the co founder of Dow Jones and Company worked with a business colleague Edward Jones, a statistician, to come up with an index that monitors the industrial sector. This index demonstrates the daily stock market trading session progress of thirty of the largest companies that are publicly traded within the U.S.

Ironically, most of the present day thirty companies listed in this index no longer have much or even anything to do with the historical definition of heavy industry. The components in the average are weighted by price and scaled in order to adjust for the impacts of stock splits and varying other forms of adjustments. This means that the total value that you see in the daily representation of the Dow Jones does not prove to be the true average of the different company stock prices.

Instead, it is the total of such company prices that are added up and then divided by a special divisor. This divisor is a number that is adjusted any time one of the company stocks underlying it pays a dividend or engages in a stock split. In this way, the index presents a constant value that is not altered by the external factors of the component stocks.

The Dow Jones Industrial Average remains one of the most heavily followed and carefully watched indices in the American stock market, along with peers the S&P 500 Index, the NASDAQ composite, and the Russell 2000 Index. The founder Dow intended for the index to monitor the American industrial sector's actual performance. Even so, the index is constantly affected by much more than simply the economic and corporate reports issued. It responds to both foreign and domestic incidents and political episodes like terrorism and war, as well as any natural disasters that might cause economic damage.

The Dow Jones Industrial Average's thirty components simultaneously trade on either the New York Stock Exchange Euronext or the NASDAQ OMX, which are the two largest American stock market outfits. Derivatives based on Dow components trade via the Chicago Board Options Exchange, as well as with the Chicago Mercantile Exchange Group. The latter is the largest futures exchange outfit on earth, and it presently owns fully ninety percent of the Dow Jones founded indexing business, along with this Industrial Average.

Investors who are interested in gaining the ability to track the progress of the Dow Jones Industrial average have several choices. There are index funds that buy the components of the index so that you do not have to own all thirty companies yourself. You might also invest in the Dow 30 by purchasing shares of the Exchange Traded Fund known as the Diamonds ETF. This trades under the AMEX exchange via the symbol DIA. Finally, you could by options and futures contracts based on the performance of the Dow Jones Average on the Chicago Board of Trade.

Dow Theory

Dow Theory is a method for picking successful stock trades. At over a hundred years old, it may be the oldest system for selecting stocks that is still utilized. This is why investors often refer to it as the grandfather of stock selection theory.

Charles Dow created his Dow Theory in a series of Wall Street Journal editorials he wrote from 1900 to 1902. He laid down the basic fundamentals of his theory in these articles. They explained how the stock markets worked. Charles Dow also created two of the main indexes for the stock markets that the markets still use today. These are the Dow Jones Industrial Average and the precursor to the Dow Jones Transportation Index (the Dow Jones Rail Index). Charles died in 1902. His death left this work to be completed by other followers who published several books on the subject over the next sixty years.

Dow Theory is still important to markets and investors today. People study the theory to understand how several of the main indexes work. Investors also have created a number of systems based on Dow Theory over the years as well. The principles of technical analysis are rooted in Dow Theory ideas. Technical analysis centers on reading charts. These technicians use information in the charts to predict future stock prices.

Six basic ideas underpin Dow Theory. Some investors have attempted to discount these concepts over the years. Over time they generally prove to be true despite the skeptics.

The first one states that the market considers all information with its price levels. This means that stock prices reflect past, present, and even future information. The market takes everything into account including inflation, interest rates, soon to be released earnings announcements, the emotions of investors, and even future event risk.

The second idea says that three trends make up the market actions. These include primary trends, secondary trends, and minor trends. The primary trends usually last over a year. Secondary trends hold for several weeks to several months. They run counter to primary trends. Minor trends occupy less than three weeks.

The third Dow Theory concept claims that three main phases make up the primary trends. The accumulate phase starts the market prices moving up. The mass participation phase is where average investors buy into the market and drive prices significantly higher. This is the longest lasting phase in any market. The excess phase is where the market becomes overbought. Bigger, more knowledgeable investors begin to sell their shares to new investors ahead of a downturn in this phase.

A fourth idea states that two market indexes must agree on the trend change. It is not just any two indexes that have to concur. Bull markets and bear markets only switch when the Dow Industrial average and Dow Transports average agree together on the change in the trend.

Dow Theory's fifth tenet is that volume confirms the trend. Volume represents the number of shares that change hands. Without major volume appearing on any significant move against a trend, the trend is usually still intact. Volume should be greater when price is moving in the direction of the trend. When price goes against the trend, volume should be less.

The final idea of Dow Theory claims that a trend continues until there is a clear reversal. It requires overwhelming evidence to convincingly reverse the trend. Trading against the trend will usually hurt investors. This makes the popular statement "the trend is your friend" more than just a catchy stock market slogan. It also proves to be a significant philosophy behind Dow Theory.

Earnings Per Share (EPS)

Earnings per share refer to the given total of earnings that a company has for every share of the firm's stock that is outstanding. There are several formulas for calculating earnings per share. These depend on which segment of earnings are being considered. The FASB, or Financial Accounting Standards Board, makes corporations report such earnings per share on their income statement for all of the major components of such statements including discontinued operations, continuing operations, extraordinary items, and net income.

To figure up the basic net earnings per share formula, you only have to divide the profit for the year by the average number of common shares of stock. With discontinued operations, it is only a matter of taking the discontinued operations income and dividing it by the average number of common stock shares outstanding. Continuing operations earnings per share equal the continuing operations income over the average number of common shares. Extraordinary items works with the income from extraordinary items and divides it by the weighted average number of common shares.

Besides the basic earnings per share numbers, there are three different types of earnings per share. Last year's earning per share are the Trailing EPS. These are the only completely known earnings for a company. The Current earnings per share are the ones for this year. These are partially projections in the end until the last quarterly numbers are released. Finally, Forward earnings per share are earnings numbers for the future. These are entirely based on predictions.

Earnings per share calculations do not take into account preferred dividends on categories besides net income and continued operations. Such continuing operations and even net income earnings per share calculations turn out to be more complex as preferred share dividends are taken off of the top of net income before the earnings per share is actually calculated. Since preferred stock shares have the right to income payments ahead of common stock payments, any money that is given out as preferred dividends is cash which can not be considered to be potentially available for giving out to every share of the commonly held stock.

Preferred dividends for the present year are generally the only ones that are taken off of such income. There is a prevalent exception to this. If preferred shares prove to be cumulative then this means that dividends for the entire year are taken off, regardless of if they have been declared yet or not. Dividends that the company is behind on paying are not contemplated when the earnings per share is calculated.

Earnings per share as a financial measuring stick for a company are extremely important. In theory, this forms the underlying basis for the value of the stock in question. Another critical measurement of stock price is price to earnings value, also known as the PE ratio. This PE ratio is determined by taking the earnings per share and dividing them into the price of the stock. Earnings per share are useful in measuring up one corporation against another one, if they are involved in the same business segment or industry. They do not tell you if the stock is a good buy or not. They also do not reveal what the overall market thinks about the company. This is where the PE ratio is more useful.

Efficient Market Hypothesis (EMH)

The efficient market hypothesis is also known by its acronym EMH. It refers to an investment theory which claims that investors can not outperform the stock markets practically on a consistent basis. This is because the efficiencies created by the inner workings of the stock market mean present day share prices will always reflect and incorporate all relevant and practical information.

The idea states that stocks will practically always sell for their true fair value on the various stock exchanges. This infers that the typical investor can not efficiently buy undervalued shares or sell them at overly high prices. This is why it is theoretically impossible for investors to better the ultimate return of the stock markets no matter how expertly they select stocks or how well they time the markets. Efficient market hypothesis claims that the only means of outperforming the markets is through buying investments with higher risk and therefore coming with accompanying better returns.

Despite the fact that this efficient market hypothesis remains a foundation of modern day financial theories, it is still regarded with suspicion and controversy. Many investors and especially stock picking fund managers consistently defy it and try to select their own stocks. Those who concur with the EMH theory state that stock pickers are wasting their time in an effort to track down undervalued shares, or in predicting market trends, using either technical or fundamental analysis.

Clearly the economists and other scholarly individuals can hold up a significant amount of evidence that supports the efficient market hypothesis. Despite this, a broad range and variety of arguments against it still exist. Legendary investing stock pickers like Warren Buffet have managed to outperform the markets year in and year out over many decades. This should not be consistently possible at all by the arguments and logic of the EMH.

Other critics of the efficient market hypothesis hold up such Black Swan Events as the Black Monday 1987 crash in the stock markets. On this particular occasion, the DJIA Dow Jones Industrial Average plunged by in excess of 20 percent in only one day. This does raise a valid point about stock prices and how efficiently they are always valued when they can suddenly fall by a fifth of their value in only hours.

Believers in this efficient market hypothesis argue that markets are both efficient and random. This means that investors should be able to make their best consistent returns by choosing to invest in low fee, unmanaged, broadly representative portfolios. Morningstar Inc., the famous market research firm has compiled a great amount of data to support this assertion. They compiled the returns of active fund managers in every category. Then they held these up versus an index of relevant funds or ETF exchange traded funds. The study concluded that for any year to year period, there were merely two different groups of active fund managers who managed to consistently outperform the passively held funds over half the time. The two that outperformed were the diversified emerging markets funds and the small growth funds.

As far as all of the remaining categories such as U.S. large value, U.S. large blend, and U.S large growth (and most others), those who invested in either ETFs or lower cost index funds would have made higher returns. It is true that a small percentage of the active fund managers do manage to realize superior performances versus the passively managed funds at times and points. The problem that this presents for individual investors lies in predicting which fund managers will do this. Fewer than a quarter of the best performing active fund managers can outperform their passive manager benchmark funds consistently. Certainly Warren Buffet counts as one of those most successful few. It helps to explain his enduring popularity and success with investors for decades now.

Election Stock Market (ESM)

Election stock markets refer to financial markets whose contracts track the predicted and actual outcome of national elections. They are also called election prediction markets. Investors who participate in such futures contract forms of exchanges invest real money, purchase and sell contracts which are listed, take on the risk of losing their invested funds, and make profits on their positions. Such ESMs work much like traditional futures exchanges and commodity exchanges that cover future time deliveries of livestock, grains, and precious metals.

The real function and mission of such Election stock markets lies in correctly predicting the outcome of a national or provincial election. It might aim to forecast the popular vote shares or numbers of seats which the political parties obtain in legislative or alternatively parliamentary elections. Those markets that are effective prove to be highly reliable at contemplating information even before it becomes available in opinion polls. Such polls often require a few days to do and compile. The various traders in such an exchange tend to put aside their personal bias politically as they have real financial incentive to correctly share their honest opinion.

There are two other purposes for these Election stock markets. Naturally they are intended as a means of teaching people about elections and futures markets. Besides this though, the professors and universities that run them also rely on them for useful research surrounding election forecasting and the behavior of the electorate.

There are two such universities which have run these Election stock markets for more than a decade in North America. The main one in the United States is the Iowa Electronic Markets, founded and run by the Tippie College of Business of the University of Iowa. This market focuses its efforts on tracking mainly the congressional and presidential elections.

The University of British Columbia and its Sauder School of Business runs the Canadian-based UBC Election Stock Market. UBC concentrates on both provincial and federal elections for Canada. Both operate as not for profit enterprises for the purpose of research. Because of this, neither of them charges trading fees or commissions for trades. They generally limit the investment amounts to a range of between five hundred U.S. dollars and one thousand Canadian dollars.

In the last few years, new prediction markets which are privately operated have appeared. These markets do assess commissions and fees to pay for their costs of operation and for profit. Some charge net profits' commissions while others levy a per transaction fee. Among the commercial markets are The Washington Stock Exchange and Irish-based Intrade Prediction Markets. Each of these follows predictions for a wide-ranging series of geopolitical events. The commercially operated markets bring in significantly more volume and investment since they do not place arbitrary limits on an investors' participation.

Two main payout concepts exist with these Election stock markets. In the first model, the system proves to be a winner takes all type of market. One winning contract will pay the promised full face value amount (commonly one dollar) while all others will be worth zero. A party winning a full majority or plurality or a yes or no referendum are examples of this structured scenario.

In the other model, there are partial payouts on a few contracts which result from the percentage proportions on a given result. This percentage will commonly be multiplied by the standard dollar to determine the proportional payout. Two typical examples of this are a popular vote market share and a percentage of seats result for a given political party. The payouts would be figured according to the popular vote percentage share for the party in question. Traders often make money by purchasing those contracts which they feel are undervalued or by selling others which they believe to be overvalued.

Emerging Markets Index

Emerging Markets Index refers to the MSCI Emerging Markets Index. Morgan Stanley Capital International (more commonly known by its own acronym MSCI) created this index in order to follow the equity market performance of the world's global emerging markets. This capitalization index is compiled as a float-adjusted one made up of indices following 24 emerging economies. These include the United Arab Emirates (UAE), Turkey, Thailand, Taiwan, South Africa, Russia, Qatar, Poland, Philippines, Peru, Pakistan, Mexico, Malaysia, South Korea, Indonesia, India, Hungary, Greece, Egypt, Czech Republic, Colombia, China, Chile, and Brazil.

It was in 1988 that Morgan Stanley actually launched this world-leading Emerging Markets Index. At the time, it was comprised of only 10 nations which represented less than one percent of the total global markets' capitalization. Nowadays, the MSCI Emerging Markets Index consists of a full 24 nations that represent a more impressive ten percent of global market capitalization. The Index is similarly offered on a range of regions and market sizes or segments. It covers roughly 85 percent of the free-floating adjusted market capitalization for all of these 24 countries.

Such markets have long been counted as somewhat risky because of their added economic, political problems, and currency factor risks. No one recommends them for investors who prefer security and safety first and foremost. Those investors who become involved in these markets have to understand that there will be often higher but always volatile returns involved with the investment. Larger profits come at the tradeoff of risks of considerable losses. The advantage to such emerging markets lies in their usually lower correlation with the world's leading developed stock markets. This means that they are an ideal component of a well-diversified portfolio which helps to decrease all around portfolio risk and similarly increase overall portfolio returns.

In no small part because of its expansion to cover all of the world's leading developing markets, the MSCI Emerging Markets Index has become the world's leading benchmark for category performance according to many different mutual funds which specialize in emerging market growth.

There are many followers of this Index by the diversified emerging market funds and portfolios like JPMorgan Emerging Markets Equity Fund. This is a managed pool which is heavily exposed to the MSCI EMI (as of the close of market March 31st in 2016). They had 6.5 percent in the consumer discretionary sector and another 5.5 percent in the investment company sector. They utilize this index as their performance benchmark.

The fund's return according to NAV net asset value has been successful at closely tracking along the index even though there are distinctive differences between the two holdings. For example, the JPMorgan fund managed a 2.88 percent yearly return on an average basis all the way through March of 2016. This compared favorably to the correlating return of the index at only 14 basis points beneath it.

The index can be easily directly invested in thanks to the iShares MSCI Emerging Markets ETF exchange traded fund. It actually owns the basket of securities comprising more than 90 percent of the index holdings by weighting. Among its top ten holdings per May 30th of 2016, it held South Korean electronics powerhouse Samsung Electronics Company Limited and Chinese technology giant Tencent Holdings Limited. A number of strategists see greater opportunity in the emerging markets as a large percentage of their citizens are beginning their historic meteoric ascent from lower classes to the consumption-heavy middle classes in the coming few years.

It is important to note that the BRIC countries of Brazil, Russia, India, and China comprise 47 percent of the MSCI Emerging Markets Index. This includes index holdings with a hefty 28 percent exposure to Chinese firms, nine percent to Indian companies, seven percent to Brazilian corporations, and three percent to Russian firms.

Energy Commodities

The term energy commodities refers to a variety of coal, oil, and gasoline derived products. These include such energy sources as coal, Brent Sea Oil, gasoline, heating oil, and natural gas. These energy resources prove to be essential in daily life. This makes consumers most aware of such commodities. Besides being among the most heavily used, they are also typically among those which are most widely traded.

These energy commodities find use in so many industrial applications that they maintain a strong investment appeal. Their prices have the ability to rise substantially over shorter time frames when demand picks up or supply drops. Energy is also a major component in inflation indices around the world, which makes investments in energy an effective hedge against rising prices. Higher oil and gasoline costs translate to higher prices in general throughout the U.S. and world economies.

Investors who are interested in investing in these different types of energy commodities have a variety of choices of investment vehicle and commodities. There are Exchange Traded Funds and Notes (ETFs and ETNs), futures and options contracts, and energy sector company stocks from which to choose.

Brent Sea Oil turns out to be the major oil benchmark in the world. It is the one to which around two-third of worldwide oil trade is tied and is especially relied upon in the EMEA region (Europe, Middle East, and Africa). This indicator represents a sweet form of crude oil, though it is not as sweet as the American benchmark WTI (West Texas Intermediate) crude oil. Brent oil is used to produce gasoline and mid purity distillates like diesel and kerosene. Crude oil finds applications in a wide range or consumer products that underpin modern day life, including plastics. Crude must first be refined in order to be turned into most useful products like gasoline or heating oil.

Coal is responsible for providing the energy for half of all the electricity generated on earth. It is usually obtained through open pit mining or via underground shaft mining. Major coal deposits exist in the Midwestern and Eastern United States as well as regions of Russia and China. Coal is principally utilized in generating electricity. Almost 40% of all energy production in the world comes from coal. In the last few years, coal has become less important in developed countries and more critical in developing nations like China who need cheap fuel. It is also useful for steel production because of the incredibly hot temperatures it produces which are critical for creating the purest steel.

Gasoline proves to be among the most critical of the energy commodities, especially for the American transportation industry. The American market makes up over 40% of all demand for gasoline. Emerging markets are utilizing an increasingly larger share of this energy resource.

Heating Oil finds its main uses in boilers and furnaces as the fuel source for warming businesses and homes. It is most heavily employed in places in the Northeastern United States and the United Kingdom and Ireland. Natural gas can be hard to access in some of these markets or too expensive to use in places where it is very cold.

Natural Gas is among the most important fuels for generating power. It is particularly popular in the cooling and heating systems throughout the United States. Natural gas powers either steam or gas turbines to create electricity. It is increasingly preferred over oil and coal as it is a much cleaner energy source that produces fewer greenhouse gas emissions. It has been made more practical for transporting thanks to LNG Liquid Natural Gas terminals that work with a CNG Compressed Natural Gas form.

Equities

Equities are another name for stocks and similar types of investments. Stocks turn out to be financial instruments that represent ownership, or equity position, within a given corporation. As such, they give an owner a stake in a representative share of the company's profits and assets. Such ownership in a given firm is determined by taking the total numbers of shares in the company's equities that the individual owns, and dividing it by the actual number of shares that exist.

The majority of these equities similarly give voting rights that provide representative votes in some decisions that the company makes. Not every company issues equities; only corporations engage in the practice, while limited partnerships and sole proprietorships do not. Equities can be further divided into smaller categories based on the market capitalization, or size, of the company in question.

Because they often yield greater returns over significant periods of time, they are typically characterized by higher amounts of risk than are bonds and money market funds. Because of these unique potential returns and associated risks, equities are generally considered to be their own class of assets that are utilized to a degree in putting together investment portfolios with proper diversification. Many different kinds of equities exist, including domestic equities, emerging market equities, developed market equities, and Real Estate Investment Trusts.

Domestic Equities prove to be those stocks for the publicly traded corporations that principally conduct their business in the same country in which the investor lives. When a person holds such equities, they receive their share of dividends that the corporation pays. Equities come with a higher degree of risk than do bonds, as bond holders have a greater claim on a corporation's assets should liquidation follow bankruptcy. Equity holders are commonly wiped out in such liquidation.

Emerging Market Equities are equities in corporations that are based in countries that are still developing their economies. Included in these are China, Brazil, and India. These nations feature economies that are commonly volatile and lack many protections for investors, like auditing and laws or monitoring of securities that are found in the industrialized countries.

Developed Market Equities are equities in firms that work primarily outside of an investor's home country but still in an industrialized country. For Americans, this mostly translates to European country companies, as well as those in places such as Japan, Australia, and New Zealand. Such companies and economies in these nations prove to be more stable than those in developing countries.

Real Estate Investment Trusts, also known as REIT's, are equity funds that invest in residential and commercial real estate. Because they receive lease and rent payments off of their investments, these typically pay greater percentage returns in dividends. These higher distributions mean that REIT's are much like a combination of fixed income and typical equity investments. This means that they commonly feature greater risk along with better anticipated returns than do the majority of fixed income investments.

Equity Securities

Equity securities prove to be those asset classes which feature shares of stock in a given corporation. Investors hold these as reported by a company's official balance sheet. Corporations issue such securities in an effort to raise business capital via the financial markets. They use this money for significant company life events, such as for product development, merger and acquisition activity, or internal expansion. The funds are seldom for daily operating needs.

When investors buy equity securities, they gain a partial stake in the underlying firm. This is a primary alternative to turning to the bond markets to borrow money in taking on debt via the publicly traded bond markets. When a company first issues such equity securities, this is called an IPO initial public offering. Companies often raise enormous amounts of cash in this means, since investors are always hunting for new stock issues that will enable them to possess a part of a new and exciting opportunity.

The total number of shares that an IPO released varies wildly. It comes down to the amounts which the companies obtain permission to issue in their financial documents which they file with the regulatory overseer for their area. Corporations are allowed to sell a specific amount of stock shares in a given price range on the actual IPO day. After these shares have been dealt out to the public via the financial markets, the price of their equity will go up and down on the stock markets every trading day. This movement all depends on the perception of investors and the accompanying demand for the shares on any given day.

It is not common for such a firm to issue its entire inventory of available stock shares in a single offering. Rather than do this, they commonly reserve a certain quantity of shares to be issued at a later date in a second offering. This is called a follow on offering or secondary offering. The management of a company would elect to do this as they know they will likely need to raise fresh additional capital in the future in order to pay for hoped for expansionary plans.

When corporations continue to issue out their equity securities via the financial exchanges there is a downside for the existing shareholders and company investors. As additional shares are available to be bought, the pre-existing stake holders have their equity stake diluted as a percentage of the total. As an example, a major share holder could possess a huge quantity of shares that equate to fully 10 percent of all outstanding company shares which can be traded. Should the company choose to boost the total number of shares which are tradable, the equity of the shareholders will immediately drop in terms of the percentage ownership of all available shares.

The main alternative to issuing equity securities lies in issuing debt securities These publicly issued bonds offered via the bond markets by a company (or even government) raise money by taking on debt which must be repaid one day, known as the maturity date. Investors who buy debt instruments like these become de facto creditors of the bond issuing entities. The main disadvantage to such issuance in debt is that the company issuing has to provide continuous interest payments to the bond holders throughout the life of the bond contract. The company is able to maintain its ownership in itself in exchange for this trade off of interest payments.

Ethereum Currency (Ether)

Ethereum Currency, often simply called Ether tokens, proves to be the much-needed fuel element for the Ethereum operating platform and system. As such, Ether is also a type of payment that platform clients can make to the machines which execute the smart contracts, or operations auto requested between two parties. Ether is simultaneously the financial incentive to make certain that the developers create high-quality applications so that the network stays healthy. Individuals must be compensated for contributing resources to the platform and network. It ensures both efficient programming and quality final products created using the Ethereum block chain, since wasteful code is more expensive to deploy.

Ether is the principal crypto currency rival to industry titan Bitcoin. Unlike Bitcoin though, whose maximum issue is a total of 18 million BTC, Ether does not have such a limited total issue. The parties who signed on to the 2014 presale terms of Ethereum currency dictated that the ether token issue would be limited to a strict 18 million tokens each year. Issuance may be strictly fixed, but total supply increases substantially every annum. The idea is that eventually there will be so many Ether tokens that the amount lost every year will merely be replaced by the new up to 18 million issued tokens. In other words, at some point in the foreseeable future, an equilibrium in total numbers of Ether in existence would be reached finally.

The creators of Ethereum currency do not see themselves as a young upstart rival to big brother crypto currency Bitcoin. In fact, they give credit to bitcoin for developing both the block chain technology and the idea for a virtual currency in the first place. The founders of Ether regard themselves as a complementary force in the so-called digital ecosystem. To them, such Ether tokens are merely crypto-fuel which can be employed to compensate for computation. They did not intend it to become a transactional currency, share, asset, or any other element.

To prove this point, the Ether system creators tout the many different means of utilizing Bitcoins in the Ethereum ecosystem. It can be traded literally for ETH tokens. There are a number of different third party firms whose goal and efforts are to see the seamless exchange of Bitcoins for Ether tokens become a reality as soon as can be.

This would allow for holders of BTC to be able to execute smart contracts with Ether tokens. They could then immediately transfer back to BTC to ensure that their currency remained within the Bitcoin network and stayed valued in BTC. Latest versions of the physical wallets come with auto converters from BTC to ETH tokens.

Ethereum currency is similarly an ideal means of performing complicated trading within multiple groups. Once all participating parties obtain a Bitcoin price source in common, it is easy for them to develop a currency based on ethereum. The value in this case could be simply and effectively pegged to the Bitcoin market value. It would allow for individuals to trade back and forth between BTC and ETH tokens with a guarantee they would be able to receive back their original quantity of Bitcoins all the while they were completely compatible with the smart contracts pioneered and championed by Ethereum.

Finally, Bitcoins may be relayed in order to create a convertible two way peg. Using the Bitcoin relay, one may easily side chain from one Bitcoin into ether tokens. It allows for people to hardwire a Bitcoin into a smart contract which is literally tied to an associated ethereum contract. Such an ethereum token could then be issued which was backed by the hardwired Bitcoin in the smart contract itself.

EUREX Exchange

EUREX is a state of the art options and futures exchange which Deutsche Borse of Germany jointly operated with SWX the Swiss Exchange until 2012. At this point, Deutsche Borse acquired the remaining shares of the EUREX exchange from SWX. The exchange operates offices in nine global locations including in Frankfurt, London, Chicago, Zurich, and Paris.

This international exchange specializes in providing trading on derivatives based in Europe. As such, it turns out to be the biggest European options and futures market. Products across nine asset classes trade on the exchange. These range from Swiss and German debt instruments to individual stock and stock indexes of European companies and exchanges.

EUREX clearing handles the clearing of every transaction carried out on the exchange. In this way, it serves as a multi asset class clearing central counterparty for the considerable product range. It also clears products that trade over the counter.

The exchange itself has become enormous. The Futures Industry Association said in its 2015 annual survey that the EUREX exchange holds the position of third biggest derivatives exchange based on the volume of contracts it trades. Its headquarters is located in Eschborn, Germany near Frankfurt, the financial capital of Germany. The operators of the exchange are the EUREX Frankfurt AG and EUREX Zürich AG. Both publicly traded companies are now entirely owned by Deutsche Börse, the German stock exchange operator.

The EUREX Exchange offered something almost unique when it began functioning in 1998. In both the United States and Great Britain, open outcry trading still dominated markets. EUREX came along as among the first exchanges in the world to provide a trading platform which was completely electronic instead of the more traditional pit or open outcry trading so prevalent at that time. Using this method of trading, buyers and sellers perform transactions via remote locations that are connected by the electronic network and trading platform.

The exchange launched its present day platform the T7 trading architecture in 2013. This system advanced the electronic trading of derivatives significantly. Deutsche Börse Group developed it. Using this dependable system, over 7,700 different traders operating in more than 35 countries are connected so that they can trade in excess of seven million contracts each market day.

The EUREX Exchange won several major impressive awards for 2016. *Global Capital* presented it with the "European Exchange of the Year" honor for the second year in a row. It received this nod for its broad range of products that hedge risk throughout nine alternative and traditional asset classes, as well as for its impressive offerings of equity index products and volatility derivatives. *Financial News* also honored EUREX with the 2016 Best Derivatives Trading Platform. This is also its second consecutive year to win this award.

EUREX gradually enabled Deutsche Börse to wrest control of the Bund German bonds futures trading away from London. Up till the late 1990s, the London Financial Futures Exchange dominated trading in this segment. This back and forth struggle for control of this important market became known as the "Battle of the Bund."

Euro Stoxx 50 Index

The Euro Stoxx 50 Index proves to be the leading European Blue-chip like index that comprises securities of mega companies from the Euro Zone. This index offers investors and financial institutions a vehicle for following and investing in the Blue chip type of sector leaders for the zone. It includes 50 stocks (as the name implies) drawn from 11 different Euro Zone member nations. These are economically important zone nations Spain, Portugal, the Netherlands, Luxembourg, Italy, Ireland, Germany, France, Finland, Belgium, and Austria.

This Euro Stoxx 50 Index has been licensed out to a wide range of financial institutions to be the basis of a great variety of investment products like ETF Exchange Traded Funds, Options on futures, Futures contracts, and structured products around the globe. Besides this master index of the Euro Stoxx 50 Index, it is subdivided into other indices. These include the following: Euro Stoxx 50 Subindex France, Euro Stoxx 50 Subindex Italy, and Euro Stoxx 50 subindex Spain which covers the national big 50 companies by market capitalization in each off the economic powerhouse countries of France, Italy, and Spain, respectively.

The operator of this important pan-Euro Zone Euro Stoxx 50 Index and business is the company STOXX Limited on behalf of Deutsche Boerse Group. They also offer international tradable and creative index concepts on other indices to numerous countries throughout the world. As of the end of June 2016, STOXX 50 and DAX have worked with iShares to create and offer two new exchange traded funds traded in Hong Kong. iShares exchange traded funds family are both managed and marketed by the BlackRock investment firm. They started trading these two new Euro STOXX 50 Index ETFs on the Hong Kong Stock Exchange at the conclusion of June 2016.

The components in the Euro Stoxx 50 Index are updated several times a year as appropriate to changing market capitalizations. As of the end of December 2016, the components included French firms oil and gas producer Total, health care and pharmaceuticals maker Sanofi, European and Global banking giant BNP Paribas, international insurance titan AXA, luxury personal household goods maker LVMH Moet, cosmetics international leader L'Oreal, chemical maker Air Liquide, industrial goods and services maker Schneider Electric, banking giant GRP Societe Generale, food and largest yogurt maker Danone Group, aircraft maker Airbus, construction materials producer Vinci, telecommunications provider Orange, industrial goods and services producer Safran, health care company Essilor International, construction and materials producer Saint Gobain, Real Estate company Unibail-Rodamco, Utilties giant Engie, and international media conglomerate Vivendi.

German components of the index were electronics and industrial goods giant Siemens, chemicals and pharmaceutical titan Bayer, leading technology firm SAP, chemicals international leader BASF, re-insurance leader Allianz, luxury car maker Daimler, telecommunications leader Deutsche Telekom, industrial goods and services provider Deutsche Post, healthcare leader Fresenius, luxury car maker BMW, insurance firm Muenchener Rueck, internationally known shoe and clothing manufacturer Adidas, utilities giant E.On, world's largest auto maker Volkswagen, and largest German financial institution Deutsche Bank.

Spanish components in the index were international banking conglomerates BCO Santander and BCO Bilbao Vizcaya Argentaria, telecommunications international behemoth Telefonica, utilities leader Iberdrola, and retailer Industria de Diseno Textil SA.

Dutch companies in the index include electronics and industrial goods maker Philips, Anglo-Dutch consumer products giant UniLever, financial services investment leader ING, technology leader ASML Holdings, and retailer Ahold Delhaize.

Italian components of the index were oil and gas producer and distributor ENI, largest Italian bank Intesa SanPaolo, and national utility company ENEL. The Irish component is construction and materials maker CRH. The Belgian component is alcohol and food giant Anheuser-Busch InBev. The Finish component is technology and cell phone maker manufacturer Nokia.

Exchange Rate Mechanism (ERM)

Exchange Rate Mechanisms are systems that were established to maintain a certain range of exchange for currencies as measured against other currencies. These ERMs can be run in three different ways. On one extreme they can float freely. This permits the systems to trade without the central banks and governments intervening.

The fixed Exchange rate mechanisms will do whatever it takes to maintain rates pegged at a specific value. In between these two extremes are the managed ERMs. The best known example of one of these is the European Exchange Rate Mechanism known as ERM II. It is in use today for those countries who wish to become a part of the EU monetary union.

The European Economic Community formally introduced the European ERM system to the world on March 13, 1979. It was a part of the EMS European Monetary System. The goal of this new system centered on attaining monetary stability throughout Europe by reducing the variable exchange rates. This was set up to prepare the way for the Economic and Monetary Union. It also paved the way for the Euro single currency introduction that formally occurred on January 1, 1999.

The Europeans changed their system once the Euro became adopted. They introduced ERM II as a way to link together those EU countries who were not a part of the eurozone with the euro. They did this to boost extra eurozone currencies' stability. A second goal was to create a means of evaluating the countries who wished to join the eurozone. In 2016 only a single currency uses the ERM II. This is the Danish krone.

The European ERM ceased to exist in 1999. This was the point after the eurozone country European Currency Units exchange rates became frozen and the Euro began trading against them. ERM II then replaced the initial ERM. At first the Greek drachma remained in the ERM II alongside the Danish currency. This changed when Greece adopted the Euro in 2001. Currencies within the newer system may float in a fairly tight range of plus or minus 15% of their central exchange rate versus the euro. Denmark does better than this. Its Danmarks Nationalbank maintains a 2.25% range versus the central rate of DKK 7.46038.

In order for other countries that wish to join the Euro to participate, they are required to be a part of the ERM II system for minimally two years before they can become members of the eurozone. This means that at some point, a number of currencies for member states that joined the EU will have to be in the system. This includes the Swedish krona, Polish zloty, Hungarian forint, Czech Republic koruna, the Romanian leu, Bulgarian lev, and Croatian kuna. Each of these is supposed to join the system according to their individual treaties of accession.

In the case of Sweden, the situation is more complicated. The country held a referendum on becoming a part of the mechanism to which the citizens voted no. The European Central Bank still expects that Sweden will join the system and eventually adopt the euro. This is because they did not negotiate for an opt out of the currency as did the U.K. and Denmark. The Maastricht Treaty requires that EU member states all eventually join the exchange rate mechanism.

Britain participated in the mechanism from 1990 until September of 1992. On September 16, 1992 the British famously crashed out of the system on what became known as Black Wednesday because of manipulation of the pound by currency speculators led by Hedge Fund Billionaire George Soros.

Expense Ratio

Expense ratio relates to the costs that a mutual fund incurs as it trades and does normal business. Typical mutual fund expense ratios include a number of different costs. Among these are management fees, transaction costs, custody costs, marketing fees, legal expenses, and transfer agent fees.

Management fees comprise those charges that the fund pays to the company which handles the portfolio management. They invest the fund's money as per the direction of the mutual fund board of directors. Management costs are typically the largest single portion of the mutual fund's expenses.

These fees commonly range from as little as .5% to as much as 2%. Lower fees are usually more advantageous for investors. This is because every dollar that goes to the management of the fund is not increasing the share holders' wealth. Some mutual fund types charge a higher amount in fees. International or global mutual funds will usually cost more than simple domestic market mutual funds. They justify these greater charges by the difficulty of managing an international portfolio.

Transaction costs include the fees that the fund pays to stock brokers. These are negotiated to extremely low rates such as a penny per share or even lower thanks to the enormous volumes that mutual funds trade. Those funds that are constantly purchasing and selling investments create significantly greater transacting costs for themselves and their investors. Higher turnover rates like this also can lead to larger capital gains taxes and other costs.

The investment holdings of a mutual fund must be kept by a custodian bank. This creates custody costs where these banks register the bonds, stocks, and other investments for the fund. Some of the banks do this electronically and others keep actual stock certificates in their vault storage.

Custodian banks also collect interest and dividend payments, maintain accounting for the various positions so gain/loss info is readily available to management, and handle stock splits and other transaction issues. These custodian costs prove to be a less significant percentage of expense ratios for the mutual funds.

Marketing fees for mutual funds come out of the money that the investors pool. This money is utilized to advertise the fund so they can raise additional investment dollars. More money in the fund means more management fees for the portfolio managers. These 12b-1 marketing fees are money that does not benefit an investor after the fund exceeds $100 million in net assets. A very small number of brokers actually refund such fees to their investors.

There are some legal expenses that mutual funds must incur in the course of normal operating business. These include for paperwork they are required by law to file for regulators like the SEC, specific licenses, incorporation, and other legal procedures. The majority of funds count such costs as a small amount of their overall expense ratio.

Transfer agent costs cover the expenses that arise when a shareholder cashes out or buys into the fund. Transfer agents must handle various account statements, paperwork, and money in the process. These agents take care of all the mundane daily paperwork for purchases, redemptions, and processing which keep the fund and other capital markets working.

There are various other costs that are not included in the mutual fund expense ratio but many experts feel should be. These include mutual fund sales loads. These fees are simply commissions that go into the pocket of the institution, company, or stockbroker that persuaded you to buy the mutual fund in the first place. Because of these and other high costs of many mutual fund expense ratios, some people prefer low cost index funds that involve very low management costs.

Face Value

Face Value represents the dollar value of a given security as the issuer states it officially. It is also otherwise known as the nominal value. Where stocks are concerned, this is the certificate-displayed original value of the stock. With bonds, this amounts to the dollar amount which will be paid back to the bond holder when the bond matures. This amount for bonds is usually $1,000 par value. Where bonds are concerned, this value is also called par value or sometimes only "par." Par value is very important with bonds, while it means little to stock investors.

Par value is two completely different concepts when dealing with bonds versus stocks. With bonds, this refers to the full amount which the company will return to the bondholder at the time of maturity. This assumes that the issuer does not default on its bond principal. Despite this set face value to be returned at maturity, bonds which trade on the secondary market have market values which fluctuate every trading day based largely on the prevailing interest rates.

As an example, when interest rates prove to be greater than the coupon rate on the bond, the issue will be sold on the secondary market at a discount to par value. This means that the price will be lower than the par. At the same time, when interest rates turn out to be lower than the coupon rate of the bond, the bond sells for a premium, at higher than par. The par value still guarantees a fixed principal return in any case. Yet this value is considered to be a bad indicator of the current worth for the bond, given the fact that very few bonds actually trade for par on the secondary market.

Bond holders can make additional profits over their fixed interest rate. This opportunity lies in buying the bond at below face value, then holding it to receive the par at maturity date. This gap between sub-par purchase price on the secondary market and the par value at maturity becomes pure profit to the bond holder if they hold the bond until that eventual date is reached.

The face value where stocks are concerned is quite different from that par with bonds. The importance of stock shares' par value as stated on their shares pertains to the legal amount of capital which the business must maintain. It is a fact that only cash the company has in excess of this total amount (number of shares times the share par value) may be paid out in the form of dividends to the investors. In practice this means that the face value of the shares serves as a type of corporate cash reserve.

The law does not mandate how much the stated par value has to be when it is issued. Businesses could sidestep the reserve requirement effect by applying laughably low values to the share certificates. Examples of two prominent companies illustrate this strategy well. AT&T shares have only $1 per common share listed as their par value. Stock giant Apple shares trading at hundreds of dollars apiece list a par value of merely $0.00001 per share, a ridiculous face value amount in practice.

This is why a stock or even bond's face value rarely if ever determines the true market value of the relevant issue, especially with stocks. The market value is only based upon the market forces of supply and demand. This is decided in practice by how much investors will willingly pay for buying and selling shares on a given security at a particular snap shot moment in time. If market conditions are right, the par value and actual market value at any given moment may have little or nothing to do with each other.

With bonds and their markets, it is all about the prevailing interest rates and how they correlate to the coupon rate of the bond. This will generally decide whether the bond sells at, above, or below its par value. With zero coupon bonds, investors do not receive any interest besides buying the bond for less than its face value. These are sold for less than par as the sole means for investors to realize any profits in this case.

Factoring

Factoring refers to a financial transaction which is considered to be debtor finance. In such an arrangement, companies actually sell off their invoices or accounts receivable to a third party factor for a discount. There is a major reason why a company would be interested in doing this. They may require cash for immediate needs which cannot wait for the accounts receivables to be effectively paid. When exporters engage in selling off their receivables in international trade finance, this is alternatively known as Forfaiting.

Factoring itself is typically also called invoice factoring, accounts receivable factoring, and accounts receivable financing. The foremost trade association for factoring proves to be the Commercial Finance Association. It handles both factoring transactions as well as asset based lending.

It is important to differentiate between factoring and invoice discounting. With factoring, receivables are actually sold off. Invoice discounting refers to a form of borrowing that utilizes for collateral on the loan the various accounts receivable assets. This is not the case in the United Kingdom however. Discounting is a type of factoring in the British market, which merely pertains to assigning receivables. This means that in Great Britain, this activity is also not deemed to be a form of borrowing. Confidentiality proves to be the principle difference between invoice discounting and factoring in the United Kingdom.

Four main events cover the factoring transaction. Each of these must be accountant-recorded by the individual financial professional who bears the responsibility for recording the transaction in its entirety. In the first step, the factor receives its fee. Next the interest expense must be paid out to the factor for advancing money on the transaction.

In the third step, the seller must allocate a certain percentage of the fees as bad debt expense. This relates to those receivables which the seller does not have confidence in being collectible. Finally, the seller will have to arrange a merchandise returns amount in the form of a "factor's holdback receivable." This category also covers any potential other gains or losses the seller will be forced to concede to the process of the invoice collecting.

There will be times when the charges the seller pays out to the factor will cover considerations such as extra credit risk, a discount fee, and additional services rendered by the factor. The final profit for the factor will amount to the ultimate difference between the amount it paid to obtain the invoices on accounts receivable and the actual money it finally recovers from the debtors. Any money which the factor loses because of non-payment is subtracted from this profit total.

With industries like clothing and textiles, companies which are completely financially sound will factor off their accounts. This results from the particular historical means of financing production in this industry. It permits the firm to cover its current cash needs and allows companies to operate with lesser cash balances. This leaves a larger amount of cash free for investing in future growth opportunities of the firm.

This debt factoring also serves a useful purpose as a means of improving cash flow control for those firms that find themselves in the unenviable position of possessing many accounts receivable that have various terms of credit which must be actively managed. Such a firm will often sell off its invoices at the appropriate discount because it decides that it will benefit financially in utilizing the resulting proceeds to improve growth. This serves them better than in acting as a de facto bank to their various clients.

This effectively means that factoring will happen at any point in any industry where the return rate for the proceeds put into future production is higher than the costs to factor out the receivable accounts. This is why the difference in money spent to factor must be carefully evaluated to ascertain if the value of producing additional goods will be higher than the money the company pays to work with the factor. A side but still important consideration revolves around how much cash the company possesses on hand for its operations and future growth potential.

Federal Trade Commission (FTC)

The FTC Federal Trade Commission proves to be the agency responsible for protecting the American consumers. They strive to stop tricky, fraudulent, and unfair practices in business in the nation's marketplaces. They also disburse valuable information to consumers that helps them to recognize, stop, and sidestep these frauds.

The FTC accepts consumer complaints by phone, email, their website, and through the mail. They take these complaints and enter them into a database that is called the Consumer Sentinel Network. This secure online tool is utilized for investigation purposes by literally hundreds of criminal and civil agencies for law enforcement throughout the United States and overseas.

What the FTC would like to do is to stop these types of deceptive and non-competitive business dealings before they hurt consumers. They are also attempting to improve consumer opportunities so that they are better informed about and comprehend the nature of competition. The agency attempts to perform all of these tasks without putting too many burdens and restrictions on businesses activities that are legitimate.

Congress created the FTC back in 1914. Originally its mandate lay in stopping unfair means of competition in trade and business caused by the trusts. They were a part of the government's stated goal to bust up these trusts. Congress has given them more authority to monitor and fight practices that were against fair competition over the years by passing other laws.

The government enacted another law in 1938 that was broadly addressed to stop any deceptive or unfair practices and acts. They have continued to receive direction and discretion to govern a number of other laws that protect consumers over the subsequent years. Among these are the Pay Per Call Rule, the Telemarketing Sales Rule, and the Equal Credit Opportunity Act. Congress passed another law in 1975 that gave the Federal Trade Commission the ability to come up with rules that regulated trade throughout the industries.

The FTC has a vision for the American economy. They want to see one that has healthy competition between producers. They also desire to see consumers able to obtain correct information. Ultimately the government agency looks for all of this to create low priced and superior quality goods. They encourage innovation, efficiency in business, and choice for consumers.

This agency carries out its vision with three strategic goals. It starts with them protecting consumers by heading off trickery and deception in the business and consumer marketplace. They desire to keep competition going strong. In this role, they stop mergers and business dealings that they believe are against competition. They also work to increase their own performance with consistently improving and excellent managerial, individual, and organizational efforts.

All of these goals and efforts combine to make the FTC one of the government agencies that most impacts each American citizen's economic and personal life. They are the only government entity that possesses a mandate for both competition jurisdiction and consumer protection in large segments of the U.S. economy. They go after aggressive and effectual enforcement of the laws.

The FTC shares its knowledge with international, state, and federal groups and agencies. The group creates research tools at a variety of conferences, workshops, and hearings every year. They also develop and distribute easy to understand educational materials for business and consumer needs in the transforming technological and global market.

The FTC carries out its work through its Bureaus of Economics, Competition, and Consumer Protection. They receive assistance from the Office of General Counsel. Seven regional offices around the country help them to carry out their mandate.

Financial Contagion

Financial contagion generally refers to the transferable characteristics of the shock of one nation's asset market to translate to asset prices in a different (but at least somewhat related) independent nation's financial markets. It is important to realize that this is possible at all because of several different kinds of shocks. Among the most accepted, important, and common of these are information shocks and liquidity shocks.

Information shocks transpire when those investors who are especially well informed, or informed investors, obtain information which they are able to rapidly and effectively utilize in picking out the best possible investment portfolios. Liquidity shocks on the other hand happen as liquidity traders transact in order to attain the necessary inventory for themselves and their client's immediate liquidity concerns.

Both of these kinds of financial contagion shocks operate in a few different ways, impacting the relevant and affected markets. The chief affected segments are in expectations and portfolio balance components of the changing price. As far as expectations components go, the price change occurs because those investors who are not well informed, or the uninformed investors, catch up their individual asset value and price anticipation to the trades which the informed investors have already executed and had filled. Portfolio balance components in price change quantifies the asset price changes which occur because portfolios are being naturally rebalanced by the uninformed investors as they understand that the prices of the various assets in question do not accurately or adequately reflect the new information which concerns these said assets.

The so-called information effect happens as either liquidity trading or informed investors' informational advantage reverberates throughout a range of international markets. This can rapidly lead to price changes from a single market reflecting information on assets in various other markets and other countries' markets. As the informed investors' knowledge travels to correlated interdependent yet fully independent markets, the uninformed investors from one market see the prices changing in other separate markets and then accordingly rush to place trades in their own national markets.

As liquidity trading reverberates throughout different markets, the price changes of a single market will also impact the assessment of uninformed investors regarding asset prices in other markets. It does not even require that financial markets between different individual sovereign countries be closely or directly linked via the macroeconomic fundamentals for the shocks to effectively transmit from one national market to the other. It may take some time for this to actually happen, but eventually it only requires the indirect sharing of macroeconomic variables in order for such financial contagion transmission to effectively occur.

This goes a long way to explain how financial contagion has so easily transferred between those diverse markets which are even weakly connected in the past, as with Asian markets, European markets, and Latin American national markets. The biggest lesson and warning message from financial contagion analysis proves to be that the inequality of information possessed by informed versus uninformed investors magnifies the effects of international market contagion.

Financial Times Stock Exchange (FTSE)

The Financial Times Stock Exchange represents an enormous group of indices owned by the London Stock Exchange. The acronym originated in the days when it was half owned by the Financial Times newspaper and the LSE. Now this group is an entirely owned subsidiary of only the London Stock Exchange.

When individuals use the word FTSE, they are most commonly referring to the most important benchmark index of the group the FTSE 100. These 100 companies are the hundred largest British companies which the London Stock Exchange lists. As such the Blue Chip companies of the British economy represent the biggest companies by market capitalization in the U.K. Besides this FTSE 100 index, the group produces the FTSE 250, the 350, the Small Cap, and the All-Share.

The FTSE 250 companies are those next 250 largest companies after the FTSE 100. Combining the 250 and the 100 yields the 350 index. Merging the 350 and Small Cap provides the All Share Index.

London Stock Exchange launched the FTSE 100 on January 3, 1984. The companies in the index are calculated for size based on their market capitalization, or number of existing shares times the price per share. The group recalculates the indices every quarter to adjust for any of the companies in the 250 index that have moved up to the 100 index and those in the 100 group that have dropped to the 250 group.

Besides this, they have to remove companies that have been taken over or merged with others. The index must also be updated for name changes, as happened with British Gas becoming BG Group and Centrica, Midland Bank becoming HSBC, and Commercial Union Assurance becoming Aviva. Name changes, mergers, and takeovers are changed as soon as they become effective.

FTSE 100 updates its composite companies based on those which rise to a position in the top 90 largest companies on the London Stock Exchange. Those which fall to the 111th position or lower are dropped. They maintain this overlapping band so that there will not be too much change in the index in any given quarter. The group is concerned about the stability of the index and the rate of change because it forces investment companies and funds to rebalance when the benchmark 100 index changes. This is an expensive process for the large investors that the group tries to mitigate.

The 100 index and other benchmark indices are calculated up every 15 seconds throughout the trading days. The values are published in real time all day. The indices are open from 8am to 4:30pm on all weekdays that are not market holidays.

FTSE 100 is considered to be a good barometer for geopolitical and economic events throughout the world. When the major global markets soar, it does as well. When they plummet, it falls in sympathy. The largest single point drop for the 100 index happened on the day following Black Monday in the U.S. on October 20th of 1987. On this occasion, the 100 index fell 12.22% in a single trading session.

FTSE is not only a series of British stock indices. The group also produces and compiles every day more than 100,000 additional indices around the globe. Among these are the Global Equity, Italy's MIB, the China A50 and 50, the Portugal 20, and the TWSE Taiwan. In 2015 the group merged with Russell to become the FTSE Russell Group. This gave it reach into a number of American stock market indices like the Russell 2000.

Fire Sale

A fire sale is a phrase with a variety of interesting meanings. The term originated in reference to the reduced sales price for goods which were damaged in a fire of a shop or business. Since then, it has come to refer to any event which forces a business to move its assets or inventory goods for prices that are substantially discounted. The reason the business would be forced to engage in such a practice is because they are in a bind through some type of serious and often-times fatal financial distress.

Where financial markets are concerned, the phrase fire sale also refers to any securities (stocks, bonds, or other financial instruments and investments) which trade at a deep discount to their intrinsic value. This could occur in extended and painful bear market phases in the equities markets.

There are a number of examples which help to clarify the several different meanings of this concept of a fire sale. Take a department store as a prime example. When the department store company has to close its doors because of a bankruptcy event, the store might offer such a sale. In this specific scenario, the department store will offer its inventory of goods at what would normally be considered ridiculously low prices.

They do this so that they can liquidate the entirety of their in stock inventory. Since the store is closing up for good, they must be rid of each item in the store's inventory. The only means of effectively accomplishing this lies in providing prices so drastically reduced that bargain hunters will be lured in to purchase the stock. When the prices offered on the merchandise are so good as to be irresistible, then this qualifies as a fire sale.

Where securities are concerned, there are always examples of a fire sale of a given stock issue. Any time a particular equity security sells for far less than the value it is perceived to be worth, this qualifies as such a sale. Look at a clear example to consider. When the Dow Jones Industrial Average cratered by a full thousand points within the day, Proctor and Gamble (ticker symbol PG) crashed and burned by a quarter of its value on a temporary basis. This led investors and analysts to declare that there had been a real fire sale on the share of Proctor and Gamble that particular day. In this particular scenario, the phrase for this kind of a sale signifies that the asset in question possesses significantly greater value than the price for which its owner is suddenly willing to sell it.

These stock or bond securities which appear to be offered for this dramatic sale often provide an appealing risk to reward payoff possibility for the types of buyers known as value investors. This is because the asset is not likely to experience significantly further deterioration in valuation, yet the profit potential to the upside could possible prove to be impressive. The truth is that there is no single set of metrics for valuing whether or not a particular stock is actually selling for a ridiculously low price. One factor that many analysts can agree on is that if a stock is being valued at multiple year lows in the price, then it is generally considered to be a huge bargain.

As an example, stocks which are trading continuously for 14 times earning multiples would likely be fire sales when they trade for a far lower multiple of earnings of a mere seven. For this to be true in all scenarios though, the fundamentals for the given company and its stock must remain more or less unchanged. In other words, they can not simply have deteriorated appreciably in the meanwhile.

Flash Crash

The Flash Crash has also been called the 2010 Flash Crash and the Crash of 2:45. It occurred on May 6 in 2010. This stock market collapse occurred in the United States and caused a trillion dollars of equity to be temporarily wiped out. It began officially at 2:32 EST. The crash happened over only the next 36 minutes.

During this crash, major stock indices including the Dow Jones Industrial Average, the S&P 500, and the NASDAQ composite fell apart and then rebounded with unparalleled speed and volatility. At one moment, the DJIA set its largest point drop within a single day to that time. It fell 998.5 points representing over 9% of its value.

Most of this drop happened in only minutes. The index then went on to recover a substantial portion of the drop a little later. Up to this point, this represented the second biggest point swing in a single day at 1010 points.

Trading volume exploded briefly as volatility increased. The prices of stock indices, individual stocks, futures on the indices, options, and ETF exchange traded funds were all over the board. In 2014, the CFTC Commodities Futures Trading Commission released a report that called this just over thirty minute crash among the most chaotic points in all of the history of global financial markets.

The government responded by putting a number of new regulations into play after the 2010 Flash Crash. Despite this fact, they were insufficient to stop another such rapid crash on August 24, 2015. During this second episode, bids on literally dozens of stocks and ETFs plunged to as little as a single penny per share as ETFs decoupled from their underlying value, per the Wall Street Journal article of December 6, 2015. As a result of this second incident, regulators placed ETFs under additional scrutiny. This also led to the analysts at Morningstar stating that legislation from the Depression era was governing the digital age technology of ETFs.

It took the Department of Justice almost five years to charge an individual with criminal misconduct that contributed massively to the original flash crash. They charged the trader Navinder Singh Sarao with 22 counts of market manipulation and fraud. Apparently he had utilized spoofing algorithms to trick the exchanges.

Immediately before the crash unfolded, Sarao had put in orders for thousands of the stock index futures contracts known as E-mini S&P 500 contracts. These orders constituted $200 million in bets that the markets would then decline. Before the orders were cancelled by his algorithm, it modified or replaced them 19,000 times. Thanks to this individual action, the government and regulators banned front running, layering, and the spoofing of orders.

In the investigation that the CFTC conducted, they came to the conclusion that Sarao bore substantial responsibility for the imbalances of the orders in derivatives markets. These impacted the stock markets and made the crash so much more severe. The small time trader Sarao was operating from his parent's house in the suburban part of west London when he carried out these actions. He had started manipulating the markets back in 2009 when he purchased and modified trading software that would permit him to quickly and automatically place and cancel his orders.

A later CFTC report in May 2014 determined that the high frequency traders who were assigned much of the blame for the flash crash did not cause it themselves. They did contribute to the severity of it as their orders were taken before those of other participants in the market.

Follow-On Public Offer (FPO)

A Follow-On Public Offer is also known by its official acronym FPO. This occurs when a public company which is already listed on a stock market exchange issues additional shares to investors. Such FPOs are useful and practical for those firms which wish to raise extra equity capital from the capital markets via stock issues. These methods are popular with publically traded corporations.

Such firms like to avail themselves of these FPO issues by selling more shares to investors. They have to complete an offer document in order to accomplish this. FPOs are never to be confused with IPOs. IPOs refer to the initial public offering a company uses to issue equity shares to the public for the very first time. FPOs are instead supplementary issues which they make once the firm is already exchange-established and -trading.

There are two main types of Follow-on public offerings available to companies today. The first kind dilutes existing investors. The Board of Directors must agree to boost the level of shares floating. It raises money for paying down debt or internally growing the company business. It ultimately raises the numbers of outstanding shares as well.

The second kind of FPO proves to be non diluting. It is the preferred method when the major shareholders or corporate directors elect to sell their own personal shares of the company stock. Since no new shares become created, it does not dilute the holdings of existing investors in the company. This is generally known as a secondary market offering. Neither the firm nor the present shareholders gain an advantage from this type of method.

Because there are two different means of selling shares with such Follow-On Public Offers, this makes it extremely crucial to know who the stock sellers are on any given offering transaction. This way, investors are able to learn quickly and easily if the new offering will prove to be net dilutive or not.

Such Follow-On Public Offerings prove to be increasingly commonplace within the world of investing. Corporations appreciate that they can quickly and easily collect additional fresh capital to utilize for any common purpose they deem appropriate or expedient. Their share price might drop as a result of such an FPO announcement. This upsets shareholders who are the main losers in such a scenario. Many times these secondary share offerings will be made at prices that are lower than the present market prices. In any case, they will almost certainly dilute the power and voting rights of their presently existing shares of company stock.

It always helps to look at some tangible examples to better grasp a challenging concept such as this one. Back in the year 2013, corporations deployed enough Follow-On Public Offers to raise an impressive $201.7 billion in additional equity. This was the greatest single-year amount that they raised for four years. Facebook outperformed in this respect by selling off an additional $3.9 billion worth of shares. This made them among the biggest single beneficiaries of the FPOs for that year.

Investment banks love secondary offerings. They benefit directly from them since they receive a portion of the fee structure pricing. In that same year of 2013, leading American investment banking operation Goldman Sachs handled $24.7 billion in secondary offerings to be the number one FPO underwriter.

The year 2015 subsequently saw a great number of firms which had only gone public a year earlier decide to issue Follow-On Public Offerings. Shake Shack proved to be one of these. They announced their secondary offering and witnessed their shares decline as a result. The stock plunged an eye-watering 16 percent on the news that a major secondary offering was in the works for a price lower than the then-current share price. Naturally, investors in Shake Shack were unhappy, but they were completely powerless to prevent the deal from going through.

FOREX Markets

FOREX markets are the world wide foreign exchange markets. They are called FX markets as well. FOREX markets are different from all of the other major financial markets in that they are over the counter and decentralized. They exist for the purpose of trading currencies.

Unlike with other markets, the FOREX markets are also open twenty-four hours a day during the week and on Sunday, since the different financial centers around the globe serve as trading bases for a variety of buyers and sellers. This foreign exchange market is the place where supply and demand mostly decides the different currencies' values for nations around the world.

The main point and reason for the FOREX markets are to help out investment and trade internationally through permitting businesses to easily change one currency to the other one that they require. In practice, individuals or businesses actually buy one amount of foreign currency through paying for it with a given amount of a different currency.

As an example, Canadian businesses may import British goods by paying for them in British Pounds, even though their income and base currency are Canadian dollars. The foreign exchange markets allow for investors to speculate on the rising and falling values of various currencies as well. It also makes the infamous carry trade possible, where investors are able to borrow currencies with low yields or interest rates and use them to purchase higher interest rate yielding currencies. Critics have said that the FOREX markets also hurt some countries' competitiveness against other countries.

This market is extremely popular and unique for a variety of reasons. It possesses the greatest trading volume on earth, managing in the three to four trillion dollar range every single trading day. This gives it enormous liquidity. It is also geographically centered all over the world, from Wellington in New Zealand to London in Great Britain to New York in the United States. Traders love that the market runs fully twenty-four hours per day except for on the weekends, when it reopens Sunday afternoon.

Finally, an enormous degree of leverage, that can be as much as two hundred to one, allows for even people with small accounts to make potentially enormous gains. Because of all of these factors and its world wide trading base, the FOREX markets have been called the ones where perfect competition is most evident. This is the case even though central banks sometimes intervene directly in these markets to increase or decrease the value of their currency relative to a trading partners' or trading competitors' currency value.

FTSE 100 Index

The FTSE 100 Index proves to be the trading world designation for the largest index managed by the FTSE Group out of London in the United Kingdom. FTSE is actually jointly owned by parent companies the Financial Times and the London Stock Exchange. This mash up of FT from Financial Times and SE from London Stock Exchange is how they arrive at the acronym FTSE. In general when analysts refer to the FTSE, they mean the FTSE 100 Index itself. This is actually a misnomer, since there are literally thousands of different FTSE indices the company owns and operates around the globe on numerous different national stock exchanges on every continent.

This FTSE 100 Index has been called the globe's most heavily referenced and most popular stock market index throughout the world. In practice, it represents around 80 percent of the entire market capitalization of the heavily multinational London Stock Exchange. The weighting system the FTSE company utilizes means that the bigger a corporation is, the larger a share of the index it occupies, thanks to it being a market capitalization-weighted index. This index is real time calculated all trading day long. The firm updates and publishes it continuously throughout the open market hours on an every 15 seconds basis.

Many analysts and investors rely on the FTSE 100 Index as some sort of prosperity indicator for British companies and the United Kingdom economy in general. This is actually a misnomer. It is all thanks to a significant constituency of the representative firms from the index being headquartered in other nations throughout the globe. It means that the index's daily movements do not truly reflect the strength of the British economy and corporations. Instead, the secondary index of the group, the FTSE 250 is more accurate a bell weather for British businesses and the economy. This is because a far smaller representation of international corporations populates the 250 index. It makes it a much better indicator for Great Britain generally speaking.

FTSE the company decides every quarter which are the 100 largest member companies on the LSE. Their tradition is to calculate this on the Wednesday after the first Friday of the month for March, June, September, and December, respectively. They utilize the business day close values from the night before to decide if any constituents should be replaced.

It is no exaggeration to call the FTSE 100 Index the Blue Chip index of the London Stock Exchange. These are the largest and most economically powerful and far-reaching corporations from Great Britain and around the world (ex the United States) in many cases.

The constituent members of the FTSE 100 as of time of publication were as follows: 3I Group, Associated British Foods, Admiral Group, Anglo American, Antofagasta, Ashtead Group, AstraZeneca, Aviva, Babcock International, BAE Systems, Barclays, Barratt Development, BHP Billiton, BP, British American Tobacco, British Land, BT Group, Bunzl, Burberry Group, Carnival, Centrica, Coca Cola HBC AG, Compass Group, Convatec, CRH, Croda International, DCC, Diageo, Direct Line, Easy Jet, Experian, Fresnillo, GKN, GlaxoSmithKline, Glencore, Hammerson, Hargreaves Lans, Hikma, HSBC Bank Holdings, Imperial Brands, Informa, Intercontinental Hotels, Intertek Group, International Consolidated Airlines, INTU Properties, ITV, Johnson Matthey, Kingfisher, Land Securities, Legal & General, Lloyds Group, London Stock Exchange, Marks & Spencer, Medi clinic, Merlin, Micro Focus, Mondi, William Morrison, National Grid, Next, Old Mutual, Paddy Power Betting, Pearson, Persimmon, Provident Financial, Prudential, Randgold Res., RDS A Shares, RDS B Shares, Reckitt Benison Group, RELX, Rentokil International, Rio Tinto, Rolls Royce Holdings, Royal Bank of Scotland, Royal Mail, RSA Insurance, Sage Group, J. Sainsbury, Schroders, Scottish Mort, Severn Trent, Shire Pharmaceuticals, Sky PLC, Smith & Nephew, Smiths Group, Smurfit Kap., SSE, St. James's Place, Standard Chartered, Standard Life, Taylor Wimpey, Tesco, TUI AG, Unilever, United Utilities, Vodafone Group, Whitbread, Wolseley, Worldpay Group, and WPP Group (the world's leading advertising company giant).

FTSE 250

FTSE 250 is a broad-based stock index maintained by the FTSE company. This company is much like Standard and Poor's in that they both concentrate their efforts on calculating indices. The FTSE is not made up of any stock exchange, though among its co-owners is the famed and historic London Stock Exchange (LSE). The other co-owner of the company is its namesake the Financial Times newspaper publishing empire.

Easily the best known of the FTSE indices is the FTSE 100. There are many thousands of indices owned, produced, and calculated by FTSE, but only one is the blue chip index of all British and international company and economy stocks based on the LSE. The second most important and widely cited index from the company is this FTSE 250. This one is made up of the 101st to 351st largest companies in the U.K. As these firms tend to be much more British and far less international than those making up the FTSE 100, they are gauged to be a superior measurement of how the British economy and U.K. based firms are actually performing.

The FTSE 250 index list is altered four times a year on a quarterly basis. This occurs reliably every March, June, September, and December month. The index itself is continuously calculated instantly in real time. The owner of the index publishes it every minute accordingly online and through financial news and media outlet feeds.

As of November 7, 2016, the 350 different constituent companies which comprise the FTSE 250 are as follows: 3i Infrastructure, AA, Aberdeen Asset Management, Aberforth Smaller Companies Trust, Acacia Mining, Aggreko, Aldermore Group, Alliance Trust, Allied Minds, Amec Foster Wheeler, AO World, Ascential, Ashmore Group, Assura, WS Atkins, Auto Trader Group, Aveva, Balfour Beatty, Bankers Investment Trust, Barr, A.G., BBA Aviation, Beazley Group, Bellway, Berendsen, Berkeley Group Holdings, Bank of Georgia Holdings, BH Macro, Big Yellow Group, B & M European Retail Value, Bodycote, Booker Group, Bovis Homes Group, Brewin Dolphin Holdings, British Empire Trust, Britvic, Brown N, BTG, Cairn Energy, Caledonia Investments, Capital & Counties Properties, Card Factory, Carillion, Centamin, Cineworld, City of London Investment Trust, Clarkson, Close Brothers Group, CLS Holdings, CMC Markets, Cobham,

Computacenter, Countryside Properties, Countrywide, Cranswick, Crest Nicholson, CYBG, Daejan Holdings, Dairy Crest, Debenhams, Dechra Pharmaceuticals, Derwent London, DFS, Dignity, Diploma, Domino's Pizza, Drax Group, Dunelm Group, Edinburgh Investment Trust, Electra Private Equity, Electrocomponents, Elementis, Entertainment One, Essentra, Esure, Euromoney Institutional Investor, Evraz, F&C Commercial Property Trust, Fidelity China Special Situations, Fidelity European Values, Fidessa Group, Finsbury Growth & Income Trust, FirstGroup, Fisher, James & Sons, Foreign & Colonial Investment Trust, G4S, Galliford Try, GCP Infrastructure Investments, Genesis Emerging Markets Fund, Genus, Go-Ahead Group, Grafton Group, Grainger, Great Portland Estates, Greencoat UK Wind, Greencore, Greene King, Greggs, GVC Holdings, Halfords Group, Halma, Hansteen Holdings, HarbourVest Global Private Equity, Hastings Group, Hays, Henderson Group, HICL Infrastructure Company, Hill & Smith, Hiscox, Hochschild Mining, Homeserve, Howden Joinery, Hunting, Ibstock, ICAP, IG Group Holdings, IMI, Inchcape, Indivior, Inmarsat, Intermediate Capital Group, International Personal Finance, International Public Partnerships, Investec, IP Group, Jardine Lloyd Thompson, JD Sports, John Laing Group, John Laing Infrastructure Fund, JPMorgan American Investment Trust, JPMorgan Emerging Markets Investment Trust, JPMorgan Indian Investment Trust, JRP Group, Jupiter Fund Management, Just Eat, KAZ Minerals, Keller, Kennedy Wilson Europe Real Estate, Kier Group, Ladbrokes Coral, Laird, Lancashire Holdings, LondonMetric Property, Man Group, Marshalls, Marston's, McCarthy & Stone, Meggitt, Mercantile Investment Trust, Metro Bank, Millennium & Copthorne Hotels, Mitchells & Butlers, Mitie, Moneysupermarket.com Group, Monks Investment Trust, Morgan Advanced Materials, Murray International Trust, National Express Group, NB Global, NCC Group, NMC Health, Ocado Group, OneSavings Bank, P2P Global Investments, PageGroup, Paragon Group of Companies, PayPoint, Paysafe, Pennon Group, Perpetual Income & Growth Investment Trust, Personal Assets Trust, Petra Diamonds, Petrofac, Pets at Home, Phoenix Group Holdings, Playtech, Polar Capital Technology Trust, Polypipe, PZ Cussons, QinetiQ, Rank Group, Rathbone Brothers, Redefine International, Redrow, Regus, Renewables Infrastructure Group, Renishaw, Rentokil Initial, Restaurant Group, Rightmove, RIT Capital Partners, Riverstone Energy, Rotork, RPC Group, Safestore, Saga, Savills, Scottish Investment Trust, Scottish Mortgage Investment Trust, Segro, Senior, Serco, Shaftesbury, Shawbrook Bank, SIG plc, Smith (DS), Smurfit Kappa Group, Softcat, Sophos,

Spectris, Spirax-Sarco Engineering, Spire Healthcare, Sports Direct, SSP Group, Stagecoach Group, St. Modwen Properties, SuperGroup, SVG Capital, Synthomer, TalkTalk Group, Tate & Lyle, Ted Baker, Telecom Plus, Temple Bar Investment Trust, Templeton Emerging Markets Investment Trust, Thomas Cook Group, Tritax Big Box REIT, TR Property Investment Trust (two listings, both ordinary & sigma shares), Tullett Prebon, Tullow Oil, UBM, UDG Healthcare, UK Commercial Property Trust, Ultra Electronics Holdings, Unite Group, Vectura Group, Vedanta Resources, Vesuvius, Victrex, Virgin Money, Weir Group, Wetherspoon (J D), W H Smith, William Hill, Witan Investment Trust, Wizz Air, Woodford Patient Capital Trust, Wood Group, Workspace Group, Worldwide Healthcare Trust, and Zoopla.

Fund Manager

Fund managers are the individuals, investment companies, or sometimes banks that handle a mutual fund's investment decisions. These decision makers are charged with earning as much profit for their fund as they reasonably can while still following the risk parameters that the mutual fund discloses.

Fund managers are compensated differently than stock brokers who earn commissions. These managers receive their compensation based on the total dollar amounts under the management of the mutual fund. An advantage to this form of payment is that it provides motivation for fund managers to increase overall assets. A more successful manager will attract more investors and money and achieve greater returns. The management fee that the fund levies pays the fund manager. This fee appears on fund financials under the expense ratio.

A mutual fund's board of directors hires the fund manager. Fund shareholders themselves select the board of directors. These fund managers wear many hats. They oversee all of the investments that the mutual fund undertakes. They must set and manage annual meetings. They must also be responsible for the mutual fund's customer service efforts and many different elements of fund compliance. Compliance roles include offering a fund prospectus, negotiating commission rates with brokers, issuing proxies, and other important periodic and daily tasks.

Fund managers generally hire staff to help them with these many roles. Sometimes they contract out some or all of these services to another company. In practice most mutual funds are owned by families of mutual fund companies. In these cases, these companies provide their fund managers with these services at a cost.

A number of mutual funds have single managers in charge of the fund. The majority of larger funds have significant sized staffs that the fund manager leads. In such cases, these leadership positions are more like investment managers than fund managers. The biggest funds have a few fund managers who share the responsibilities and decisions. Entire investment firms act as fund managers to some mutual funds.

A fund manager is an important person to consider when investors are looking at mutual funds. One of the most important characteristics of a successful mutual fund concerns how long the fund manager has been present. Funds which boast a fund manager who has been with them a long time have a distinct advantage.

If a fund claims significant changes in its fund management, this is generally looked at as a negative factor. It might indicate that there have been problems in the fund with the performance. It could also imply that the fund manager has not properly carried out compliance and other critical issues in the daily running of the fund. Alternatively, a change in fund manager could simply mean that the fund has overhauled its investment strategy and changed its emphasis.

Hedge funds also employ fund managers. A hedge fund manager is far less restricted in the investments that he or she can pursue than is a mutual fund manager. This is because there is much less regulation for hedge funds than for mutual funds.

The hedge fund managers receive their income according to a different compensation scheme. Mutual fund managers earn their fees however the fund performs. Hedge fund managers instead are rewarded with a percentage of their earned returns. They also receive a small management fee that commonly runs between one and four percent of the fund's net asset value.

Investors who do not like paying managers for poor performance appreciate this structure for paying hedge fund managers. The disadvantage to it concerns risk. Hedge fund managers could pursue more aggressive and risky strategies to make greater returns because of their fee structure.

Future Value

Future Value refers to a current asset's anticipated value at a given specific date of the future. Such a forecast will be dependent on the rate of growth rate that the company assumes over time. As an example, a company may assume a certain guaranteed rate of growth. This would allow them to state that a $10,000 investment they make now will have a value of $100,000 twenty years from now. This would have the FV of the original $10,000 investment at $100,000. This equation takes for granted that the rate of growth will be approximately consistent and constant. It also assumes that the upfront payment is an untouched one throughout the life of the literal investment in question.

Such a Future Value calculation permits managers and analysts alike to anticipate with hopefully some accuracy the profits they can forecast earning in comparing varying investments. The weakness is that the quantity of growth which the investment generates cannot be predicted with one hundred percent certainty. Still, the returns on the investment if it were sunk into stocks versus a new product launch or other revenue accruing project will likely be vastly different from one another, which mean that the accountants will stay busy extrapolating multiple base case scenario possibilities.

It can be quite complex to accurately ascertain the future value of a given asset. This of course varies per the asset class. Such FV calculations assume that the growth rate will remain consistently stable. This is easy to determine with great accuracy when analysts are considering money put into a fixed rate of interest CD or savings account. Investments they make in securities such as stocks will provide a higher degree of volatility and fluctuating rate of return. This makes it exceedingly difficult to prognosticate with accuracy. Where the core idea is concerned though, compound and simple interest rates reflect the easiest to understand examples of utilizing a FV calculation.

These future value calculations might be compiled in two different ways, depending on the interest accruing. Look at the simple interest calculation approach. The formula for when the base case assumes simple interest is FV equals Initial principle times the result of one plus the interest rate multiplied by time in years.

It is always most illuminating to look at a tangible example on challenging concepts such as this one. Consider a $100,000 investment that the firm keeps in a simple time deposit CD account that yields five percent on a simple annual interest payment basis. In this scenario, the future value of the $100,000 would be $100,000 times (one plus .05 times five) for a final result of $125,000.

It becomes more challenging when compounded interest is taken into consideration. Under the compounding interest base case, the rate has to be reapplied on every year's cumulative account balance. Using the same example as above, if the investment in its first year realizes a five percent interest, this is $5,000 in interest. The next year, the total account value would be base of $105,000 before interest begins to accrue. Now the five percent rate would be applied to the $105,000 instead of the old $100,000 initial total. At five percent interest again, this would yield an interest dollar amount of $5,250. The calculations continue as such until the final year is reached. This means that the formula for investment earnings on a compounded interest basis is Future Value equals Initial investment times the final result of one plus the interest rate raised to the power of the time value.

Futures

Futures prove to be financial derivatives that are also called forward contracts. Such a futures contract gives a seller the obligation to deliver an asset, such as a commodity, to the buyer at a pre set date. These contracts are heavily traded on major produced commodities like wheat, gold, oil, coffee, and sugar. They also exist for underlying financial instruments that include government bonds, stock market indexes, and foreign currencies.

The history of futures goes back to Ancient Greece where the first recorded example is detailed about an olive press arrangement that philosopher Thales entered into. Futures contracts become commonplace at trade fairs throughout Europe by the 1100's. Merchants did not feel secure traveling with significant amounts of goods, so they would only bring display samples along and then sell merchandise that they would deliver in greater quantities at future dates.

Futures contracts created an enormous bubble in the 1600's with the Dutch Tulip Mania that caused tulip bulbs to skyrocket to unthinkable levels. In this speculative bubble, the majority of money that was exchanged turned out to be for tulip futures and not the tulips themselves. The first futures exchange in the United States opened in 1868 as the Chicago Board of Trade, where copper, pork bellies, and wheat were traded in futures contracts.

In the early years of the 1970's, futures trading grew explosively in volume. Pricing models created by Myron Scholes and Fischer Black permitted the quick pricing of futures and options on them. Investors could easily speculate on commodities prices through these futures. As the demand for the futures skyrocketed, additional significant futures exchanges opened and expanded around the world, especially in Chicago, London, and New York.

Futures trading could not happen effectively without the exchanges. Futures contracts are spelled out in terms of the asset that underlies them, the date of delivery, the last day of contract trading, transaction currency, and size of ticks or minimum permissible price changes. Exchanges have developed into major and predictable markets through their standardizing of all of these various factors for many different kinds of futures contracts.

Trading futures contracts involves major leverage. This means that they carry tremendous opportunities as well as risks. Futures, with their ability to control enormous quantities of commodities and financials, have been the root causes for many collapses. Enron and Barings Bank were both brought down by financial futures. Perhaps the most famous futures meltdown involved the Long Term Capital Management group.

Even though this company had the inventors of the futures pricing models Scholes and Black working for them, the company lost money in the futures markets so quickly that the Federal Reserve Bank had to become involved and bail out the company to stop the whole financial system of the Untied States from collapsing.

Futures Contracts

Futures contracts are legally binding agreements which two parties usually enter into on a futures exchange trading floor or electronic platform. They spell out the particulars for selling or buying specific financial instruments or commodities for a pre-set price at an exact moment in the future. Such contracts have become standardized to make it easy to trade them on the various futures exchanges. They provide information on the quantity and quality of the commodity, though this depends on the nature of the underlying asset.

Futures contracts can be settled in two ways. Some of them require actual physical delivery of the commodity specified. Others simply settle between the two parties in cash. These contracts specify all important characteristics for the item which the parties are trading. This makes them different from the word "futures" that more generally refers to the markets in which these commodities and instruments trade.

There are two actual types of participants in the futures markets who utilize such futures contracts. These are speculators and hedgers. Individual traders and managers of portfolios can use them to place speculative bets on the direction of price movements for the given asset that underlies the contracts. Hedgers involve buyers or producers of the contact asset itself attempting to lock in the price for which they will later buy or sell their commodity.

There are many different commodities and assets for which futures contracts exist. The most obvious of these are hard assets such as precious metals, industrial metals, natural gas, crude oil and other energy products, grains, seeds, livestock, oils, and carbon credits. Literally dozens of the more significant stock market indices around the globe have these contracts available to trade. Some major individual stocks have their own futures contract on their shares as well. The major interest rates and most important currency pairs also have such contracts and markets to trade.

Futures contracts which require physical delivery do not often result in such physical delivery. Many investors in these contracts trade them and sell them before the date of delivery. They can roll them forward by selling the imminent to expire contract and buying a further month out to replace them.

For producers of a good, these contracts provide a unique solution to the problem of fluctuating prices. Oil producers are classic examples. They might intend to produce a million barrels of oil to deliver in precisely a year. If the price is $50 for a barrel today, and the producer does not want to risk prices falling lower, it could lock it in. Oil prices have become so volatile that they could be substantially lower or higher a year from now. By selling a futures contract, the producer gives up the opportunity to possibly sell the oil for more in a year. It also eliminates the risk of receiving a lower amount.

Mathematical models actually determine the prices of futures contracts. They consider the present day spot price, time until maturity, risk free return rates, dividends, dividend yields, convenience yields, and storage costs. This might mean with oil prices at $50 that a one year futures contract sells for $53. The producer receives a guarantee for $53 million and will have to provide the 1 million barrels of oil on the exact delivery date. It will obtain this $53 per barrel price despite the spot prices at which the markets are trading on that date.

Futures Exchange

A futures exchange refers to a central clearing marketplace that allows for futures contracts as well as options on such futures contracts to be traded. Thanks to the rapid increase in electronic trading of futures, this term also finds use regarding futures trading activities directly.

There are the two most important futures exchanges in the world today. The biggest in the United States is the Chicago Mercantile Exchange, or CME. This one became established in the last years of the 1890s. In the early days, the only futures contracts available were agricultural products' futures.

This changed rapidly in the 1970s. Currency futures appeared on the major currency pairs after the breakdown of the Breton Woods Agreement. The futures exchanges of today are massive by comparison. They allow for investors to hedge all sorts of financial products and commodities. These range from stock indices and individual stocks to energies, precious and base metals, soft commodities such as orange juice and soybeans, interest rate products, and even credit default swaps.

In today's futures exchange, it is hedging financial instruments and products which create the significant majority of activity in futures markets. Today the futures exchange markets carry an important responsibility for global financial system operations, efficient functioning, and activity. The international nature of this global futures exchange has given rise to the world's first truly international futures market, the ICE Intercontinental Exchange.

ICE is massive and important in not only futures markets. They own and operate 12 different exchanges around the world, including NYSE EuroNext, which controls the famed and venerable New York Stock Exchange and EuroNext exchange (owning the Paris and Dutch stock exchanges, among others). In Europe, this is a serious rival to the historic LSE London Stock Exchange and continental powerhouse the German Deutsche Bourse. The ICE today counts 12,000 listed futures contracts as well as securities. It trades 5.2 million futures contracts every day, as well as $1.8 billion in cash equities every day.

In energies, the Intercontinental Exchange Futures commands almost half of all the traded crude and refined oil futures contracts volume for the entire planet. It is also the location of the most highly liquid market for the European interest rates short term contracts. It controls a wide variety of global benchmarks in agriculture, energies, foreign exchange, and equity indices.

ICE only launched its international futures exchange back in 2000 with the advent of their electronic trading platform. This makes it among the newer futures exchanges in the world, and yet it is a dominant international player still. Their high tech-powered rise increased the access to and transparency of the Over the Counter traded energy markets as well as the new global futures markets exchange they opened shortly thereafter. It was 2001 when they expanded to energy futures with their acquisition of the International Petroleum Exchange.

In 2002, ICE expanded heavily into Europe by opening up their ICE Clear Europe. This represented the first new clearing house in the United Kingdom in a full century. By 2007, the Intercontinental Exchange had cemented its global position in energy trade by acquiring both the NYBOT New York Board of Trade and the Canadian-based Winnipeg Commodity Exchange.

The end result today is an entire ecosystem made up of futures and equities markets, clearing houses throughout the world, listing and data centers and services, and technology-driven solutions which together work to create a full, free, and transparent accessibility to the worldwide futures, energy, derivatives, and capital markets.

Between ICE Futures U.S.'s operations and endeavors within the United States, the futures exchange is enabling and empowering markets which allow for an effective risk management throughout the world economy. Their product offerings and solutions encompass a diverse and broad variety of futures contracts. These span internationally traded equity indexes and futures; credit derivative futures; FX futures; North American oil, power, and natural gas futures; and soft commodities and agriculture futures including sugar, cotton, coffee, and cocoa.

Gold Certificate

A Gold Certificate refers to the world's original paper bank notes. Beginning back in the 1600s, such certificates based on gold became first issued by various goldsmiths in both London and Amsterdam to their customers who would deposit their gold bullion with them for safe keeping. Such gold certificates became proof of the ownership of gold. After some time elapsed, such certificates became passed from one hand to the next in transactions much like cash. It avoided the inconvenience of needing to withdraw and physically transfer over the gold bullion which was bulky and expensive to ship and protect.

By the middle of the 1800s, the U.S. Treasury started offering gold certificates which people might then exchange with them for gold from within the Treasury vaults. They actually circulated as legal tender in the United States all the way through 1933. At this point, the American federal government outlawed the ownership of private gold within the U.S.

Even though they are no longer legal tender anywhere in the world nowadays, gold certificates still exist today. A few Swiss and German banks keep issuing them. Gold pool investment programs in the United States and Australia also issue such certificates. As in the earliest days of the certificates, the gold certificates today represent an ownership stake in a specific amount of gold bullion coins or bars in a vault. The gold owner receives the certificates and is then able to avoid the very considerable costs of gold trading, delivery, insurance, and storage.

Investors seem to have an ongoing love affair with gold certificates four hundred years later after they first appeared. They provide a feeling of comfort from an expensive piece of paper that stands for something of actual tangible value. Yet the critics of the concept abound. They claim that there can be many issues with such certificates. The issuer might have mistakenly issued a duplicate certificate or over issued them by accident. There are also hard to tell fakes and forgeries, poor administration, elimination of older certificates, changes of address issues, and more which can cause them to be worthless or contested.

In their defense, such certificates are now mostly also updated online in accessible databases as the gold pool publishes a daily list of gold owners which is easily accessible via the Internet and proves who owns what from the gold vault hoard. This method often utilizes nicknames to maintain the privacy and anonymity of gold ownership, which is extremely important to many holders of gold today.

The problem with gold certificates nowadays is that they represent unallocated gold claims to convert real gold into ownership through physical allocation when the investor surrenders the certificate and pays the considerable costs of transfer. Many investors and analysts do not like unallocated gold because of these limitations. Those who own unallocated gold are actually creditors to the gold pool since the gold ownership is merely a balance sheet item when all is said and done. This exposes the certificate holders to the potential insolvency of the company which owns and manages the actual gold pool over the longer term.

This is not to say that some government-guaranteed gold pools do not issue good gold certificates which investors can bank on today. The best known, most respected, and safest of these is undoubtedly the Perth Mint Certificate Program. They issue good certificates for gold coins and bullion bars which are actually there inventoried and audited independently in the vault and can be claimed upon demand and surrendering of the appropriate certificates.

Government Bonds

Government bonds are debt instruments that governments issue to pay for government expenditures. Within the United States, federal government issues include savings bonds, treasury notes, treasury bonds, and TIPS Treasury inflation protected securities. Investors should carefully consider the risks that different countries' governments possess before they invest in their bonds. Among these international government risks are political risk, country risk, interest rate risk, and inflation risk. Governments generally have less credit risk, though not always.

Savings bonds are a type of United States government bonds that the Treasury department sells. They are available in an electronic form. The Treasury offers them directly from their website, or individuals can buy them from the majority of financial institutions and banks. When savings bonds reach maturity, the investors get back the bond's face value along with interest which accrued. These savings bonds may not be redeemed the first year of issue. Any investors who redeem them in their first five years of issue lose three months interest for cashing out too early.

The Treasury of the United States also issues intermediate time frame bonds known as Treasury notes or T-Notes. These notes provide interest payments semiannually at a coupon rate which is fixed. These notes typically are denominated in $1,000 face values. Those with three or two year maturity dates come in $5,000 denominations. Before 1984, T-Notes were callable and gave the Treasury the right to buy them back given specific conditions.

The U.S. government's longest term bonds are Treasury Bonds, or T-Bonds. These have maturity dates ranging from ten to 30 years time. They also provide interest payments on a semiannual basis and come in $1,000 denominated values. These T-bonds are important because they pay for federal budget shortfalls, are a form of monetary policy, and ensure the country is able to regulate its money supply. As all bond issuers, the Treasury department looks at return and risk requirements on the market when it goes to raise capital so that it can be as efficient as possible. This helps to explain the different kinds of Treasury securities and government bonds they offer.

U.S. government bonds have generally been considered to be without risk, which is why they trade so easily in extremely large and liquid markets. The downside to this is that they offer considerably lower returns than do other bonds. TIPS do provide protection against inflation so that any inflation increases will not exceed the interest rate of the bond. The prices of government bonds are based on current interest rates. This means that the fixed rate bonds will decline in value as the interest rates rise, since there is lost opportunity to obtain newer bonds at higher interest rates. Similarly, if interest rates fall, the bond's values will rise.

The federal government is able to control the money supply in part by its issue of the government bonds. If they wish to increase the money supply, they can simply buy back their own bonds. These funds then find their way to a bank and expand the money supply as banks keep small reserves and loan the rest out (in the money multiplier effect). The government is also able to lower the money supply by selling additional bonds which takes money out of circulation. If the government were to retire the funds received from the sale of these bonds, it would reduce the available money supply. More often than not, the U.S. government spends the money.

Hedge Account

A hedge account is an account established with a hedge fund. There are several reasons why a person or business would be interested in setting up a hedge account. These mostly center on the desire for investments that commonly produce higher profits or the wish to hedge, or protect, a business' operations from certain unpredictable and undesirable swings in market prices. Businesses can open up their own hedge accounts in various futures and commodities markets to protect themselves from these business impacting price movements in important related commodities.

A person who is interested in opening a hedge account will have to make application to a hedge fund. Hedge funds are typically restrictive in the types of funds that they will accept from an investor. The investor will have to prove certain income levels or asset base holdings that demonstrate that they are capable of bearing the substantial losses that could result from trades in a hedge account. They must also have liquid cash that they can tie up for long periods of time, since most hedge funds do not allow immediate on demand withdrawals.

Funds that are invested with them could be tied up for a year or longer, and minimum waiting periods apply. Because of all of these reasons, hedge funds are typically looking for people as investors who have in excess of a million dollars of liquid net worth.

Hedge accounts can also be accounts that businesses use to offset the changes in commodities' prices. A company's products may be heavily dependent on prices such as sugar and cocoa if they are a chocolate company, oil and other energy prices if they use energy intensive processes or are shipping companies, or even industrial metals such as copper if they produce wires or cables. Gold and silver mining companies, along with oil producers, routinely hedge their quantities of precious metals and energies that they expect to produce to protect against anticipated declining prices. By locking in the present price for these goods and commodities that they require or will produce later on in the year, they can insulate themselves from price swings that move against them.

This can mean the difference between having to raise prices and risk losing market share or selling goods at a much lower profit margin. Because of this, many major multinational companies around the world routinely protect themselves and their operations through the use of hedge accounts. Some of them even have individuals or departments that oversee these operations.

For a business to set up such a hedge account is not difficult. They only have to open a commodities account with one of the major commodities exchanges, such as the Chicago Mercantile Exchange, the Chicago Board of Trade, New York Mercantile Exchange, or the New York Board of Trade. These accounts can be used by companies for speculating on the price movements of underlying commodities as well, and not only for hedging their operations. In this case, care has to be taken, as the leverage provided by hedge accounts, such as commodities accounts, is enough to bring down a company overnight if they are irresponsible with the trades in the account.

Hedge Fund

A hedge fund is an investment fund which are commonly only open to a specific group of investors. These investors pay a large performance fee each year, commonly a certain percent of their funds under management, to the manager of the hedge fund. Hedge funds are very minimally regulated and are therefore are able to participate in a wide array of investments and investment strategies.

Literally every single hedge fund pursues its own strategy of investing that will establish the kinds of investments that it seeks. Hedge funds commonly go for a wide range of investments in which they may buy or sell short shares and positions. Stocks, commodities, and bonds are some of these asset classes with which they work.

As you would anticipate from the name, hedge funds typically try to offset some of the risks in their portfolios by employing a number of risk hedging strategies. These mostly revolve around the use of derivatives, or financial instruments with values that depend on anticipated price movements in the future of an asset to which they are linked, as well as short selling investments.

Most countries only allow certain types of wealthy and professional investors to open a hedge fund account. Regulators may not heavily oversee the activities of hedge funds, but they do govern who is allowed to participate. As a result, traditional investment funds' rules and regulations mostly do not apply to hedge funds.

Actual net asset values of hedge funds often tally into the many billions of dollars. The funds' gross assets held commonly prove to be massively higher as a result of their using leverage on their money invested. In particular niche markets like distressed debt, high yield ratings, and derivatives trading, hedge funds are the dominant players.

Investors get involved in hedge funds in search of higher than normal market returns. When times are good, many hedge funds yield even twenty percent annual investment returns. The nature of their hedging strategies is supposed to protect them from terrible losses, such as were seen in the financial crisis from 2007-2010.

The hedge fund industry is opaque and difficult to measure accurately. This is partially as a result of the significant expansion of the industry, as well as an inconsistent definition of what makes a hedge fund. Prior to the peak of hedge funds in the summer of 2008, it is believed that hedge funds might have overseen as much as two and a half trillion dollars. The credit crunch hit many hedge funds particularly hard, and their assets under management have declined sharply as a result of both losses, as well as requests for withdrawals by investors. In 2010, it is believed that hedge funds once again represent in excess of two trillion dollars in assets under management.

The largest hedge funds in the world are JP Morgan Chase, with over $53 billion under management; Bridgewater Associates, having more than $43 billion in assets under management; Paulson and Company, with more than $32 billion in assets; Brevan Howard that has greater than $27 billion in assets; and Soros Fund Management, which boasts around $27 billion in assets under management.

Hedging

In the world of finance, hedging is the act of putting together a hedge. Hedging involves building up a position in one market whose goal is try to counteract risk from changes in price in another market's position that is the opposite. The ultimate goal is to diminish or eliminate the business or person's possibilities of risk that they wish to avoid. A number of specific vehicles exist to help with hedging. These typically include forward contracts, swaps, insurance policies, options, derivatives, and products sold over the counter. Futures contracts prove to be the most popular version of hedging instruments.

In the 1800's, futures markets open to the public came into existence. These were set up to permit a standardized form of effective, viable, and open hedging of commodity prices in agriculture. In the intervening century, these have grown to include all manners of futures contracts that allow individuals and businesses to hedge precious metals, energy, changes in interest rates, and movements in foreign currencies.

There are countless examples of individuals who might be interested in hedging. Commercial farmers are common types of people who practice hedging. Prices for agricultural crops like wheat change all the time as the demand and supply for them fluctuates. Sometimes these price changes are significant in one direction or the other. With the present prices and crop predictions at harvest time, a commercial farmer might determine that planting wheat for the season is smart.

The problem that he encounters is that these predicted prices are simply forecasts. After the farmer plants his wheat crop, he has tied himself to it for the whole growing season. Should the real price of wheat soar in between the time that the farmer plants and harvests his crop then he might make a great amount of money that he did not count on, yet should the real price decline by the time the harvest is in then the farmer might be ruined completely.

To remove the risk from his wheat crop equation, the farmer can set up a hedge. He does this hedging by selling a certain quantity of futures contracts for wheat. These should be sold at an amount equal to the wheat crop size that he expects when he plants it. In such a way, the commercial farmer fixes his price of wheat at planting time. His hedging contract proves to be a pledge to furnish a particular quantity of wheat bushels to a certain place on a fixed date in time at a guaranteed price. Now the farmer is hedged against changes in the prices of wheat. He does not have to worry anymore about the wheat prices and whether they are falling or rising, since he has been promised a fixed price in his hedging wheat futures contract. The possibility of him being totally ruined by falling wheat prices is completely removed from the realm of possibility. At the same time, he has lost the opportunity of realizing extra money as a result of rising wheat prices when harvest time arrives. These are the upsides and the downsides to hedging; both the positives and the negatives of uncertainty are eliminated.

High Frequency Trading (HFT)

High frequency trading turns out to be a platform for program-based trades. It works with super computers that are able to run huge quantities of trading orders at incredibly rapid speeds. This HFT works with complicated algorithms. These analyze a wide range of markets and then place a number fast-paced orders depending on the conditions in the markets. The secret of the trading algorithms lies in their speed. Those traders who have the quickest trade executions usually make more money than do traders who have slower trade executions.

This high frequency trading has not always been mainstream or even possible. It grew in popularity as some of the exchanges began to provide incentives for corporations that could increase the stock market's liquidity.

As an example, the NYSE New York Stock Exchange works with a number of liquidity providers. These are known as SLPs Supplemental Liquidity Providers. The strive to provide better liquidity and more competition for the exchange and its already existing quotes.

The companies that participate in this program earn either a rebate or a fee when they increase the liquidity. This amount turned out to be $0.0019 in mid 2016 for securities that are listed on the NYSE or NYSE MKT. It may not sound like an enormous amount of money. It adds up to major profits quickly as some of these companies are engaged in millions of transactions on busy days.

The NYSE and other exchanges introduced this SLP program for a specific reason. After Lehman Brothers collapsed back in 2008, liquidity turned into an enormous concern for market participants. The SLP provided the solution to low liquidity. It also made high frequency trading a major part of the stock market in only a few years.

High frequency trading offers some significant benefits to the stock exchanges and financial markets. The most significant one centers on the significantly better liquidity that the programs provide. It has reduced bid ask spreads substantially. Larger spreads are more or less a thing of the past.

Some exchanges tested the benefits by trying to place fees on the HFT. The spreads then increased as fewer trades occurred. The Canadian government started charging fees for high frequency trading on Canadian markets. A study concluded that the end result was 9% higher bid to ask spreads.

There are many who dislike high frequency trading as well. Opponents are harsh in their criticism. Many broker dealers have been eliminated by the computer programs. The human element has been removed from many decisions on the exchanges.

When errors occur, the critics are quick to point out that human interactions could have prevented them. Part of the problem in the speed is that the programs are making decisions in literally thousandths of a second. This can lead to huge moves in the market with no apparent explanation or reason.

The best example of the mistakes that can lead to enormous and scary stock market moves happened on May 6, 2010 during the Flash Crash. The DJIA Dow Jones Industrial Average experienced its biggest drop of all time on an intraday basis. The Dow plunged over 1,000 points and dropped a full 10% in only twenty minutes. It then recovered back much of the loss in the next few hours. When the government investigated the issue, they found an enormous order which had caused the sell off to begin. The HFT computer algorithms did all the rest.

Another criticism concerns large corporate profiting at the expense of the smaller retail investors. The trade off is superior liquidity. Unfortunately, much of this turns out to be phantom liquidity. It is there for the market at one moment and then gone in another. This keeps the traders from benefiting from the liquidity.

High Yield Bonds

High Yield Bonds turn out to be bonds that possess a lower credit rating and higher yield than those corporate, municipal, and sovereign government bonds which are of investment grade. Thanks to the greater risk of them defaulting, such bonds yield a higher return than the bonds which are qualified investment grade issues. Those companies that issue high yielding debt are usually capital intensive companies and startup firms that already possess higher debt ratios. Investors often refer to such bonds as junk bonds.

The two principal corporate rating credit agencies determine the breakdown of what qualifies as a High Yield Bond and what does not. When Moody's rates a bond with lower than a "Baa" rating, or Standard and Poor's (S&P) rates then with an under "BBB" rating, then they become known as junk bonds. At the same time, all of those bonds which enjoy higher ratings than these (or the same rating at least) investors will consider to be investment grade. There are credit ratings that cover such categories as presently in default, or "D." Those kinds of bonds holding "C" ratings and below also have high probabilities for defaulting. In order to compensate the investors who take them on for the significant risks they run of not receiving either their original principal back or accrued interest payments by the maturity date, the yields must be offered at extremely high interest rates.

Despite the negative label of "junk bond," these High Yield Bonds remain popular and heavily bought by global investors. The majority of these investors choose to diversify for safety sake by utilizing either a junk bond ETF exchange traded fund or a High Yield Bonds mutual fund. The spread between the yields on the higher yielding and investment grade types of bonds constantly fluctuates on the markets. The at the time condition of the global and national economies impacts this. Industry-specific and individual corporate events also play a part in the differences between the various kinds of bonds' interest rates.

In general though, High Yield Bonds' investors can count on receiving a good 150 to 300 basis points more in yield as measured against the investment quality bonds in any particular time frame. This is why mutual funds and ETFs make imminent sense as an effective means of gaining exposure to the greater yields without taking on the unnecessary risk of a single issuer's bonds defaulting and costing the investors all or most of their original investing principal.

In the last few years, various central bankers throughout the globe have decided to inject enormous amounts of liquidity into their individual economies so that credit will remain cheaply and easily available. This includes the European Central Bank, the U.S. Federal Reserve, and the Bank of Japan. It has created the side effect of causing borrowing costs to drop and lenders to experience significantly lower returns.

By February of 2016, an incredible $9 trillion in sovereign government debt bonds provided yields of only from zero percent to one percent. Seven trillion of the sovereign bonds delivered negative real yields once adjusted for anticipated levels of inflation. It means that holding such bonds cost investors money, or provided them a real losing return.

In typical economic environments, this would drive intelligent investors to competing markets that provide better return rates. Higher yield bond markets have stayed volatile though. Distressed debts which pay minimally a yield higher than 1,000 basis points greater than a comparably maturing Treasury bond were notably affected. Energy company high yielding debt bond prices collapsed by approximately 20 percent in 2015 as a consequence of the problems in the energy sector which resulted from plummeting energy prices.

High Yield Preferred Stocks

Preferred stocks are a special type of stocks that many companies issue. These types of stocks provide investors with a different level of ownership in a given company. A preferred stock holder obtains a higher priority on the earnings and assets of a company than a common stock holder would enjoy. These preferred stocks also pay a higher dividend that has to be given out before any dividends can be paid to the common stock holders.

As such, they represent a hybrid type of security on the stock markets. They are like common stocks in that they are bought and sold as stocks and represent ownership in a company. These stocks can also trade up and down in price like a common stock. Unlike a common stock, they do not come with any rights to vote for a company board of directors or items on a company ballot at the annual meeting.

They are also like bonds in that they pay a higher dividend that must be paid out unless the company lacks the earnings to pay these holders. In this way preferred stocks have elements of bonds with their fixed rate of dividends. Every preferred stock comes with its own unique details that are set when the company issues the stock.

Preferred stocks are often higher yielding issues. They are most commonly issued by companies that are in industries such as financials, real estate investment trusts, utilities, industrials, and conglomerates. Despite this higher yield that makes them like bonds, they can be traded on the major stock exchanges. They are typically found on exchanges including the NASDAQ and the New York Stock Exchange.

As preferred stocks are a type of equity legally, they show up as equity on any company balance sheet. Both common and preferred stock holders are owners in the company. There are several advantages to preferred stocks that investors like about them.

In the past, individual retail investors were less aware of preferred stocks, but this is changing. Part of the reason they have gained in popularity surrounds market volatility. As common stocks have seen wild price swings in recent years, investors have been looking for more stable instruments in which they can invest.

Preferred stocks fit this need as they tend to be more stable in price than do common stocks. With more baby boomers looking for investments that provide higher yields, this has brought preferred stocks into the spotlight. The retirees gain the advantage of better yields and the opportunity for the price to increase in the issues as well.

Preferred stocks are not new. They have existed from the time when modern day investing began. Institutional investors have known about and invested in them for many decades. Many individual investors did not because they lacked the information they required to select and trade them.

In the past, individuals did not have any lists of preferred stocks from which to pick. The information available was difficult to come up with before the Internet made this kind of information much more readily available. Now there are tools smaller individual investors can find that provide calendar searches for ex-dividend dates.

There are also screening filters that allow individuals to narrow down their search for the best high yielding dividend preferred stocks. Preferred stocks represent another way to diversify an investor's portfolio and earn higher yields on dividends at the same time.

Holdings

Holdings refer to the asset contents in a given portfolio which an entity or individual possesses. Pension funds and mutual funds are good examples of organizations that have holdings. These positions can include all sorts of different investment assets and classes. Among these are stocks, mutual funds, bonds, futures, options, ETF exchange traded funds, and private equity assets.

It is both the kinds and amounts of such holdings in any portfolios that determine how well-diversified the portfolio actually proves to be. Well-diversified portfolios often include various sectors of stocks, bonds from a range of maturities and companies, and a variety of other investments that do not correlate with either stocks or bonds. Alternatively, only a few positions in several stocks that come from only one sector would be indicative of poorly diversified portfolios.

It is actually the mix and amount of various asset classes in any portfolio that will substantially determine what its total rate of return will be. The biggest positions will exert a larger impact on the return of a portfolio than marginal or tinier holdings in such a portfolio will. Many investors make it a practice to closely scrutinize the lists of positions which the world's most successful money managers maintain in an effort to follow their trades.

Such investors try to imitate the trading prowess of these superior results money managers in a variety of ways. It might be the manager has purchased stocks, in which case the imitating investors will try to stake out a similar company position. If these managers sell out of a stake, the investors will similarly sell off their assets in the company. The problem with such a follower strategy is that there is often substantial lag time between that point where the money managers make their moves and when this information becomes public domain knowledge.

There is another variation on the idea of mutual funds, hedge funds, and pension funds. This is the concept of holding companies. Such organizations are groups where the investors organize their positions and assets as an LLC Limited Liability Company. The reasons for this are varied. It might be they wish to decrease their own risk exposure, pool their investment dollars with fellow investors, and/or reduce their taxes as much as possible. Such companies rarely operate their own businesses directly. Instead, they are generally only a vehicle utilized to own various investments and companies.

Probably the best-known example of such an LLC company is the internationally followed Berkshire Hathaway, Inc. This Warren Buffet-dominated Omaha, Nebraska- based corporation originally began as a clothing textiles' manufacturing firm. Over the last numbers of decades, the corporation has solely existed as Warren Buffet's personal vehicle to buy out, maintain, and sell out his numerous and wide-ranging investments in various companies. Among the greatest and most significant positions which Berkshire owns are large stakes in the Coca-Cola Company, Dairy Queen Inc, and their wholly controlled subsidiary GEICO Government Employees Insurance Company.

The simplest way to envision these holdings is to mentally picture a large bucket, which represents the mutual fund. Every rock within the bucket stands for an individual bond or stock position. When analysts add up all of the rocks (as stocks or bonds), this equals the aggregate numbers of all holdings.

Figuring out the best mix of these holdings is the challenge that mutual funds, pension funds, and hedge funds all grapple with on a regular basis. It all comes down to the type of fund which they represent. Those bond funds or index funds would anticipate having many positions. This could mean from hundreds to thousands of different bonds and stocks. With the majority of other funds, too many or too few positions is risky and dangerous. Those funds that hold merely 30 positions would be subject to extreme volatility and single stock risks. If they had 500 to 600 different stocks or bonds then the fund would be as large as many indices like the S&P 500.

Index Funds

Index funds are typically exchange traded funds or mutual funds. Their goal is to reproduce the actual movements of an underlying index for a particular financial market. They do this no matter what is happening in the overall stock markets.

There are several means of tracking such an index. One way of doing this is by purchasing and holding all of the index securities to the same proportion as they are represented in the index. Another way of accomplishing this is by doing a statistical sample of the market and then acquiring securities that are representative of it. A great number of the index funds are based on a computer model that accepts little to no input from people in its decision making of the securities bought and sold. This qualifies as a type of passive management when the index fund is run this way.

These index funds do not have active management. This allows them to benefit from possessing lesser fees and taxes in their accounts that are taxable. The low fees that are charged do come off of the investment returns that are otherwise mostly matching those of the index. Besides this, exactly matching an index is not possible since the sampling and mirroring models of this index will never be one hundred percent right. Such variances between an index performance and that of the fund are referred to as the tracking error, or more conversationally as a jitter.

A wide variety of index funds exist for you to choose from these days. They are offered by a number of different investment managers as well. Among the more typically seen indices are the FTSE 100, the S&P 500, and the Nikkei 225. Other indexes have been created that are so called research indexes for creating asset pricing models. Kenneth French and Eugene Fama created one known as the Three Factor Model. This Fama-French three factor model is actually utilized by Dimensional Fund Advisers to come up with their various index funds. Other, newer indexes have been created that are known as fundamentally based indexes. These find their basis in factors like earnings, dividends, sales, and book values of companies.

The underlying concept for developing index funds comes from the EMH, or efficient market hypothesis. This hypothesis claims that because stock analysts and fund managers are always searching for stocks that will do better than the whole market, this efficient competition among them translates to current information on a company's affairs being swiftly factored into the price of the stock. Because of this, it is generally accepted that knowing which stocks will do better than the over all market in advance is exceedingly hard. Developing a market index then makes sense as the inefficiencies and risks inherent in picking out individual stocks can be simply eliminated through purchasing the index fund itself.

Initial Coin Offering (ICO)

An Initial Coin Offering refers to a non-regulated process in which the funds for new crypto-currency projects become raised. This is also popularly known by its acronym of ICO. These ICOs allow for entrepreneurs to sidestep the heavily regulated process of raising capital through more traditional means involving banks, venture capital, angel investors, or IPOs initial public offerings on stock exchanges.

With any ICO offer campaign, at least some of the crypto-currency will be sold off to those backers of the venture who become involved early. They receive this in compensation for providing traditional currency or alternative currency investment from the likes of Bitcoin. These ICOs are also known as IPCOs, or Initial Public Coin Offerings sometimes.

The process for engaging in an Initial Coin Offering is straightforward and relatively easy to do. The startup outfit begins by producing and releasing a whitepaper-based plan that reveals all of the key details on the venture. These include the needs this operation will meet when it is up and running, what percentage of the new virtual currency project pioneers will keep, what kinds of funding is allowed, the amount of cash required to make the venture a success, and what time duration the campaign will run.

In this campaign, the investors and supports of the new initiative will purchase part of the alternative coins of the new venture with real or virtual money. Such alt coins will be called tokens. They function in much the same way as do shares of stock which corporations sell their investors during an IPO initial public offering.

In cases where the funds raised are not sufficient to carry out the project requirements as set out by the firm in the white paper plan, invested sums will be given back to the investors as the ICO becomes a failure. Yet in those many cases where the funding objective are attained within the set out duration, then the money will be utilized to fund the new enterprise (or to finish it in other cases).

Naturally the upfront investors have their own motivation in purchasing such crypto-coins in the project. This is because they believe that the operation will be a success following launch. This would lead to a potentially massive gain in the value of their tokens.

One highly successful ICO proved to be the platform for the introduction of smart contracts to the world, known as Ethereum. Its coin tokens are called Ether. The Ethereum project came out in 2014. The ICO garnered $18 million worth of Bitcoins for the project's completion. This meant that the Ether tokens cost forty cents apiece. Following the live launch of Ethereum in 2015 and growing success in 2016, Ether roared higher to more than $14. In 2017, it has even topped $400 each at one point. Early investors who held to $400 realized gains of an eye-watering over 1,000 percent in less than five years.

It is true that many ICO events go off successfully. These Initial Coin Offerings are in fact highly disruptive and innovative means of fundraising. Yet they are not a serious rival to traditional stocks by a long shot. Many ICO campaigns have been deemed to be fraud. Without the imperative regulation provided by the SEC Securities Exchange Commission, their volume is likely to remain a tiny fraction of that done in IPOs on traditional exchanges for at least the foreseeable future.

ICOs have suffered from official national opposition which has hindered them as well. The People's Bank of China fully banned all ICOs in September of 2017. They declared them to be financially unstable and disruptive to an orderly economy. Banks were forbidden to provide any services having anything to do with ICOs. At the same time, these new tokens were no longer allowed to be utilized as a currency on Chinese markets. It caused the Bitcoin and Ether enthusiasts to realize that crypto-currency regulation is in the future cards. This temporarily crushed the prices of both main alternative currencies as investors realized what a serious setback it represents.

Insider Trading

Insider trading is a generally negative phrase, though it can also refer to a legal activity. The illegal and better known version if it involves a person purchasing or selling a security when they have information that is not publicly available on the stock. The timing involved in such a trade often determines if it is legal or illegal.

If the critical information has not yet been released to the public, then it is not legally allowed. This is because the government determined to level the playing field in investing. Trading securities when investors have special knowledge is not fair to those traders who do not have the ability to access this information.

A person who tips off other individuals is also participating in illegal insider trading. This is the case if the tipster possesses valuable and relevant information that is not available to the public. Fines and jail time can be given to those who pass along illegal insider information. The responsible body for policing this type of illegal trading is the SEC Securities and Exchange Commission. They maintain and enforce rules that protect average investors from the results of illegal insider trading.

Legal insider trading happens all the time. It is not as well known as the illegal version. A legal trade from an insider occurs when company directors buy or sell shares that they fully disclose according to the rules. This occurs every week. The transactions must be electronically turned in to the SEC in a manner that is timely. Not only must they be sent in to the SEC, the company of the person involved must disclose this transaction information on their official website.

Congress passed the Securities Exchange Act of 1934 to address this issue. This first important step pertained to company stock transactions and legal disclosure. Major owners of securities and directors of the company as well had to disclose their positions, any transactions, and any time the ownership changed hands.

Several forms allow corporate insiders to legally disclose their stock affairs. Form 3 permits them to initially file that they have a company stake.

Directors use Form 4 to make a disclosure on company stock transactions two days or less after the sale or purchase. They utilize Form 5 for earlier transactions or for transactions that become deferred until later.

It is not only company or corporate directors who are able to be tried and convicted for insider trading. Stock brokers and their clients can also be accused of this crime. Martha Stewart is a classic example of a brokerage client who the courts found guilty for placing insider trades back in 2003.

Martha Stewart received a tip from her Merrill Lynch stockbroker Peter Bacanovic concerning her shares of ImClone, a bio-pharmaceutical company. She used this information to sell her shares. Her broker had obtained this information that the Chief Executive Officer of ImClone Samuel Waksal liquidated all of his position in the corporation.

Waksal learned that the Food and Drug Administration was not going to approve his company's cancer drug Erbitux. After the two sales occurred, the FDA officially and publicly rejected the ImClone treatment drug. This caused a major selloff in the company stock of 16% in a single trading day. Stewart had saved a stock loss of $45,673 by selling out early.

The problem was that her sale had been based on the tip that CEO Waksal had sold all of his shares. This had not been publicly disclosed. Waksal became convicted and received a seven year jail sentence. Martha Steward was also convicted and forced to serve out five months in jail. She also received a number of months of house arrest and then probation.

Institutional Investor

Institutional investors turn out to be organizations or occasionally individuals which buy and sell securities in huge enough quantities and currency totals. They benefit from lower fees and commissions as well as special treatment from the market makers.

These large and powerful deep pocketed investors experience fewer regulations from the regulatory agencies as well since they naturally assume that they have a larger knowledge base and are sophisticated enough to protect themselves in their investing strategies. There are many different kinds of investors who qualify as institutional investors. Some of them are life insurance firms and pension funds.

These entities derive their money from a variety of sources, but in all cases they pool the funds in order to buy and sell real estate, stock and bond securities, and other alternative types of investment classes such as loans, commodities, precious metals, and artwork.

There are many different kinds of institutional investors such as hedge funds, pension funds, insurance companies, sovereign wealth funds, commercial banks, investment advisors, Real Estate Investment Trusts, mutual funds, and university endowments. Other operating firms that choose to invest their extra capital in such asset classes are also covered by the term. Some institutional investors are activist. This means that they may interfere with the internal workings and governance of the firm by using their substantial voting rights in the companies in which they own larger stakes to influence corporate decisions, investments, and behavior.

Institutional investors act as intermediaries between smaller retail investors and corporations. They are also significant sources of critical capital for the financial markets. Since they pool together their member investment dollars or Euros, these larger and more powerful investors effectively lessen the cost of capital to entrepreneurs at the same time as the efficiently diversify their clients' portfolios. Since they can impact the behavior of companies as well, this helps to reduce agency costs.

Institutional investors have several significant and game changing advantages over smaller, weaker retail investors. They possess enormous resources to invest as well as specialty knowledge that pertains to a variety of different investment options. Many of these choices are not even available to traditional retail investors at all. They also have longer term investing horizons as they are not limited to accumulation and distribution requirements of individual investors who will want to transition to retirement at some point.

Such institutions turn out to be the biggest movers and shakers within both supply and demand segments in the securities markets. This means that they transact the overwhelming majority of all trades on the major stock and bond market exchanges. Their choices and actions substantially impact the prices and bid/asks of most securities on the various markets.

This has led a number of retail investors to attempt to level the proverbial playing field of investing by researching the various filings of holdings the institutions make with the SEC Securities and Exchange Commission to learn what different securities they ought to invest in for their own individual portfolios and trades.

Some of these institutional investors are critically important in specific types of countries. For example, those countries which are oil rich and exporting nations generally contain one or more massive sovereign wealth funds which possess a lion's share of the investable wealth of the nation. These are usually government controlled and administered institutional funds and investors.

They can amass even hundreds of billions of investable dollars, as have the Norwegian, Abu Dhabi, Saudi Arabian, Qatari, and Kuwaiti funds. In developed nations, it is the pension funds and insurance companies which control a substantial portion of the excess and readily deployable and investable capital.

Intraday

Intraday refers to trades that occur during the normal course of the day. These price movements are especially important for traders who practice short term trading. They attempt to earn profits trading repeatedly throughout the one day trading session. Sometimes the term is utilized to refer to securities which engage in normal trading on the stock exchanges throughout the regular hours' session. This would include ETFs exchange traded funds and company stocks.

On the other hand, investors must purchase mutual funds from dealers directly. Their transactions typically occur after the stock market exchanges close for the day. This happens because the mutual funds must calculate their closing NAV Net Asset Value before they can lock in the buying and selling prices for their fund shares each market day.

Intraday also can be employed to explain a new low or high for a given security. It is always illuminating to consider a real example of such concepts. When dealers or analysts refer to a new Intraday low, they signify that the security touched a new low as compared to its other price points throughout the day in a single trading session. There are many cases where such an intraday low or high is the same as the final closing price for the given security.

Short term traders are always interested in these single day price movements. They watch them carefully with computer power-generated real time charts. This helps them to ascertain the right points to trade in and out in an effort to make money on the short term volatility and movements in the underlying issue stock prices. These shorter term time frame traders generally deploy 60, 30, 15, five, and one minute charts as they are trading in a single session and day. They might employ the five and one minute charts for scalping, while they would utilize the 60 and 30 minute charts for holding periods of a longer several hours.

There are a range of advantages and disadvantages to such Intraday trading. The greatest benefit to it lies in the fact that any unforeseen after market news can not impact the prices of the securities themselves. As an example, consider a surprise earnings report or important economic data release. There are also broker downgrades and upgrades which might happen after the market has closed or before it even opens. By only trading stocks on a throughout the day basis, short term and scalping traders avoid these pitfalls which can cause dramatic price swings and shocks. Intraday trading also permits tighter stop loss orders, greater opportunities for learning, and higher leverage limitations.

Disadvantages in such trading are that there is not always enough time for various stock prices to gain sufficiently in profit. Commission costs are also significantly higher as the traders on a short term basis are often in and out of positions repeatedly throughout he day, raising the costs of trading.

Short term traders are not without their effective strategies that help them to realize profits on an intraday basis. Some of them are range trading in which they work off of resistance and support levels in order to decide sell and buy entry and exit points. There are also scalping trades that seek to earn a large number of profits on minute changes in the price of the securities in question. News-based trading seeks to gain advantage on the increased volatility levels surrounding announced news which may make for interesting and exciting trading opportunities on an intraday basis. Finally, there are high frequency trading strategies. These employ expensive and complicated computer algorithms to take advantage of tiny inefficiencies in the single day trading markets.

Investment Trusts

An investment trust represent a type of collective investment pool generally utilized in Great Britain. These closed end funds are established as public limited companies within the United Kingdom primarily. Analysts have stated that the British investment trust was a forerunner of the American-promoted investment company.

In truth the name is somewhat of a misnomer. These investment trusts are not actually legal trust entities whatsoever. Instead they are a legal company or even individual. The reason this is important is because of the fiduciary responsibilities that trustees owe their membership.

When the fund is first established, a pool of all investors' funds becomes created. The investors then received a set amount of the fixed total number of shares that the trust floats on the launch date. Boards usually hand over the responsibility of the fund management into the care of a professional fund manager. This manager will then invest the fund's money into a vast range of individual shares of different corporations. This provides the fund investors with a massive diversification into a number of different companies that they could not possibly afford to do using their own limited resources.

These investment trusts may not have any employees, but instead count just a board of directors which is made up of exclusively non-executive directors. This has begun to change over the last few years as competition in the form of other funds emerged. Thanks to commercial property trusts and private equity groups utilizing the investment trust structure for holding vehicles, the structure of the staff and boards has changed in some cases.

Shares of investment trusts trade on various stock exchanges as do shares of typical publicly held corporations. What makes the value of these shares of the investment trusts interesting is that the offered price per share is not always the same as what the underlying share value should be based on the portfolio which the trust holds. When this happens, analysts say that the trust itself trades for a discount or a premium to its actual NAV net asset value.

This sector of the investment trust experienced significant trouble in the years from 2000 through 2003. This was because there was no set compensation plan for the industry. They then came up with guidelines for compensation packages and this cleared up many of the issues overshadowing the space.

One should not confuse investment trusts and unit (investment) trusts. There are some key differences between the two. The manager of an investment trust has the carte blanche legal ability to borrow funds in order to buy shares in company stocks. The managers of unit trusts (which are open ended funds) may not do this without first having a process for risk management established that makes rules on the ways the leverage will be considered and permitted. Such gearing can boost gains earned on investments yet also dramatically expands the risk to investors.

These investment trusts have a history going back around 150 years. The first one established was the 1868 founded Foreign & Colonial Investment Trust. Its stated goal was to "give the investor of moderate means the same advantages as the large capitalists in diminishing the risk of spreading the investment over a number of stocks."

The investment trust is classified in a breakdown by similar characteristics. This permits prospective investors to compare and contrast the various trusts within a certain category more effectively. The trusts are also further broken down according to the kinds of shares they issue. Traditional investment trusts possess only the single class of ordinary shares and enjoy an unending investment vehicle lifespan.

With the rival Splits, or Split Capital Investment Trusts, the structure proves to be more complex. They issues several varying share classes so that investors can match the shares up with their own investment objectives. The majority of such Splits begin with a preset investment life span that the fund determines when it launches. They call this the wind up date. The average wind up date of such a Split Capital Investment Trust occurs between five and ten years from the fund establishment.

Junk Bonds

Junk bonds are almost the same as regular bonds with an important difference. They are lower rated for credit worthiness. This is why in order to understand junk bonds, individuals first must comprehend the basics of traditional bonds.

Like traditional bonds, junk bonds are promises from organizations or companies to pay back the holder the amount of money which they borrow. This amount is known as the principal. Terms of such bonds involve several elements. The maturity date is the time when the borrower will repay the bond holder. There will also be an interest rate that the bond holder receives, or a coupon. Junk bonds are unlike those traditional ones because the credit quality of the issuing organization is lower.

Every kind of bond is rated according to its credit quality. Bonds can all be categorized in one of two types. Investment grade bonds possess medium to low risk. Their credit ratings are commonly in the range of from AAA to BBB. The downside to these bonds is that they do not provide much in the way of interest returns. Their advantage is that they have significantly lower chances of the borrower being unable to make interest payments.

Junk bonds on the other hand offer higher interest yields to their bond holders. Issuers do this because they do not have any other way to finance their needs. With a lower credit rating, they can not borrow capital at a more favorable price. The ratings on such junk bonds are often BB or less from Standard & Poor's or Ba or less by Moody's rating agency. Bond ratings such as these can be considered like a report card for the credit rating of the company in question. Riskier firms receive lower ratings while safe blue-chip companies earn higher ratings.

Junk bonds typically pay an average yield that is from 4% to 6% higher than U.S. Treasury yields. These types of bonds are placed into one of two categories. These are fallen angels and rising stars. Fallen angels bonds used to be considered at an investment grade. They were cut to junk bond level as the company that issued them saw its credit quality decline.

Rising stars are the opposites of fallen angels. This means the rating of the bond has risen. As the underlying issuer's credit quality improves, so does the rating of the bond. Rising stars are often still considered to be junk bonds. They are on track to rise to investment quality.

Junk bonds are risky for more reasons than the chances of not receiving one or more interest payments. There is the possibility of not receiving the original principal back. This type of investing also needs a great amount of skills in analyzing data like special credit. Because of these risk factors and specialized skills that are needed, institutional investors massively dominate the market.

A better way for individuals to become involved with junk bonds is through high yield bond funds. Professionals research and manage the holdings of these funds. The risks associated with a single bond defaulting are greatly reduced. They do this by diversifying into a variety of companies and types of bonds. High yield bond funds often require investors to stay invested for minimally a year or two.

When the yield of junk bonds declines below the typical 4% to 6% spread above Treasuries, investors should be careful. The risk does not become less in these cases. It is that the returns no longer justify the dangers in the junk bonds. Investors also should carefully consider the junk bond default rates. These can be tracked for free on Moody's website.

Margin Call

Margin Call refers to a demand from a broker that the account holding investor (who is utilizing margin) deposit additional funds or securities in order to restore the margin account to a minimum preset maintenance margin level. This could occur with a stock, futures, or commodities margin account. Such margin calls happen as the account value falls to a ratio which that specific brokerage deems unacceptable. Many brokerage houses use their own unique formulas to determine the amount at which they will issue such a call for more funds or securities.

Investors get into this unpleasant position when one or many of their securities they have purchased (utilizing money they borrowed from the brokerage) drops to a specified value point. That is when the call goes out from the broker for more money to restore the account to an acceptable minimum value. Investors will have two choices. They could comply with the request for additional funds and make an urgent deposit. Otherwise, they could sell off some or all of the positions in the account to reduce the need for minimum margin maintenance or raise the account equity position. The third choice of completely disregarding or ignoring the margin call would result in the broker force-selling positions to reduce this maintenance amount required.

Margin calls would not be necessary at all if investors did not buy securities, futures, or commodities with a combination of their own cash plus money they borrow off of the broker. This is why many experts recommend not utilizing such margin accounts unless an investor is a both seasoned and experienced trader.

Investors have equity in these margin-purchased investments. This amount equals the securities market value less the funds they originally borrowed to complete the purchase in the first place. If and when this equity of the account holder drops to lower than the brokerage-set percentage requirement of maintenance margin, then such a margin call becomes issued. Such maintenance margins do vary somewhat significantly from one broker to the next.

The constant is the Federal minimum maintenance margin requirements.

These are set at a lowest common requirement of 25 percent, regardless of who the responsible broker is. The brokers can choose to utilize a higher margin maintenance level than this amount, but they can not ever reduce their own limit to less than the 25 percent set by the Feds. Brokers can decide to change their maintenance level higher or lower than their present set one with little to no advance warning or notice, so long as they do not drop it below the government-mandated minimum amount. Raising their margin maintenance requirements may also result in creating a margin call.

Looking at a tangible example helps to clarify the concept and make it more understandable. Investors might purchase $50,000 worth of stocks via a combination of $25,000 of their own funds and through borrowing the balance $25,000 off of the brokerage firm. Assume that this particular broker chooses to utilize the government-set minimum of 25 percent maintenance margin. The investor has no choice but to honor this.

When the investors open the trade, at that point the equity positions of the investments prove to be $25,000 (or $50,000 minus the $25,000 borrowed). This makes the investor equity percentage an even 50 percent (using the $25,000 equity divided by the $50,000 original securities market value). This is twice the required minimum 25 percent margin maintenance.

Yet a week later, our investors suffer a drastic decline in the value of their securities, which precipitously drop to $30,000. The investors' equity is now down to a mere $5,000 (or $30,000 minus the $25,000 borrowed). Yet the brokerage (and government regulations which are the same in this scenario) requires that they keep a minimally $7,500 worth of equity for the account to remain margin-eligible (which is 25 percent of the borrowed amount of $30,000).

It means that there is presently a $2,500 deficit ($7,500 requirement minus the $5,000 actual market value). The broker will then issue a margin call for $2,500 in additional cash to be deposited immediately. Should the investors refuse or take their time, then the broker is legally bound and permitted to sell off some of the securities to reach the minimum $7,500 in account equity value.

Margin Trading

Margin trading is the practice of buying investments on margin. This is accomplished through borrowing money from your broker in order to buy stocks. Another way of understanding margin trading is taking out a loan from your broker to buy greater amounts of stock shares.

Margin trading generally requires a margin account. Margin accounts differ from cash accounts that only allow you to trade with the money that your account contains. Brokers have to get a signature from you in order to open up a new margin account. This could be as an extension of your existing account and account opening forms or as a separate and new agreement. Minimum investments of $2,000 are necessary to open such a margin account. Some brokers insist on larger amounts. Whatever the final margin requirement deposit is, it is called the minimum margin.

After the margin account is up and running, you are able to purchase as much as fifty percent of a stock with margin trading money. The money that you use to buy your part of the stock is called initial margin. Margining up to the full fifty percent is entirely optional. You might borrow only fifteen or twenty percent instead.

Margin trading loans can be held for as long a period as you wish, assuming that you continue to meet the margin obligations. A stock maintenance margin has to be maintained while the loan is outstanding too. This maintenance margin is the lowest account balance that can be held by the account in advance of the broker making you deposit additional funds. If you do not meet this minimum or resulting margin call for extra funds, then the broker has the right to sell your stocks in order to reduce your outstanding loan.

Borrowing money from your broker is not done for the sake of charity. Interest has to be paid on the loan. Also, the marginable securities in the account become tied up as collateral. Unless you pay down the loan, interest charges will be applied to the loan balance. These interest amounts can significantly increase the debt level in the account with time. Higher debt levels in your account lead to still higher interest charges. Because of this, buying stocks on margin is typically utilized only for shorter time frame investments. This is true since the greater amount of time that you hold the margin loan in the investment, the higher a return you will require in order to break even on the margin trade. When you maintain such a margin based investment over a long time frame, it becomes difficult to turn a profit after the expenses are cleared.

It is also important to remember that not every stock qualifies for purchase using margin. The rules pertaining to which stocks can be purchased with margin are set by the Federal Reserve Board. In general though, Initial Public Offerings, penny stocks, or over the counter traded stocks are not allowed to be purchased utilizing margin as a result of the daily volatility and trading risks associated with such kinds of stocks. Besides this, each brokerage can restrict whichever other stocks that they wish.

Market Sentiment

Market sentiment refers to the all around attitude investors have with regards to a certain financial market or specific security. It is the tone and feeling in a market. This is displayed via the price movement and activity of various securities which trade in a given market. Some have called it the market crowd psychology or investor sentiment. Rising prices in a market are indicative of bullish market sentiment, while declining prices indicate the sentiment in a market is bearish.

What makes market sentiment so interesting is that it is sometimes not based on the underlying fundamentals of the security or market in question. At times it instead is based on emotion and greed rather than actual business valuations and fundamentals.

This market sentiment matters immensely to both technical analysts and to day traders. These individuals read technical indicators in order to measure shorter term price movements which the attitudes of investors can cause in a given security. They attempt to profit from these price fluctuations. Such sentiment also is important for contrarian investors. They prefer to place trades in the opposite direction of any prevailing sentiment. When all other investors are buying, a contrarian will use this sentiment to instead sell.

In general, market sentiment is referred to as either bullish or bearish. As the bulls have control, the stock prices are running up and away. As the bears are dominant, prices of stocks are declining or even plunging. Since the markets are subject to and driven from the emotion of the collective traders, the sentiment of the markets is often not correlated to the underlying fundamental values. This means that market sentiment is more about group emotions and feelings while the fundamental value is more about the actual business performance.

Traders realize profits when they find those stocks which are either undervalued or overvalued because of their market sentiment. Traders and investors alike utilize different indicators to attempt to ascertain what the sentiment of the markets actually is. This helps them to decide which stocks are the best ones for them to trade. There are a number of these helpful indicators. Among the more popular ones are the following: VIX CBOE

Volatility Index, Bullish Percentage, 52 Weeks High to Low Sentiment Ratio, 200 Days Moving Average, and 50 Days Moving Average.

The Fear Index, or VIX, runs off of the option prices. Such options prove to be like insurance contracts. A rise in the VIX means that traders see the need for more insurance within the markets. When traders instead feel like there should be more risk, this reveals a greater amount of price movement. Traders can simply compare the present VIX against the historical moving averages of it to decide if it is actually lower or higher.

Bullish Percentage quantifies the numbers of stocks that have bullish patterns. It relies on point and figure charts to do this. Typical markets will demonstrate a 50 percent bullish percentage. If the figure turns out to be at least 80 percent or greater than this, then the sentiment of the markets is highly bullish. Another way of saying this is that the market is actually overbought. Similarly if the figure is 20 percent or less than this amount, it signals the sentiment of the market is bearish. This makes it oversold. Traders can simply sell as the market is too overbought and buy as the markets are oversold.

High To Low Sentiment indicators will take the stocks which have made 52 week long highs and compare these against those stocks which have just made 52 week long lows. If stock prices trade around the lows universally, then the trading community is bearish in its sentiment on the markets. Conversely, if the stock prices trade near or at their highs, the same traders are instead showing their bullish market sentiments.

Modern Portfolio Theory

Modern portfolio theory proves to be a model for investing invented by Harry Markowtiz. He outlined many of the ideas in his 1950s book Portfolio Selection. The economist and mathematician claimed that investors could successfully reduce their amount of market risk and still maximize their portfolio returns for that given level of investments. This is actually accomplished by mixing different risk level investments together. If the various investment risks are not correlated, then risky investments with higher returns can actually reduce overall risk in a portfolio.

This Modern Portfolio Theory has come to dominate and become heavily utilized throughout the financial advising industry. Most investors would appreciate the goal of it to reach the greatest potential returns over the long term without having to suffer excessive amounts of market risk in the short term.

Everyone would like to be able to decrease market fluctuations in their portfolios. The way it is possible is by diversifying. The theory demonstrates how investors are able to take individual investments which have high risk and combine them with a few other kinds of investments that are lower risk. The end result is a balance that delivers a better return while providing lower risk than the more volatile investments in the portfolio feature.

Examples of how this works abound throughout the markets. Stocks usually have more risk in the markets than do bonds. Combining bonds with stocks can lower the risk of the stocks and still deliver an acceptable return. With individual stocks, international stocks along with smaller cap stocks carry a greater risk than do the larger cap stocks. If an investor includes all three types of these then the return will be above average while the risk is only average. This works as measured over longer time frames and compared to major benchmarks like the S&P 500.

The theory itself can actually become a little complicated as it mathematically compares different kinds of investments against each other. This does not change an inescapable truth. Markotwitz claimed that no matter how well an investor balances out the portfolio, there are still limitations. In order to secure a greater return on average, investors will have to be willing to accept more risk. The opposite of this is true as well. If an investor wants fewer fluctuations in the portfolio from one month or year to the next, then he or she will have to be stand for lower returns over the long term in order to accomplish this.

There are variations on Modern Portfolio Theory that are used by a wide range of financial advisors and investors. One of these is tactical asset allocation. It takes the parts of MPT that have to do with diversification and re-balancing and applies them to investing.

There are a number of critics to MPT who charge that it is not the best means of investing. Many of these prefer technical analysis methods and like to use trends and market psychology in their strategies. Others put down the buy and hold principle that underlies the Modern Portfolio Theory.

These critics continue to make the argument that market behaviors and trends can be timed. They state that balanced asset allocating misses out on the ability to capture big moves and avoid corrections. The problem with these charges is that market timing is not easy. Countless investors have failed at timing the markets. The majority of them lack the knowledge, temperament, and time to be effective at it consistently.

Moving Averages

Moving Averages are an indicator that is heavily used in technical analysis. They represent average prices spread out over a period of time. They are more useful because the changes in price action are smoothed out as any random price movements become filtered out.

There are a number of different variations. Two of them prove to be the most commonly used. These are the simple moving average, or SMA, and the exponential moving average, or EMA. A simple moving average is a straight average compiled over a certain number of different time periods. With the Exponential Moving Average, prices that are more recent tend to have a greater amount of weight given to them than prices that are farther back.

Moving Averages are most commonly used to find the direction of the overall trend. They also help to set the levels of resistance and support. Moving averages are also heavily used to create a number of other technical indicators. One of the better known that is based upon the moving averages is the MACD, or Moving Average Convergence Divergence.

Moving Averages tend to be lagging indicators themselves. This is because programs and charts derived them from historical prices. They are useful even despite this lagging nature. The longer a time frame that an individual considers with a moving average, the bigger the lag will be. For example, 200 day moving averages would lag significantly more than 100 day moving averages and even more than 20 day moving averages.

Different Moving Average time frames are employed depending on the trading needs. Investors who are practicing short term trading will be most interested in shorter time-frame Moving Averages. Investors who pursue long term trading will find longer time frame moving averages to be more helpful.

Many different traders and investors find the 200 Day Moving Average to be a useful and significant benchmark and tool. When there are breaks to the top or bottom it sends major trading signals.

For example, if a 200 day moving average acting as a support were convincingly broken, then the underlying security would likely continue moving down. Conversely, if the same important moving average was functioning as a resistance point, then a break of this average to the topside would likely signal the instrument would continue moving up significantly.

Moving Averages deliver a variety of critical signals for trading by themselves. When two of them cross, it can be even more significant. Moving Averages that are going up demonstrate that the instrument or security is trending higher as part of an uptrend. A Moving Average that declined would show the security to be trending lower and involved in a downtrend.

A bullish crossover is another confirmation of movement to the upside. This happens as a shorter time frame Moving Average crosses over and above another Moving Average that is longer term. Similarly, a bearish crossover signals that there is more momentum to the downside. It happens as the shorter time frame Moving Average makes the cross beneath a Moving Average which is longer term.

Another important usage surrounds supports and resistances. When stocks or other securities are trending up, moving averages function as supports. A shorter term uptrend would look to 20 Day Simple MAs. These are a part of Bollinger Band indicators as an example. The longer term uptrend often looks for support at the popular 200 Day Moving Average.

Conversely when securities trend downwards, these moving averages act as resistances. An interesting point about 200 Day Moving Averages is that they are so widely followed that they work in many cases either as support or resistance simply because so many people watch and give them significance.

Net Asset Value

The Net Asset Value refers to a mutual fund and its per share value. It is also known by its acronym NAV. Exchange traded funds, or ETFs, can also be referenced by the NAV. These values which the companies themselves compute for investors only provide a snap shot of the NAV at a particular time and date. In either security type, the fund's per share dollar value arises from the aggregate value of every security within its portfolio minus any liabilities the fund may owe. Finally this is expressed over the total number of outstanding shares in order to arrive at the shares' ultimate NAV.

Where mutual funds are concerned, the Net Asset Value is derived one time every trading day. They utilize the closing market prices for every security within the fund's holdings in order to determine this. Once this is done, the fund is able to settle all sell and buy orders which are outstanding on the shares. These prices will be set by the NAV of the mutual fund in question for the value per the trade date. Investors will always be required to wait to the next day in order to obtain their actual trade-in or trade-out price.

Because mutual funds do pay out nearly all their capital gains and income, such NAV changes are never the optimal gauge for the performance of the given fund. Instead these are better determined by looking at the yearly aggregate return, or total return.

With ETFs, these are actually closed end types of funds. This means that they actually trade more like stocks do. The shares of these Exchange Traded Funds therefore constantly trade at the market value. It might be a literal value which is higher than the NAV. This would be trading at a premium to the Net Asset Value. It could similarly trade under the NAV. This would mean the prices were trading at a discount to the NAV.

With these ETFs, the Net Asset Value becomes computed once at the markets' close so that the fund can correctly report the ETF values. During the day however, these are figured differently than the mutual fund computations. This is because the ETFs will compile the during-the-day NAV in real time at numerous points in every minute of the trading day.

It is helpful to consider an example of how the mutual funds compute their Net Asset Value calculations. The formula is actually very straightforward. It is simply that the NAV is equal to the mutual fund's assets less its liabilities with the difference divided by the total number of shares outstanding. The assets in the case of mutual funds include cash equivalents and cash, accrued income, and receivables. The main portion of their assets commonly are their investments, which will be priced per the end of the day closing values. Liabilities equate to the complete longer-term and shorter-term money owed, along with each accrued expense. Among these expenses will be utilities, salaries of the staff of the fund, and various operational costs for running such a fund.

Consider that the fictitious Diamond Stocks Mutual Fund counted $200 million in investments, figured utilizing the end of day closing prices of all their assets. Besides this, it has $14 million in cash equivalents and cash and another $8 million in receivables in total. The daily accrued income amounts to $150,000. Besides this, Diamond Stocks owes $26 million in its shorter-term liabilities and has $4 million of longer-term liabilities. The daily accrued expenses amount to $20,000. With 10 million outstanding shares, the net asset value would equate to $19.21 in the case of the Diamond Stocks Mutual Fund.

New York Mercantile Exchange (NYMEX)

The New York Mercantile Exchange proves to be the biggest physical commodity exchange for futures buying, selling, and trading in the world. Since they merged, it is comprised of both the NYMEX Division and the COMEX Division. At NYMEX, traders are able to trade platinum, palladium, and energy markets.

COMEX is where they trade FTSE 100 index options as well as silver, gold, and copper futures. NYMEX still keeps a place for the open outcry system where traders shout and make hand gestures to indicate their purchases. This operates only during the day time. After normal business hours, the electronic trading system takes over for the night.

The NYMEX origins go back to an association of Manhattan dairy merchants. In 1872, a group of them came together and formed the Butter and Cheese Exchange of New York. Once eggs joined the various dairy businesses handled on the exchange, they changed the name to Butter, Cheese, and Egg Exchange. By 1882 they had added canned goods, dried fruits, and poultry to the offerings. The name received its final change to reflect the broader product offerings as the New York Mercantile Exchange at this time.

Though COMEX Commodities Exchange and NYMEX used to be separately owned and run exchanges, they merged together to become two divisions of the NYMEX Holdings, Inc. back in 1994. They listed on the New York Stock Exchange on November 17, 2006 trading under the NMX ticker symbol.

In March of 2008, the CME Group of Chicago committed to a conclusive agreement to buy NYMEX holdings for $11.2 billion combination in cash and stock offerings. In August of 2008 the deal finished and NYMEX and COMEX began to function as DCM Designated Contract Markets for the CME Group. They joined sister exchanges the Chicago Board of Trade and Chicago Mercantile Exchange as part of the four DCMs.

In 2006, the New York Mercantile Exchange became almost entirely electronically traded. NYMEX keeps a smaller venue operating for those traders who prefer to engage in the open outcry historic and sentimental form of trading. There they utilize complicated hand signals and shouting while standing on a physical trading floor to buy and sell. The hand signal system is being preserved by a project published on the subject.

NYMEX's headquarters is found in the Battery Park City area of Manhattan in Brookfield Place. They also maintain offices around the world in such cities as Washington D.C., Boston, San Francisco, Atlanta, London, Dubai, and Tokyo. The options and futures traded here on precious metals and energy commodities have developed into important tools for companies that are seeking to mitigate their risk through hedging their own positions. Because these various instruments are traded so easily and liquidly, companies are able to discern future prices and to hedge their future needs. This is why NYMEX has grown to become such a critical part of global activities in hedging and trading environments.

Today the NYMEX manages literally billions of dollars in metals, energy carrier, and other commodities that companies and traders sell and buy every day for delivery in the future. This is handled on either the physical trading floor or the electronic trading system by computers.

These prices on the exchange and its numerous transactions become the basis of pricing for individuals and companies who purchase commodities around the globe. The Commodity Futures Trading Commissions agency of the U.S. government actually regulates the NYMEX floor. Trading on the exchange is performed by independent brokers sent by specific companies.

New York Stock Exchange (NYSE)

The NYSE is the acronym for the world's largest stock exchange, the New York Stock Exchange. With a market capitalization of companies listed on it totaling at $11.92 trillion dollars in August 2010, it also possessed an average day trading value of around $153 billion in 2008. By market capitalization, the NYSE has no rivals for size.

The New York Stock Exchange is owned and operated by the NYSE Euronext company. This outfit came into being in 2007 when the NYSE merged with the completely electronic Euronext stock exchange. Four rooms make up the trading floor of the NYSE that is found at 11 Wall Street. Its main building is found at 18 Broad Street on the corners of Wall Street and Exchange Place. This building became a National Historic Landmark back in 1978, along with its sister 11 Wall Street Building.

Occasionally known as "the Big Board," the New York Stock Exchange allows for sellers and buyers of stocks to exchange shares in all of the companies that are listed for public trading. Its trading hours prove to be 9:30 AM to 4:00 PM on Monday to Friday. Holidays are spelled out in advance by the exchange itself.

The NYSE has always operated as an in person trading floor since its inception in 1792. Today, this works in an auction format that is ongoing. Floor traders here are able to make stock transactions for investors. They simply gather together surrounding the particular company post where there is a specialist broker working as auctioneer in open outcry format to get buyers and sellers together and to oversee the auction itself. This specialist works directly for the company that is an NYSE member and not the exchange itself. These specialists will commit their own money to assist the trades about ten percent of the time. Naturally, they also give out information that serves to bring together sellers and buyers.

In 1995, NYSE began making the automation transition for the auctions. This started with hand held computers that were wireless. Like this, traders were capable of executing and getting orders electronically. This ended a 203 year tradition of paper based trades.

From January 24 of 2007, most every stock on the NYSE is able to be traded on the electronic Hybrid Market. With this ability to send in customer orders for electronic confirmation immediately, orders can also be sent to the floor for auction market trade. More than eighty-two percent of the NYSE order volume came to the floor electronically in only the first three months of that first year.

Only those who own one of 1,366 actual seats on the exchange are permitted to trade shares directly on the exchange. Such seats are sold for enormous sums. The highest price paid for one amounted to $4 million in the tail end of the 1990's. The highest price ever paid adjusted for inflation proved to be $625,000 in 1929, which would amount to more than six million dollars in terms of 2010 dollars. Since the exchange became a public company, the seats have been instead sold in one year licenses.

Nikkei 225

The Nikkei is an abbreviation for Japan's foremost, best known, and most respected stock index of Japanese companies. Its full name is the Nikkei 225 Stock Average. This index is price weighted and made up of the top 225 industry leading companies which investors trade on the Tokyo Stock Exchange. The United States equivalent of this Nikkei is the Dow Jones Industrial Average.

This stock index originally came into existence as the Nikkei Dow Jones Stock Average. Investors knew it by this name during the years 1975 to 1985. Today's Nikkei 225 carries the name of the Japan Economic Newspaper "Nihon Keizai Shimbun" which is generally referred to as Nikkei. This newspaper is the sponsor for the index and its calculation. There has been a calculation of this index going back to September of 1950. There are many well known firms that make up this index. Some of the most recognized are Toyota Motor Corporation, Sony Corporation, and Canon Inc.

The Nikkei 225 proves to be Asia's oldest stock index in existence. The country founded it in its industrialization and reconstruction efforts that followed the end of World War II. Stocks which make it up are not ranked by market capitalization like in the majority of such indices around the world. Instead they are ranked and listed based on their share prices. The denominations of every stock's value are in Japanese yen. Each September the Nikkei's make up undergoes review so that necessary changes can be made effective for October.

The actual Tokyo Stock Exchange began operating in 1878. This exchange received a major boost in the heat of World War II when the Japanese government decided to merge Tokyo's Stock Exchange with five other exchanges to make a single, unified national Japanese Stock Exchange. This pan-Japanese exchange had to be shut down in August of 1945 towards the conclusion of the war. It finally opened again on May 16 in 1949 as part of the new legislation the Securities Exchange Act.

An enormous asset bubble engulfed Japan during the late 1980s. The government bore responsibility for this as they employed both monetary and fiscal stimulus programs to attempt to offset the nation's currency led recession. The yen had risen 50% in the beginning of the decade. From 1985 to 1989, both land and stock prices tripled in value. When the bubble reached its peak, Tokyo's Stock Exchange comprised an astonishing 60 percent of all capitalization for global stock exchanges.

This bubble exploded in 1990. That year alone the Nikkei 225 Index dropped by a third. This economic and stock market stagnation continued for decades so that in the midst of the Great Recession in October 2008, the Nikkei's value had dropped below 7,000. This represented an astonishing plunge of over 80 percent from the high set back in December of 1989. The government worked to re-inflate the index powerfully from June 2012 to June 2015 as it rose 150 percent. The government's economic stimulus programs coupled with efforts of the Bank of Japan assisted in this asset appreciation. Even at these loftier levels, this still proved to be almost 50 percent under the high set in 1989.

Investors who wish to invest in the index may not buy it directly. A few different ETF Exchange Traded Funds track its performance. These include the Japan iShares Nikkei 225 by Blackrock and the Nikkei 225 Exchange Traded Fund by Nomura Asset Management. Investors can trade the index via ETFs in dollars on the New York Stock Exchange by purchasing or selling shares of the Nikkei 225 Index ETF by Maxis.

Option Spreads

Option spreads are option combinations which have traders combining two different options contracts with varied strikes but identical expiration dates. They do this in a strategy to limit their overall risk. The idea behind these option spreads is relatively simple, but the possible effects of some spread constructs can become slightly more complicated.

Reducing the concept of option spreads to their most intuitive elements involves the discussion of the two legs, or option contracts, which comprise the spread itself. Putting on two legs refers to traders combining as an example a call option purchase with one which they sell at the same time. In other words, the traders who enter this strategy will take on both sides of the market when they make options spreads. It will either be in buying the one and selling the other, or selling the one and buying the other option contract.

The idea behind buying and simultaneously selling two options with the same expiration but different strikes is that this action reduces the risk. When traders sell a call and also buy a call, they are less exposed to a fall in the market or the option premium time decay thanks to the option which they sold, for which they received a premium. The net cost of the spread is therefore less than that of simply buying a call.

Another way of looking at this maneuver is that the cost of the one call is subsidized by the sale price of the one which the traders sell. The one sold is further out of the money than the one bought, which reduces the cost of the overall spread options. This effectively limits aggregate risk, exposure to the relentless time decay factor, and the penalty for the price movement potential to the downside.

Consider a real world example. If HSBC bank stock is trading at $53 per share and traders believe that the stock price will rise in the short term, they might decide to put on a bull call spread. They might construct this spread by buying a $55 strike price call at the same time as they sell a $60 strike price call. The expiration date in this example is irrelevant so long as the two call contracts have the same expiration date. In this example, the traders pay $500 for the $55 strike call and receive $250 for the $60 strike price call. The net cost of the spread position is $250 then.

In this example, the maximum risk is limited to the $250 net cost of the spread. Instead of having a $500 risk from only buying the single $55 strike price call, risk is reduced in this case by half for also selling the $60 strike price call. The trade off for this lowered risk is a reduced maximum potential profit. The reason is that as the stock price reaches $60 per share, the spread owners realize their maximum profit point. This is $500 gross realized for a $250 maximum net profit (maximum $500 gross proceeds minus the $250 spread cost). Even if the stock price were to rise to $65 per share, it would not change the profit possibility, since the sold call with a strike at $60 means that the spread owners can not capture any additional gains in the price of the stock beyond the strike price which they already sold.

If the price of the stock moves against the spread owners, they can not lose any more money than the maximum $250 net cost of the spread, regardless of how low the underlying stock price moves against them. This makes these bull call and bull put spreads very popular with options traders, since they are effective at reducing risk while still allowing for large profit potentials.

Options

Options are contracts on stocks, indexes, currencies, commodities, or debt instruments. There are two principle types. These are call options and put options. Call options give holders the ability to purchase a set amount of the underlying instrument for a specific price in a certain amount of time. This specific price is known as the strike price. Put options grant holders the ability to sell the exact amount of the underlying instrument at a fixed price in a given period of time.

With options on stocks, the set amount of the underlying shares that calls and puts cover are typically 100 shares. Option contracts have two parties to them. The first are the sellers who are also known as writers of the option. The buyers are the holders of the option.

Option values are made up of two components. These are intrinsic value and time value. Intrinsic value is the amount that the option is in the money. For an option to be in the money, the stock price must be higher than the strike price for calls. For puts, the stock price has to be lower than the strike price. The value that is left after subtracting intrinsic value is the option's time value. When an option has no intrinsic value, one hundred percent of its value is time value.

Investors can buy and sell options until they run out of time. At this point, they expire either with some intrinsic value or worthless. They can also be exercised. When an option is exercised, the seller must transfer the underlying shares to the holder of the option. When the instrument is not able to be transferred over, then the parties settle in cash instead.

Investors like this financial tool because they give buyers peace of mind. The most an option holder is able to lose is the total price that they paid when they bought the contract. If options are not exercised or sold within the given time frame, then they expire. An option that expires worthless does not involve any exchange of shares or cash.

Buyers and sellers have different potential profits with options. Profit potential is limitless for the buyers. For the sellers, the profit is limited to the price which they receive for the contract. Sellers have unlimited loss potential unless they own the underlying shares or instrument. When a seller of an option holds the underlying instrument, the option is covered.

There are two main reasons that investors buy options. These can be to gain leverage or to obtain protection. The leverage benefit means that the option holder can control a larger amount of equity for a much smaller price than it costs to actually buy the shares. This exposes the buyer to a far smaller potential loss.

Options provide protection to investors who own the shares that underlie the contract. While the owners of the option hold the contract, they gain protection against adverse price movements in their shares. This is because the contract provides the ability to obtain the stock at a certain price during the option's contract time-frame. In this case, the cost of the option is the premium that the owner pays.

There are several downsides to options. The trading costs for options are higher than with buying the underlying shares of the stock or other instrument. This is because the spread between the bid and ask is higher for options. Option commissions also cost more than do stock commissions.

Option trading is more complicated than stock trading too. Options also have to be watched more closely than do stocks generally. The time involved to trade and maintain option strategies can be significant.

Over The Counter (OTC)

OTC is the acronym for Over the Counter. In the business and financial world, Over the Counter trading is also known as trading off of the exchange. Such OTC trading goes on when financial instruments of various kinds, including stocks, commodities, bonds, or derivatives, are traded literally between the buying and selling party themselves, without having an exchange in the middle of the transaction.

Over the Counter trading can be said to be the opposite of exchange trading. Exchange trading happens in facilities or over electronic market places that are specially created for the trading of these instruments. Stock exchanges and futures exchanges are the places that exchange trading takes place and Over the Counter trading does not.

Within the United States, Over the Counter stock trading is done via market makers who ensure that there are markets in both Pink Sheet and OTCBB, or bulletin boards, securities. They do this through the utilization of quotation services that are between dealers, like Pink Quote, run by the Pink OTC Markets, and OTC Bulletin Board for the OTCBB. While Over the Counter stocks typically do not either list or trade on any form of stock exchange, stocks that are listed on exchanges may be traded on the third market over the counter.

OTCBB quoted stocks have to follow the reporting rules as set out by the United States SEC, or Securities and Exchange Commission, regulatory body. Pink Sheet stocks are not governed by such reporting requirements. Still other stocks that are traded as OTCQX meet different disclosure guidelines that they are permitted to work under in the OTC Pink sheet markets.

OTC can also relate to contracts created between two entities. In these contracts, the two parties concur on the way that a specific trade will be settled at a certain future point. These typically come from investment banks and go out to their own clients. Good examples of these types of OTC arrangements are swaps and forwards. Such contracts are typically arranged over the phone or via computer. Derivative OTC contracts fall under the governance of an agreement provided by the International Swaps and Derivatives Association. This type of OTC market is sometimes called the Fourth Market.

In the Financial Crisis of 2007-2010, many of these OTC derivative contracts created and wreaked havoc in international financial markets specifically because they were traded over the counter, and no one exactly knew what risk and credit were entailed in the contracts that totaled in the tens of trillions of dollars and were made between mysterious partners. To address this critical problem, the NYMEX, or New York Mercantile Exchange, set up a mechanism for clearing many of the most frequently traded energy derivatives that were previously traded only OTC. Now, many of these customers can simply hand over the trade to the exchange's clearing house ClearPort. This removes the dangers associated with both performance and credit risk that were previously seen in these OTC transactions. Other exchanges are endeavoring to do the same thing to try to take derivatives and credit default swap contracts away from the shadowy world of Over the Counter trading. The G20, or Group of Twenty Industrialized and Industrializing nations, is considering ways of rewarding parties for bringing such OTC derivative transactions onto regulated exchanges as well.

Penny Stocks

Penny stocks are those securities that usually trade for comparatively lower prices, off of the big stock exchanges, and with smaller market capitalizations. Many analysts and investors look at these securities as higher in risk and extremely speculative. This is because they feature significant bid and ask spreads, less liquidity, smaller followings, and lesser capitalization and disclosure requirements. Many of these smaller stocks trade on the pink sheets or OTC Bulletin Board in what is known as the "over the counter market."

Penny stocks used to be those which traded for under a dollar, but thanks to the SEC this is no longer the case. The SEC altered the definition so that all stock shares which trade for less than $5 are now considered to be a penny stock. These companies have fewer listing requirements, regulations, and filings which govern them.

It is important to remember that penny stocks best suit investors who can stand more risk. They come with greater amounts of volatility which can lead to steep losses or possibly greater returns. The lower volumes and greater amounts of risk are why the moves in these stocks can be staggering. These companies struggle with fewer resources and less cash, but sometimes achieve breakthroughs that can catapult their share prices higher. It is safer to trade or invest in penny stocks which are listed on the NASDAQ or the AMEX American Stock Exchange because these exchanges more vigorously regulate their constituent companies.

Four factors make these micro cap stocks so much riskier than traditional blue chip stocks. The information which the public has access to is usually lacking. It is harder to make well informed decisions on companies that do not provide sufficient information. Other information that is offered on such micro cap stocks can come from less than reputable sources.

Another feature that makes penny stocks so risky is that they do not have a common set of minimum standards. Neither the pink sheets nor the OTCBB require these companies to live up to minimum requirements to stay listed. They will have to file certain documents in a timely manner with the OTCBB, but not with the pink sheets. These standards traditionally offer a safety cushion that helps to protect investors. They are a benchmark for other smaller companies to achieve.

A third difficulty with these micro cap stocks is they lack history. A great number of such companies could be nearing bankruptcy or recently founded. This means that their track records are either non existent or poor at best. A lack of historical data compounds the difficulty of assessing a company's future and their stock's near and long term possibilities.

A final danger with penny stocks is their lack of liquidity. This creates two problems. An investor may not be able to sell out of the stock at an acceptable price. With low liquidity, there may be no buyer available at any price. Lower liquidity also leads to the possibility for traders to manipulate the prices of the stocks themselves. They can purchase enormous quantities of the issue, promote it themselves, and then sell it at higher prices to other investors who become stuck with it. This is called a pump and dump strategy.

Pivotal Points

Pivotal Points refers to a system for predicting stock price movements that Jesse Livermore created and developed. Time Magazine described him as the most incomparable living American trader of his day. In the 1920's, he used the system to amass a fortune that at its peak valued $100 million. As a share of the U.S. GDP of the time, this amounts to $14 billion in current dollars as measured against today's GDP.

This represented the first time that any investor had documented using Pivotal Points. Livermore famously wrote about it in his book, Reminiscences of a Stock Operator. These Pivotal Points are so useful because more than 90 years after Jesse created them investors still utilize and teach them.

Pivotal Points are the levels at which stock prices find support and resistance. In fact they are the primary levels of both support and resistance, depending on whether they are higher or lower than the price of the stock. Because of the importance of these Pivotal Points, they are the levels where the greatest price movement generally happens. There may be other resistance and support levels. Other levels are less important than the pivotal ones.

There are two principal ways that Pivotal Points are utilized today as they were in the 1920's when Livermore first created them. In the first case, investors can employ them to decide what the general market trend is. Market trend is important because it tells investors which way the market is generally moving.

Should the Pivotal Point price be broken to the upside, then the stock or market proves to be bullish. If instead the Pivotal Point is broken in a downward movement, then an individual investor considers the case to be bearish for the stock or market.

A second way to utilize the Pivotal Points is as a price level for either entering or exiting a trade. Finding the right level to open a position or close out an existing one is critical. Investors can place buy limit orders based on the Pivotal Point resistance level breaking. They might also use the Pivotal Point support level as their stop loss to exit a trade should this critical support line fail.

Nowadays it is easy to figure up Pivotal Points. Computer programs and charting software can find the levels easily. When Jesse first created them, these points had to be manually figured out with no more than a calculator, pencils, and paper. There are a number of formulas that can be used to determine them. Jesse Livermore made his own charts by hand. He looked for the levels where the stocks tended to bounce several times to find them.

Many traders today consider Pivotal Points to be shorter term use indicators. Because a number of investors use them for a single day trading, they have to recalculate them every day. Despite this fact, even day trading Pivotal Points is considered to be helpful. This is because a person can quickly calculate up important levels where there will be significant price movement.

Portfolio

In the world of business and finance, a portfolio stands for an investment collection that a person or institution holds. People and other entities put together portfolios in order to diversify their holdings to reduce risk to a manageable level. A number of different kinds of risk are mitigated through the acquisition of a few varying types of assets. A portfolio's assets might be comprised of stocks, options, bonds, bank accounts, gold certificates, warrants, futures contracts, real estate, facilities of production, and other assets that tend to hold their value.

Investment portfolios may be constructed in various ways. Financial entities will commonly do their own careful analysis of investments in putting together a portfolio. Individuals might work with the either financial firms or financial advisors that manage portfolios. Alternatively, they could put together a self directed portfolio through working with a self directed online broker such as TD Ameritrade, eTrade, or Scott Trade.

A whole field of portfolio management has arisen to help with the allocation of investment money. This management pertains to determining the types of assets that are appropriate for an individual's risk tolerance and ultimate goals. Choosing the instruments that will comprise a portfolio has much to do with knowing the kinds of instruments to buy and sell, how many of each to obtain, and the time that is most appropriate to purchase or sell them.

Such decisions are rooted in a measurement for the investments' performance. This usually pertains to risk versus return on investments and anticipated returns of the entire portfolio. With portfolio returns, various types of assets are understood to commonly return amounts of differing ranges. Portfolio management has to factor in an individual investor's own precise situation and desired results as well. There are investors who are more fearful of risk than are other investors. These kinds of investors are termed risk averse. Risk averse portfolios are significantly different in their composition than are typical portfolios.

Mutual funds have evolved the act of portfolio management almost to a science. Their fund managers came up with techniques that allow them to prioritize and ideally set their portfolio holdings. This fund management reduces risk and increases returns to maximum levels. Strategies that these managers have created for running portfolios include designing equally weighted portfolios, price weighted portfolios, capitalization weighted portfolios, and optimal portfolios in which the risk adjusted return proves to be the highest possible.

Well diversified portfolios will contain many different asset classes. These will include far more than just stocks, bonds, and mutual funds. They will feature international stocks and bonds to provide diversification away from the U.S. dollar, as well as foreign currencies and hard asset commodities such as real estate investments, and gold and silver holdings.

Portfolio Manager

Portfolio managers are individuals who invest the assets of a fund. They generally handle either an ETF exchange traded fund, a mutual fund, or a closed end fund. Their responsibility is to carry out the daily trading of the portfolio and to put into practice the fund's investment strategy.

When investors are considering different funds in which to invest, among the most critical elements to think about is the name, reputation, and track record of the portfolio manger. This is especially true if they are involved in active portfolio management as opposed to passive management. Though there are numerous active fund managers in the markets, the track records of historical performances are not encouraging. Only a small minority of them are successful in beating the main market indices.

These managers engage in portfolio management as part of their daily routines. This is the science of making difficult decisions regarding the funds objectives. They must weigh investment mix against objectives, carefully balance the fund risk versus performance, and allocate the assets for the funds customers.

The management of a given portfolio revolves around opportunities, risks, weaknesses and strengths of various categories. These include deciding between equity investments as opposed to debt instruments, international versus domestic securities, and safety as compared to growth. There are numerous trade offs involved in this type of management as a manager makes tough choices in an effort to increase returns to the optimal point for the risk the investors are willing to take.

Passive management is the form of managing a portfolio where the holdings of a fund track an index in the markets. This is most often known as index investing or indexing. Active management is the opposite form. It requires that either one manager, a few managers working together, or even a management team strive to try to outperform the market's return. They try to do this by managing the portfolio actively. They make choices and investment decisions utilizing research on individual securities and positions. Among the different actively managed funds are closed end funds and many mutual funds.

In passive management, the style is to have the holdings of the fund identically reflect the benchmark index. This is the direct opposite of an active style of management where the managers are buying and selling securities in the portfolio according to different investment strategies.

Passive managers and the followers of this particular management type hold with the efficient market hypothesis. This idea says that the markets always reflect and factor in all relevant information all of the time. It believes that picking stocks out individually is a waste of time. Followers of this premise believe that the best method for investing is to put investment funds into index funds. History shows that these funds have performed better than most of the funds which are actively managed.

Active management still has a significant following. It utilizes the human efforts of the management team, co managers, or single portfolio manager to manage the funds portfolio on a daily, weekly, and monthly basis. These active managers work with forecasts, analytical research, and their own personal experiences and judgments to engage in the buying, selling, and holding decisions of the various securities.

The sponsors of these actively managed funds and their investment companies hold that a really good manager can beat the market. This is why they employ professional fund managers to actively handle the portfolio funds. Their goal is to beat those returns of their benchmark. For a large cap stock fund this would mean outperforming the S&P 500 index. Despite the best efforts of a considerable majority of active fund managers, they have not been able to do this successfully.

Preferred Stock

Preferred stock is referred to as preference shares or preferred shares as well. Preferred stock is the name used for a particular equity security which exhibits both characteristics of a stock equity as well as an instrument of debt. Because of this, preferred stocks are commonly deemed to be hybrid types of instruments. In the claims on a company's assets in the event of default or bankruptcy, preferred stocks prove to be higher ranking than mere common stocks, yet subordinated to bonds.

Preferred stocks have a number of interesting properties. They typically come with a dividend that is often fixed. They also enjoy preference versus common stocks where dividend payments are concerned and at any liquidation of the company's assets. A downside to preferred stocks is that they do not include voting rights as do common stock shares. Some preferred stocks offer convertible features that turn them into common shares of stock at a certain time. There are preferred stocks that may be called in early at the wishes of the issuing company. All terms for a preferred stock are listed out specifically in the Certificate of Designation.

Since preferred stocks are somewhat like bonds, the big credit rating companies all rate them for quality of credit. Preferred stocks generally garner lower ratings than do bonds, as the dividends of preferred stocks are not guaranteed as are bonds' interest payments. Preferred stocks are also subordinated to all of the creditors, making them less secure.

Dividends are a key feature of preferred stocks and the main motivating factor in acquiring them. Preferred stocks come with dividend payment preference over other shares. While this does not guarantee that the stated dividends will be paid, the company has to pay such dividends to the preferred share holders before they are allowed to issue any common stock shares' dividends.

These dividends for preferred stocks might be either noncumulative or cumulative. Cumulative preferred stocks mandate that companies who neglect to cover stated dividends up to the full rate must cover them fully at a later date. In each passing dividend time frame, the dividends continue to accumulate. This might be on an annual, semi annual, or quarterly basis.

Dividends that are not paid on time are labeled dividends that have passed. These passed dividends for cumulative stocks are called dividends that are in arrears. If a stock does not possess these cumulative features, then it is called a straight preferred stock, or a noncumulative dividend stock. With these types of non cumulative preferred stocks, the dividends that become passed simply vanish for good if they are not paid on time.

Besides these preferred stock features, they have various other rights. Some types of preferred shares do include a particular group of voting rights for the approval of unusual events like the ability to issue and sell extra shares, to approve the company to be sold, or even to choose the board of directors' members. In general, preferred stocks do not have voting rights. Many preferred shares also come with a liquidation value that states what sum of money was put into the issuing corporation as the shares became issued.

Private Equity Fund

A Private Equity Fund refers to a fund that is not carried by a public stock exchange and which does not have to be regulated by the SEC Securities Exchange Commission. Private equity itself is made up of the range of investors and funds who choose to invest directly in privately held companies. They might also pursue mergers and acquisitions to cause public companies to be delisted by taking private the companies which were public.

The capital for such private equity comes from retail and institutional investors. Such funding is useful for many types of purposes. It might bolster working capital, make possible research into a new technology, provide for acquisitions of public or other privately held companies, or simply improve a given company's balance sheet.

Such private equity funds derived most of their resources from accredited investors and institutional investors. These deep pocketed entities are able to allocate enormous amounts of money into an investment (that might possibly fail) for longer term time frames. Generally these longer investment holding time frames become necessary for such private equity investments. This is because working with distressed companies or waiting on liquidity events like IPO initial public offerings or selling the private company to a public one needs time.

This private equity fund market has grown rapidly from the 1970s to date. Nowadays, funding pools can be started by private equity firms so that they can take enormous public companies private. A substantial quantity of these private equity operations engage in what analysts call LBO leveraged buyouts. With an LBO, large purchases can be affected in the markets thanks to the pooling of enormous resources. Once the transaction is completed, the private equity firms will do their very best to better the profits, prospects, and all around financial condition of the newly privatized company. Their greatest hope and plan is to resell the company back via an initial public offering or alternatively through selling the company to another larger firm.

It is worth noting that the fee arrangements of these private equity funds are different from one fund to the next. They generally start with a management fee and add a performance-based fee to the costs as well. Some firms will assess an approximately two percent management fee each year based on the value of the assets under management. They usually also get 20 percent of all profits realized when selling any companies.

When investors hand over their money to one of these private equity funds, they are throwing their lot in with an adviser that is actually a private equity firm. These funds are something like a hedge fund or mutual fund in many respects. All three of them are comprised of pooled resources that an advisor combines to utilize for investment purchases for the common good of the fund. There are differences between these types of pooled funds though.

Private equity firms will usually concentrate their efforts on longer term time framed investment possibilities. They will often look for those assets that require significant amounts of time in order to sell investments. This given investment horizon will require many times at least 10 years and sometimes significantly longer than this.

A common strategy of investing with these private equity funds proves to be engaging in minority stake investments in startups or companies which are rapidly expanding in a promising industry. Others focus solely on the previously mentioned leveraged buyouts. In either case, transparency of these funds is an issue that has been growing since 2015. The high incomes for these funds have raised questions about what they are doing with the enormous sums of money they receive.

From 2016, some states began to pursue regulations and bills that provided more clarity on what the inner workings of such private equity firms is really like. The congress has so far resisted these investigations and tried to limit the ability of the SEC Securities and Exchange Commission to access the funds' privately held proprietary information.

Proprietary Trading

Proprietary Trading refers to a type of trading in which the bank or other financial institution invests its own funds for its own benefit. They do this instead of investing the money of and for their clients and gaining a commission fee for trading for their customers. Such trading happens as a firm makes the choice to engage in market profiteering instead of existing on the tiny commissions which they realize for taking and processing others' trades.

Those banks and companies which pursue such proprietary trading feel certain they enjoy some from of competitive advantage. It is this which provides them with the confidence in their own abilities to make outsized returns versus other traditional investors.

Proprietary trading is actually a dangerous and risky type of trading. Rather than safely carrying out the orders of their clients and collecting their fair commissions, the bank traders take on real positions using the capital of the company. In other words, they will enjoy the entire profit or suffer from the brunt of the full loss of such a position. These firms will do this entirely electronically to boost their speed of execution. They will employ the firms' own leverage in order to multiply the size of their positions as well as the hoped for returns or actually realized losses which they incur.

This actually occurs because the company's own trading desk at these huge financial institutions decides they can do it for themselves. These companies are typically investment banks or brokerage firms. They will then utilize their own corporate balance sheet and capital of the company in order to make transactions in the financial or stock markets. Such trades are commonly speculative. The products in which they trade are commonly complicated and dangerous investment vehicles such as derivatives and credit default swaps.

Naturally these financial companies receive benefits from proprietary trading on their own behalf. The biggest one is that they often do enjoy higher profits, at least until a financial crisis hits like with the one in 2007-2009 that nearly overthrew most of the American, British, and continental European banking system financial institutions. With these proprietary trades, the brokerage firm or investment bank gets to keep all of the investment gains which they realize from their investments.

A second benefit which these large financial firms enjoy is that they will be capable of inventorying an impressive array of securities. It allows them to offer their speculative inventory directly to their clients who could not have obtained it any other way. It also helps the institutions to be well-supplied with securities in the event of illiquid or declining markets when it is more difficult to buy such securities on the free markets.

The last benefit pertains to the second one. With such proprietary trading, financial firms can evolve into an important market maker. They gain the ability to offer liquidity for a particular security or even range of securities through dealing in such investments. They can realize profitable spreads and fees when acting in this capacity.

The ugly truth is that this proprietary trading has led to enormous losses for the investment banks in particular. Thanks to the likes of such one time investment banking firms as Merrill Lynch, Bear Stearns, Lehman Brothers, and others engaging in such dangerously over-leveraged proprietary trading schemes before the outbreak of the financial crisis, they nearly brought down the entire financial system.

The Lehman Brothers moment refers to the point where the company failed completely. All other investment banks began to crater at this point. Bear Stearns ceased to be a going concern. Merrill Lynch the one-time largest investment bank and brokerage had to be bought out by Bank of America in order to survive. Both Morgan Stanley and Goldman Sachs, the only remaining two of the big five, were forced to change into traditional banks, backstopped by the FDIC, This helped them to stave off total collapse at the height of the Global Financial Crisis of 2008/2009.

Because of these unmitigated disasters, the Dodd-Frank Legislation and Volcker Rules were passed. These made it increasingly more difficult to engage in such trading for a financial firms' own benefits and with their leveraged balance sheets and company capital.

Put Option

Put options are financial contracts that are entered into by two parties, the buyer of the option and the seller, or writer, of the option. They are generally called simply puts. A purchaser is able to establish a long position in a put option by buying the right to actually sell the instrument that underlies the put.

This is done at a particular price called the strike price and is only valid with the options' seller for a certain amount of time. Should you as the buyer of the option choose to exercise your rights, then the seller has to purchase the associated instrument off of you at the price that was set in advance, whatever the present market price proves to be. In consideration for the buyer gaining this option, you pay an option premium amount to the seller of the option.

Put options are a form of insurance against loss. This is because they offer a guaranteed price and purchaser for a given amount of time for an associated instrument. Put option sellers also benefit when they obtain profits for selling you options that you do not choose to exercise. Options are almost never exercised if the instrument's market value stays above the strike price within the put option contract time frame.

You as a buyer of a put option also have the ability to make money. This is done by selling the associated instrument for a higher price and buying back the position for a significantly lower market price. When an option is not sold or exercised, it expires worthless, representing a total loss of the premium paid for it.

When you purchase a put, you do so with the idea that the associated asset price will decline by the expiration date. The other reason for taking on such a put option is to safe guard a position that you own in the asset or security. Purchasing a put option provides an advantage as compared to selling a stock short. The most that you can lose with a put option is the money that you have paid for it, while those who sell short have an unlimited loss potential. The downside to a put is that the gain potential is restricted to a certain amount. This turns out to be the strike price of the option minus the spot price of the associated asset and the premium that you pay for the option.

A seller or writer of a put feels confident that the associated asset price will go up or remain the same but not decline. Sellers of puts engage in this activity in order to collect premiums. A writer of a put has a limited loss equal to the strike price of the put minus the spot price and the premium that has already been obtained. Put options can similarly be utilized to reduce a risk in the option seller's investment portfolio. They can be part of complicated strategies called option spreads.

A put option that is not covered by owning the underlying security or asset is referred to as a naked put. In these types of put scenarios, the investor might hope to build up a position in the stock that underlies the options so long as they can get a cheap enough price. If you the buyer do not exercise these options, then the seller of the put gets to keep the premium that you paid for the option, representing a profit to the seller.

Should the associated stock's actual price be lower than the strike price of the option when the expiration date comes, then you as a buyer have the ability to exercise the put option in question. This makes the seller of the put option purchase the associated stock at the strike price of the option. You as a buyer would profit to the amount of the difference found between the market price of the stock and the strike price of the option. Yet, should the price of the stock prove to be higher than the strike price of the option on the expiration day, this option becomes worthless. The loss to the owner of the option is restricted to the money that you paid for it, which then becomes the profit to the put option seller.

Quota Effects

Quota Effects refer to the economic consequences of a government body imposing an import quota in a national economy. Such import quotas are the legal limitations on the quantities of specific imports that companies are allowed to bring into a given nation. As an example, the United Kingdom might decide to restrict the quantities of Japanese cars that may be imported to 1 million vehicles each year.

The simple answer to the question on effects this causes in a specific country which enforces them is that they will lower foreign imports to the benefit of domestic producers and suppliers. At the same time, this causes more complicated, unintended, and undesirable side effects. Consumers will pay higher prices for their goods, the overall economic well being of the nation may decline, and nations which have been targeted with the import quotas may choose to retaliate with quotas of their own on the imposing nation's exports.

Rising prices occur as Quota Effects come into play. It is always helpful to consider a concrete and real world example of this concept. If a nation which is a major sugar producer controls around 55 percent of the entire market, they may decide to impose sugar import quotas. This would cause the aggregate available supply of sugar in the domestic market to decrease. Additional demand for sugar would lead to sugar prices rising. The purchasing power of consumers in this nation would suffer. It may be that the domestic sugar producers are able to increase production and meet the demand. If not, the prices will stay high so long as the import quotas are in place. Demand destruction (loss of demand because prices are simply too high) may occur as well.

Increases in domestic production can also be positive Quota Effects. The national producers will have the opportunity to fill the gap of foreign sugar producers and suppliers. If the quotas have reduced the individual sugar imports from four pounds per individual to two pounds, then domestic producers of sugar will need to boost their inputs, production, and labor participation hours in order to fill in the missing two pounds of sugar per consumer. This is particularly beneficial for those domestic industry producers who have the factory capacity and employee numbers to expand their production. They only thing they might be lacking is the incentive to produce additional sugar as the foreign imports of the good are cheaper than what they can additionally produce.

Import quotas such as these also have dramatic and typically negative consequences for the large international multi-nation corporations. These companies have high priority on their international production and trade capabilities. Only the domestic consumption within their nations would not be enough to meet their production and sales targets. Look at General Motors as a classic example of this fact. For the year 2008, they produced around seven million vehicles in total which they sold. Yet a mere three million of such sales occurred within the United States. Had one of their major international country buyers chosen to impose an import quota on American cars, then they would have been forced to rapidly develop an alternative market for the cars, or to reduce production and the resulting income and profits alongside it.

The primary reason that countries resort to such import quotas is that they wish to safeguard one of their important industries from free market failure against the major international MNC players. This is the same thing as putting failing industries on government assistance to keep them going. What many economists believe is that countries should allow their failing industries to disappear and try to focus instead on ones at which they have a competitive and comparative advantage. As an example, the United States is unable to directly compete with China for clothing articles production. The U.S. should instead focus its efforts on maintaining its effective market domination in the computer software development business.

Restricted Stock

Restricted Stock refers to those company stock shares which prove to be unregistered. These are typically issued out to affiliates of the corporation such as the directors, board, company insiders, and company executives. Because this stock class is non-transferable, it can only be traded as those SEC special regulations set out. This stock class is often referred to as letter stock or Section 1244 stock. It commonly becomes available for sale under the guidelines of certain vesting schedule provisions which transpire over a few years' time in most cases.

Companies have two different types of such awards they can make in reward for faithful service which goes above and beyond the call of corporate performance and duty. These are restricted shares of stock and restricted stock units. The difference is that the units could be offered either as cash or stock shares. This will always be spelled out in the award letter or agreement. The units which are converted to stock do so at a typical one for one ratio. The underlying shares do not actually become issued until the unit fully vests. This means that the voting rights on the shares underlying the units will not yet be available. Units are also not paid dividends as they are not yet physical shares of stock. There are plans though which credit the dividend equivalents for the underlying stock to the account in any case. Taxes become due on such awards only when they fully vest.

It was actually in the years of the middle 2000s that such restricted stock shares grew in popularity and practice with companies. Corporations were made to expense out stock option grants. Insiders of the company receive restricted stock following merger and acquisition transactions, affiliate ownership, or underwriting activity to keep them from advance selling shares which could negatively impact the firm. When executives choose to leave the company, they could forfeit all shares of their non-vested restricted stock. Failing to attain set standards of performance or to measure up to corporate and personal goals are other reasons for inadvertently forfeiting their stock shares. If they run afoul of the Securities and Exchange Commission and its stringent trading restrictions, they might similarly lose their promised shares.

This matters enormously since the SEC's regulations which govern all restricted stock trading and transactions are contained within the SEC Rule 144. It lays out very clearly and specifically the ways and means for registering and publically trading any stock shares that are restricted as well as the limits placed upon volume and holding periods.

Restricted stock is also taxed under the Internal Revenue Service codes which are laid out in Section 1244 of their IRS Code. The computations and regulations are quite complicated. Holders of such stock which is restricted will have to pay capital gains or losses tax which is figured up based on the difference from the value of the underlying shares at the time of vesting and the date where the holder sells the shares. Such restricted stock shares become taxed in the year in which they vest as ordinary income. In other words, the share awards are treated as compensation. Those amounts which holders must declare to the government as income are the fair market value of the vesting date less the original exercise price of the underlying shares.

Those restricted stock share awards can be forfeited by the recipient if he or she were to leave the company earlier than their vesting. This would happen regardless of whether the separation was voluntary or involuntary in the end. Any taxes which were prepaid to the IRS on shares that had not yet vested would be non-refundable, making the matter more complicated still.

Revenue Bonds

Revenue Bonds are municipal bonds. Their payments on principal and interest come from a special project's revenue. This could be from a highway toll, toll bridge, or area stadium receipts. Whatever the specific project may be, its revenues are what support the underlying bond issues.

These revenue bonds are utilized to finance projects which will eventually produce income for the issuing authority. Generally any government agency or even government fund which they run like a business will be able to issue these types of bonds. Such bonds stand in contrast to those competing types called general obligation bonds, or GO bonds.

General obligation bonds may be paid back by drawing on a number of different tax sources. Those investors who purchase such GO bonds are relying on the "full faith and credit' by which the municipality promises to repay them with any means necessary. This makes the revenue bond issues riskier. They only can promise the revenues from a particular project. Because of this fact, the revenue bonds pay a higher interest rate than do the GO bonds.

Municipalities structure revenue bonds in a particular way. They possess maturity dates of from 20 to 30 years most of the time. The issuers offer them in standard $5,000 even increments or amounts. There are a number of these bonds which include maturity dates that stagger. This means their maturities will not be on the same day and year. Bond aficionados call these serial bonds.

A toll road is a classic example of such revenue bonds. A municipality might issue this in order to pay to construct a new toll road. The revenue which would secure this issue would be the tolls they collect in the future from those drivers who utilize the road. The construction expenses will have to be covered before the bond holders are completely paid off at maturity.

These revenue bonds became popular because the issuing authorities' debt limits are set by legislation. They may only borrow so much money according to the laws. These types of bonds allow them to side step the legal debt limit restrictions so that they can build new improvements within their jurisdiction.

This also means that government groups which rely only on only tax dollars can not issue such bonds. Public schools are one example of this. They would not be able to pay off a revenue bond since they would not have any income off of a specific project.

These revenue bonds should not be confused with combination bonds. The combination ones are usually municipal bonds with two sources of financial backing. On the one hand, they enjoy revenue off of an existing or a future project. At the same time, they are covered by the full faith and credit of the issuing municipality or agency. This makes them a true combination of both revenue and general obligation bonds. Naturally, these types of bonds are deemed to be considerably safer. Such lower perceived risk results in the agency paying a lesser interest rate than they would have to give investors on comparable revenue or even general obligation bonds.

It is helpful to consider a real world example of a revenue bond. The MTA Metropolitan Transportation Authority of New York chose to float Green Bonds back in February of 2016. MTA announced it will put this $500 million in total proceeds towards covering the costs of renewal projects on infrastructure. This includes upgrades to their various railroads. The bonds were issued by the Transportation Revenue Bond of the MTA. They received backing from the income of the MTA transportation service. This income comes from two sources, subsidies which the State of New York provides and operating revenues of the agency.

Reverse Split

A reverse split is also known as a reverse stock split. Reverse splits are used to reduce the total outstanding number of a given company's shares. This action boosts the value of its stock and the resulting earnings per share. Not everything concerning a stock changes in a reverse stock split. One thing that remains the same is the market capitalization. Market capitalization refers to the value price of the total outstanding number of shares.

A reverse split works by a certain process. In this scenario, a company involved will actually cancel out the presently existing shares for every share holder. They will replace these with a smaller number of new shares. These new shares will be issued in an exact proportion to your original stake in the company.

Such a reverse split proves to be the exact opposite of a stock split. Reverse splits can also be called stock merges, since they literally reduce the total number of outstanding shares and proportionally increase the price per share. Companies commonly issue the reverse split shares according to an easy to understand ratio. You might receive one new share for every two old shares, or possibly four new shares for every old five ones that you owned.

Looking at an example of the way that a reverse stock split actually works is helpful. Say that a company in which you own stock shares decided to affect a one for ten reverse split. If you had one thousand shares of the company, then you would only own one hundred shares of the resulting issue. This would not change the value of the shares that you held though, as the price of the shares would increase by ten times. If the shares had been worth only four dollars per share, now they would be valued at forty dollars per share.

There are several reasons why companies choose to do a reverse split of their stock shares. They might feel that the actual price per share of their stock is so low that it is not appealing to new investors. Some institutions are only allowed to buy shares that trade at a certain minimum value, such as five dollars per share or higher. Reverse stock splits can also be used to reduce the number of share holders, since they can force smaller shareholders to be cashed out, which means that they no longer possess any shares of the company. In this case, you would receive the value of your shares in cash.

There is a negative connotation associated with engaging in reverse stock splits. Because of this reason, they are not done lightly by companies. A company might find that its share price has declined so precipitously that it becomes in danger of having its shares de-listed from the stock exchange. They could quickly boost the share price with the reverse split. Stocks that have undergone a reverse split will usually have the letter D added to the end of their symbol tickers.

A board of directors for a given company is allowed to perform a reverse split without consulting with its share holders to obtain their approval. The Securities and Exchange Commission also does not have any say over such reverse stock splits. They are instead regulated by a state's corporate laws and the company's own articles of incorporation, along with the company's by laws.

Risk Arbitrage

Risk arbitrage is also known as statistical arbitrage. It is different from pure arbitrage as it involves risk or speculation. It is also far more accessible to retail traders than real arbitrage. Because of the reasonably high probability that risk arbitrage offers traders, experts generally consider it to be playing the odds. Despite the risk involved, this form of arbitrage has grown to be among the most practiced type by retail traders. Three main types of this arbitrage exist, liquidation, merger and acquisition, and pairs trading arbitrage.

Liquidation arbitrage is a kind that involves determining the liquidation value of a business' assets. If a company possesses a book value of $100 per share and trades at $70 per share, it falls under this type. If the company determines it will liquidate, there would be an opportunity to make $30 per share on the dissolution of the company. When bigger companies practice this they buy companies whose parts are worth more than the whole of the company. They then sell off the various parts or assets to make money.

Merger and acquisition arbitrage remain the most practiced form of the strategy. The goal is to find a company that is undervalued at its current share price. If it is selected by another company as a takeover target, then it presents opportunity. The offer for this target will raise the company share price to near this level. The earlier investors get in on such a prospect, the more they are likely to profit from it.

If the merger does not go on as planned, the share prices will probably drop. Speed is the necessary factor to make this type of arbitrage work. Traders who practice this type usually receive streaming market news and trade on Level II trading. When a merger deal is announced, these traders attempt to buy in before everyone else does.

An example of this type of a deal would be a company trading at $40 which received a takeover bid for $50. The share price will rapidly rise towards $50 but not reach it until the merger actually closes. It might move to $48 per share. Those who get in on it immediately have a chance to make as much as $10 per share, or a 25% return. Others who buy in at $48 only have a $2 per share arbitrage opportunity for 4%. So long as the takeover happens as planned, both parties will make their returns. If it fails in the end for some reason, they will both likely take losses. The amount they lose depends on the price they paid and how far the stock falls back down on the failed acquisition.

Pairs trading arbitrage may be less common than the other two but it is especially useful in sideways trading markets. The idea is that investors find stock pairs which trade at a high correlation. They could be unrelated or related so long as their historical trading chart demonstrates that they trade in near tandem. Usually pairs with the greatest likelihood of success turn out to be larger stocks competing in the same industry.

The goal is to wait until one of these pairs has a price divergence in the 5% to 7% range. The variance also needs to last for some significant amount of time like two or three trading days. Investors then buy the cheaper stock long and sell the more expensive one short.

The last step is to wait for the prices to approach each other again. Once the prices are back in line, this type of arbitrage closes the trade and pockets the percentages they were apart initially. If the investor both bought the one long and sold the other short, then the gains can be twice the percentage the pair was apart.

Russell 2000 Index

The Russell 2000 Index represents a British-based American stock market index which measures the actual price performance of around 2,000 small cap companies located in the United States. It is actually a portion of the far larger capitalized Russell 3000 Index, comprised of the 3,000 largest American stocks. The Russell 2000 still equates to the major benchmark for the United States' based small cap stocks today.

The way these two indices work is that the complete index is the Russell 3000. The lower capitalized 2,000 stocks in this 3000 Index are the ones comprising the Russell 2000 Index itself. FTSE Russell is the subsidiary company of the world renowned London Stock Exchange Group, based in the United Kingdom, which created and maintains the popular benchmarking index.

Without a doubt or real rival, the Russell 2000 Index proves to be the most frequently relied upon benchmark for the various families of mutual funds that present themselves in their prospectuses as small cap funds. Conversely, with large cap stock-based mutual funds, they rely on the S&P 500 index. It means that this Russell 2000 is easily the most frequently and universally referenced measurement for the aggregate performance in the mid cap to small cap company space and their corporate stock prices. Though it is the bottom 2,000 issues in the Russell 3000 Index, the market capitalization weighting of the 2,000 bottom stocks only turns out to be a mere eight percent of the overall market cap within the all around Russell 3000 Index.

The ticker symbol for the Russell 2000 is ^RUT on most platforms and trading systems. Per March 31st of 2017, the market capitalization weighted average for companies in the Russell 2000 remains about $2.3 billion, while the median market cap proves to be approximately $809 million. The biggest company in this popular market index has a market cap amounting to nearly $13.3 billion. The index first traded higher than the 1,000 point mark between May 21st and May 22nd in 2013.

A similar but not serious rival to this small cap behemoth index is the S&P 600, produced by Standard & Poor's. It is far less frequently sourced and cited, as are other competitors maintained by various rival financial providers.

One unique breakdown of the Russell 3000 and Russell 2000 indices is for a special sub index called the Russell 3000 Growth Index. Included in this special index are companies which demonstrate greater than average levels of growth. This is why this growth index is utilized as a best measurement gauge of the American growth segment stocks. In order to be included in the Russell 3000 Growth Index, they must demonstrate higher forecast earnings and greater price to book values.

The company Russell Investments has a precise procedure for determining these various indices component stocks. They screen the biggest 3,000 common stocks in the United States to form the Russell 3000 Index. The biggest 1,000 companies screened are named composite members of the Russell 1000 Index, while the subsequent 2,000 companies become members of the Russell 2000 Index. Russell Investments has strict rules on those issues which can not be included in their indices. They may not be either foreign stocks or ADR American Depository Receipts. They also can not be components of the BB bulletin board stocks or OTC pink sheet stocks.

It is interesting to note that investors who like this Russell 2000 Index have a number of options in both exchange traded funds as well as mutual funds that do their best to replicate its real performance. None of them match it perfectly though. This is because there are trading costs and expenses involved in acquiring the various 2,000 component companies, stock selection market cap imbalances, and changes to the index's constituent companies which are difficult to replicate with precision. Investors can not directly invest in the index itself, or any stock market index for that matter.

S&P 500 Index

The S&P 500 Index refers to a world famous American stock market index. It is comprised of 500 stocks today which analysts and investors view to be the leading indicator for American stocks and equities. They call this the mirror of the large cap world performance. Economists are the ones who select the components of the S&P 500.

The S&P 500 Index itself proves to be weighted based on market value. It is among the three most significant benchmarks of the American stock markets along with the Dow Jones Industrial Average and the NASDAQ Composite. There are also various other lesser known S&P indices which focus on either mid cap firms or small cap companies which boast lower market capitalizations of from $300 million to $2 billion. A wide range of investment products exist that trade on the S&P 500. Among these are both ETF exchange traded funds and index funds in which investors can speculate or invest.

Most investors consider the S&P 500 Index to be the most crucially accurate measurement of the large cap American equities performance. It is true that this index only concentrates on the bigger capitalized portion of the stock markets. Yet it is deemed to be representative of the overall market simply because it covers a substantial part of the entire U.S. stock market value.

It is the S&P Index Committee that picks out the 500 constituents of this index. This committee is comprised of a team made up of economists and analysts who work for Standard & Poor's. The professionals in this group contemplate a number of different characteristics when they decide on the 500 constituent companies that make up the index. Some of the most important considerations are liquidity, market size, and grouping of their industry.

In recent years, the S&P 500 Index has become so widely followed and popular that it has surpassed the DJIA Dow Jones Industrial Average as the preferred benchmark metric of United States' stocks. Part of the reason for its inevitable success is that the S&P 500 includes an impressive and more representative 500 different American firms versus the only 30 companies in the Dow Jones Industrials.

Besides this, another major difference exists between the two popular indices. While the S&P 500 employs a market capitalization methodology that delivers greater weight to bigger companies, DJIA utilizes a different price weighting procedure that provides greater weight to stocks which are more costly by price. Many economists and investors consider the market cap weighting method to be more true to life of the way the market itself functions.

It is difficult for individual investors to personally duplicate the S&P 500 alone. This is because the portfolio would require for them to purchase stocks from fully 500 individual companies in set quantities in order to replicate the methodology for the index. This is why it is so much easier for investors to simply buy into one of the good S&P 500 products. Some of these are the SPDR S&P 500 ETF, the Vanguard S&P 500 ETF, and the iShares S&P 500 Index ETF.

There are other S&P indices in the S&P 500 Index family. The 500 index is also a member of the S&P Global 1200 family. Besides this, there are the popular indices including the S&P Small Cap 600 Index with its smaller capitalization firms, the S&P Mid Cap 400 Index with its mid cap corporations, and the composite of the three S&P 500, 600, and 400 indices--- the S&P Composite 1500 Index.

The original name of the S&P 500 Index was the Composite Index. This arose in 1923 to track a small group of American stocks. Standard & Poor's expanded the index in 1926 to 90 stocks and finally to the present 500 in 1957.

Salvage Value

Salvage value refers to a value calculation for assets. It proves to be the estimated value for reselling assets at the conclusion of their natural and useful lives. The value is important because analysts subtract it out of the fixed assets' original costs to learn what part of this cost may be depreciated for accounting and taxation purposes. This explains why the salvage values are critical parts of depreciation calculations.

The concept of salvage values also has to do with the anticipated returns businesses or personal owners will receive when they sell off such assets at the end of their natural lives. Such values are dependent on only estimates for the value of the asset at this point in time. There is also an official salvage value which the government calculates on many assets. In the United States, it is up to the IRS Internal Revenue Service to make such a determination and provide this fixed and preset calculation value.

It is this salvage value which analysts combine with the original purchase price of the assets. They utilize this with a particular method of accounting in order to decide what the fair yearly depreciation amount for the assets in question is. Business owners have two choices in calculating the depreciation for an asset. They might employ what experts call the straight line depreciation method.

In this commonplace means of calculating, an even dollar amount in depreciation will be determined and taken as a tax deduction every year of the useful life of the given asset. There is also the competing accelerated depreciation method. With this alternative means, the firm will accept a higher amount of depreciation for the initial years of the asset's life and realize a lesser amount over the latter years of the practical life of the asset.

It is always a useful idea to look at some concrete examples of how the concept works out in real life. If a firm purchases a factory machine for $10,000, the salvage value of the machine might be $2,000 at the end of its practical five year life span. With a straight line method of annual depreciation employed, the calculations show that the $10,000 original cost minus the $2,000 salvage value results in an $8,000 depreciation value. The $8,000 depreciation value is divided by the five years practical asset life to come up with $1,600 per year in depreciation. The salvage value matters because the business will be able to sell the asset and recoup this final value amount.

With the alternative accelerated depreciation method, the company will instead depreciate the asset purchase value faster over the initial years of its practical life and slower over its latter years. A primary method for this is the DDB Double Declining Balance method. This assumes a depreciation rate which amounts to two times its straight line percentage.

Using the original factory machine example above, the yearly depreciation amount will be 40 percent per year for the initial year in this method. This amounts to a first year deduction of $3,200. Thanks to the fact that the DDB employs a double the normal rate of depreciation as does the straight line method, a greater amount of the total depreciation will be realized for the first years of this asset's life.

Another important term related to the idea of salvage value is accumulated depreciation. This represents the aggregate depreciation that has been realized from the in-service date of the asset (from when it was purchased) to the present time. Eventually the book value of the asset in question (which is the cost minus the accumulated depreciation) will equal to the ultimate salvage value. At this point, there can not be any additional depreciation realized or taken for the asset. Companies will typically sell the asset then to obtain that salvage value which they have been assuming throughout the practical life of the asset.

Securities

Securities refer to financial instruments which stand for a position of ownership in a corporation which is publically traded. These would be stock shares. They could also be a creditor-like relationship to a corporation or a government entity or agency. This security would be called a bond. They might also be an option, which is the right but not obligation to acquire and own something. A security is ultimately a financial instrument that an investor or company can sell or transfer and which represents a kind of financial holding and value. The entity or corporation which provides the security to the investors is called the issuer.

There are two principal types of securities, equities and debts. Equities refer to shareholder-held ownership of a corporation. A stock is the most common example of these equities. Equity holders may receive dividends and sell their position to another party for a capital gain when the price increases to higher than they that for which they purchased it originally.

Debt securities are proof of creditor-borrower arrangements. These stand for money which a corporation or government agency borrows and which they must repay to the creditor. The debt security has terms which outline and specify the cash amount that they have borrowed, the maturity or renewal date, and the interest rate that applies. There are many forms of these debt instruments. The most common include CDs certificates of deposit, preferred stocks, corporate and government bonds, and CMOs or CDOs which are Collateralized Mortgage Obligations or Collateralized Debt Obligations.

Besides the standard forms of debt and equity types, there are also hybrid securities. They merge features of an equity and debt security together. Equity warrants are classic examples of this type of security. These are options that a company issues which provide its holders with the ability to buy stock shares in a given time frame for a pre-determined price. Convertibles are bonds which may be transferred into stock shares of common stock in the company which issues them. Preferred shares are actual shares of stock that pay dividends or interest ahead of the common stock class of shares.

Two main organizations regulate the issuance and sale of such a security within the United States. These are the SEC Securities and Exchange Commission and the FINRA Financial Industry Regulatory Authority.

Issuers of a security like this could be one of several different types of organizations. Municipal governments can issue bonds in order to raise specific project funding. Buyers of a security might be retail investors who purchase and sell them for their own accounts. Wholesale investors are those which trade the security as a financial institution working at the instruction for their customers and clients. There are also institutional investors which are a major category of security buyers. These include insurance companies, managed funds, pension funds, and investment banks like Goldman Sachs.

The purpose of a security is to float a debt or ownership instrument so that a commercial enterprise or government agency can raise fresh capital. By selling such a security, corporations are able to create money for business purposes and acquisitions. Sometimes the demand in the market place is strong enough and the pricing arrangements are favorable enough that it makes more sense for companies to issue securities to raise money rather than choose to borrow them in the form of loans or bonds. Government entities can not issue and float stock. Instead they may only issue debt in the form of general obligation or specific revenue bonds.

Securities which companies issue in the primary market they do in the form of an IPO initial public offering. Once these shares are floated and sold, all issued shares of stock are called secondary offerings. This is the case even when they still sell them in the primary market. Companies can also privately place such securities. There are cases where both private placement and public primary market floating takes place. The secondary market is the place where such a security becomes transferred from one investor to a different investor.

Securities and Exchange Commission (SEC)

The SEC is the acronym for the Securities and Exchange Commission. This Federal government agency actually governs the buying and selling of stock securities and other types of related investments. The SEC also works to safe guard investors against impropriety and fraud. They encourage the development of the market with the end goal of keeping America in the first place as the world's leading economic giant.

The Securities and Exchange Commission came into existence in 1934. The stock market crash in 1929 prompted a tremendous regulatory response where the national government observed that it had to oversee and monitor investments within the U.S. The SEC is headquartered today in Washington D.C. Its staff is comprised of five commissioners who are appointed, as well as the personnel working in eleven different regional offices throughout the country. They work together to create, amend, and enforce the laws that regulate investments in the country.

The SEC has various critical missions. Among the most significant one is their role in ensuring that the markets are transparent. To do this, they significantly regulate securities trading within the U.S. Companies are required to turn in a variety of legal financial documents during the year so that investors may obtain a true picture of the total financial health of the firm in question.

The documents are kept on file in a database that is available to the public. Anyone who is interested is allowed to inspect them by logging on to the SEC's website and working through their system of electronic documentation. The SEC has great powers that it exercises in enforcing the rules. It is able to mandate company audits if it has suspicions of illegal behavior. Those it finds in violation of its rules may be brought by the SEC to court.

In keeping with the SEC's mandate to help safe guard investors, they monitor the trading of stocks and the individuals responsible for selling them. This means that exchanges, their dealers, and all stock brokers are required to work through the Securities and Exchange Commission. They can be subjected to inspection from time to time to be certain that they are properly taking care of their customers. Consumers have the right to report practices that are unfair to the SEC directly. If you are an investor, you ought to avail yourself of the SEC's wide range of documents on the various publicly traded corporations that they keep in their database on their website.

The SEC additionally governs companies that are interested in undergoing Initial Public Offerings in order to become public companies. Such interested firms have to file a significant quantity of documents with them first. To help them accomplish this, the SEC engages a big staff. Their document database includes regulations and directions for filing such documents. Consultation help is available if companies run into difficulties.

The SEC also promotes education. If you are an investor who wants to learn more about safe investing, then simply go to their website. They have workshops and publications on the site to help all investors. This is in addition to all of the companies' documents kept on file there.

Securities Markets

Securities Markets refer to either literal physical or virtual online places for traders and investors to buy and sell securities. These markets have been dramatically changing in the last several decades in order to best meet the requirements and wishes of investors and traders alike. Traders must have such markets which are easy to access, highly liquid, and that levy the most competitive transaction costs possible. These three core needs of traders have combined to create several different kinds of market structures around the globe. Among these are markets which are order driven, quote driven, hybrid, and brokered.

Many Securities Markets are order driven. With these markets, the sellers and buyers on the exchanges match directly up, typically using a computer system. The middle man is eliminated in such a market structure. This makes them the opposite of markets which are quote driven. Price discovery is accomplished thanks to the traders' limit orders on every security. The majority of such order-based markets utilize an auction system. Naturally sellers will be seeking the highest possible price while buyers are on the hunt for the best possible bargain. When they match, execution of trades happens.

The two kinds of such markets are the continuous auction and the call auction markets. The greatest advantage to this style of market is the massive quantities of investors and traders who will offer to sell and buy a security. This means that prices are competitive and provides superior prices for all traders. It does have a downside. When a security has only a few members trading, then liquidity is often weak. The TSX Toronto Stock Exchange of Canada represents a market that is order driven.

Securities Markets which are quote driven are also referred to as dealer markets. In such market structures, the sellers and buyers have a transacting middle man in between them in the form of a dealer or market maker. It is up to the market makers to provide the ask and bid quotes on stocks for which they are willing to sell and purchase shares. These market makers have exclusivity in their market functions (many times) and receive special privileges. Among these are low to no exchange fees, specific order book and order flow information, and the unique ability to post the stock quotes. Such markets are most common with OTC over the counter markets like the NASDAQ and London's SEAQ, the FOREX market, and the bond markets. Nowadays NASDAQ has become more of a hybrid type with elements of order-driven structures in place.

The greatest advantage to such quote-driven securities markets appears when stocks or markets are illiquid. Dealers are able to boost the traders' liquidity with their intervention, as they often keep a security inventory on hand. They get to enjoy the spread between the bids and ask as a compensation for this accommodation.

Hybrid markets are also popular structures with many Securities Markets. They are sometimes called mixed markets. The NYSE New York Stock Exchange is a well-known example of this category. Naturally this system will utilize characteristics from the two order-driven and quote-driven arrangements. When they have low liquidity periods, these markets are able to fall back on the dealer-provided liquidity to improve transactions.

A final type of Securities Markets is the brokered markets. Brokers represent middle men who engage in discovering counterparties for any trade. As customers request of a broker to help them complete an order, the brokers will go through their extensive networks in an effort to locate an appropriately matching client. These types of markets are mainly for those securities which do not have a traditional public market. Illiquid and unique securities fall into this category. Where huge block trades of highly illiquid stocks or bonds are concerned, brokered markets are employed. Direct real estate is another classic example of such a brokered type of market. Real estate brokers are the ones who fill the service of matching up a unique seller and interested buyer in this case.

Selling Short

Selling short, or short selling, is a strategy used in trading stocks. In the selling short process, you borrow the shares of the stock in question from your stock broker. You then turn around and sell the stock shares borrowed for a certain price that the market offers. Your hope is that the price of the stock will drop, so that you can buy back the stock shares for a lesser amount. This creates a profit for your transaction. The practice is buying low and selling high done in the reverse order.

If the price of the stock drops, then this process of short selling makes you money. The down side to it is that when the price of the stock instead rises, then you lose money. Detractors of selling short claim that you can subject yourself to an unlimited amount of risk, since stock prices could rise without stopping. This means that you could potentially lose more than the amount of money that you invest if a given stock that you sold short took off and ran away without you closing out the transaction. Profits are limited by the distance of the stock price to zero, since a share's price can never decline below zero.

Such selling short trades are closed out by repurchasing the shares that you sold short earlier. When it is time to close out the transaction by buying back the shares, this is called covering. The other names for this process are buy to cover or simply cover.

There are risks involved in selling short stocks. The biggest risk is that the stock could go up indefinitely. For example, you might sell short ten shares of IBM's stock at $100 per share. This means that you have put a thousand dollars into the trade. If the stock later declined to ninety, then you would realize a gain of one hundred dollars. If instead it rose to $130 before you covered it, then you would lose three hundred dollars. While the lowest that the IBM shares might decline is to zero, potentially making you as much as one thousand dollars in profits, they could also rise to three hundred dollars, losing you two thousand dollars.

Short sellers can also fall victim to a short squeeze. As the stock price that you have shorted rises, some investors who shorted it will choose to limit their losses by buying the stock back. Still other investors may have no choice but to buy back the shares in order to satisfy any margin calls on their declining valued position. All of this buying back to cover creates a bigger increase in the price of the stock. The final outcome is a large move up in the price of the stock that creates significant losses for those who continue to be short the stock.

Shareholder Value

Shareholder Value refers to the value of a company which stakeholders in the firm enjoy as a direct result of management growing revenues, earnings, and free flow cash in time. The actual value of any company comes down to the effects and results of the strategic choices that senior management makes and carries out for a firm. This includes both strong returns on their invested capital positions as well as making solid investments.

As value is built up over the longer term time frame, the price of the shares goes up and the company is able to pay out bigger cash dividends to its various stake holders. Unfortunately, the opposite is also true; share prices can fall while dividends can sometimes be cut out of dire necessity. Rising dividends is usually the sign of a healthy and growing company, while falling dividends are a sign of a weakening and sick firm.

The balance sheet of a given company will reflect a higher and growing shareholder value. This is tallied in the equity section on the corporate balance sheet. The formula for this balance sheet is stockholder's equity equates to the company assets minus the corporate liabilities. Stakeholder equity also includes retained earnings. These are the company's sum of all net income minus the cash dividends from the inception of the firm.

When the management of a company in question affects strong strategic choices which boost company earnings every year, the firm will gain the ability to either keep higher retained earnings to build up the business organically or to dole out a bigger cash dividend to its shareholders.

The EPS earnings per share of a firm can be appropriately defined as the earnings available to the shareholders divided up by the number of shares of common stock which are outstanding. This ratio proves to be the primary indicator of the shareholding value of a corporation. As the firm grows its earnings then such a ratio will also increase. It will cause the corporation to be looked on more favorably and valuably by investors.

Corporations have to raise significant amounts of capital in order to purchase assets. They utilize said assets to generate revenues.

Corporations which are effectively managed optimize their asset use in order to run the business with lesser investments in the assets. Take a concrete example to help understand this challenging concept. A plumbing firm may utilize both a truck and equipment in order to finish a residential plumbing job. The full cost of such assets amounts to $100,000. The higher the sales which the plumbing firm is capable of generating with the truck and plumbing equipment, the greater the shareholder value the company will create for its stakeholders. Companies which are valuable are able to generate higher and higher earnings using the identical amount of dollars in assets.

It is also true that creating enough cash inflows is necessary to run the business with solvency. This represents a critical shareholder value indicator. It also allows the firm to operate its company and grow the sales without having to resort to issuing additional shares of stock or borrowing additional sums of money from bondholders or alternatively from banks. Such firms are able to rapidly boost their cash flow through effectively collecting on their accounts receivables and quickly converting their existing inventory into sales.

This is why the rate of cash collection is so very important to any firm. It can be quantified via turnover ratios. Corporations will try to boost their sales without having to order and hold greater amounts of inventory or without needing to boost the typical dollar amount in actual receivables. A larger rate of accounts receivable turnover and inventory turnover will result in building up the share holders' value with time.

Shareholders

Shareholders are companies, people, or institutions which own minimally a single share of the stock in a given company. They can also be referred to as stockholders. These stockholders are not only investors, but also the owners of the corporation. As owners, they gain the advantageous results from the firm's success. This can translate into higher stock prices, dividend payouts, or hopefully both. Should the corporation not perform well, the stock holders can similarly lose value in their investments as the stock price goes down.

There is a difference between shareholders and owners of partnerships and sole proprietorships. The stakeholders in corporations do not experience personal liability for the financial and debt obligations of the corporation. Should the company in question fail, creditors can not attempt to secure payments or assets from the stockholders as they might be able to do from owners of entities which are privately held.

Corporations with shareholders have another important difference from other structures of businesses. They depend on their executive management and board of directors to handle the day to day operations. This means that the stock holders do not have much control over the daily operations of the company.

Shareholders may not have much involvement in the company's decisions, but they still have important rights. These are specified by the corporation's bylaws and charter. One of these is the right to go through the company records and financial books. Another is to sue the company for officer and director committed mistakes. Even common stock holders have the right to vote on important corporate decisions like whether to agree to a potential merger or on the makeup of the board of directors.

Shareholders have what may be their most important right when a company goes into liquidation through dissolution or bankruptcy. They have the rights to regain a representative amount of the recovered proceeds. They are in line after the secured debt holders including bondholders, preferred stock holders, and creditors, all of whom have precedence over the common stockholders.

Stock holders have several other rights which they enjoy. They receive a part of dividends which their company announces. They also gain the privilege to attend in person the annual meeting of the corporation. Here they are able to learn more regarding the performance of the firm. They can also choose to sit in on the meeting using a conference call. If these common stock holders are not able to or interested in going to the annual meeting, they can instead choose to vote through the mail or online using a vote by proxy. All of these rights which belong to preferred and common shareholders are detailed in the corporate governance policy.

A great number of corporations elect to create two classes of stock. These are common and preferred shares. The majority of stock holders purchase and hold common stocks since they are more of them and they are less expensive than preferred shares. Unlike preferred stock holders who are due to receive dividends every quarter, common shareholders must wait on the board of directors to decide if and when they will be paid a dividend in a given quarter. The directors must decide if this is an appropriate way to utilize the corporation's funds.

Preferred stockholders lack the voting rights of common shareholders. They do receive higher dividends on a more frequent basis. Their payments have to be paid at least yearly and their dividends are also guaranteed. For investors more interested in creating a reliable annual income from investments, preferred shares can be a very helpful tool.

Shares Outstanding

The Shares Outstanding refers to the quantity of shares in a given company's stock which are presently owned by all of the shareholders in total. This also includes the larger share blocks owned by the institutional investors. It also encompasses the company officers' and insider shares which are restricted ones. Every corporate balance sheet will display this number under the category title of "Capital Stock."

This key company metric is utilized in determining such important attributes of a publically traded company as their market capitalization, their CFPS cash flow per share, and their EPS earnings per share. The number of shares for a particular firm is never static, but in fact can range significantly over the years. The concept is also referred to as outstanding shares.

The only type of company shares that are not a part of this Shares Outstanding figure are the treasury stock which the company holds itself. Corporate share numbers can and do change for a variety of reasons. When firms choose to float additional shares, this raises the total numbers. They often do this in an effort to raise fresh capital via equity financing or as employees choose to exercise their employee stock option benefits. It is also possible for total number of outstanding shares to decrease over time. This especially occurs when corporations buy back their own shares from the open market using a share repurchase program. These rebought shares then become additional treasury stock for the firm.

Corporations are required by the SEC Securities and Exchange Commission to make publically available the numbers off both outstanding and issued shares. This information will not only be included in the annual reports and company balance sheets, but also in the corporate websites under the sub pages of investor relations. They can also be determined from the stock exchange websites as well. This information is similarly contained within the quarterly filings with the SEC.

When companies engage in a 2 for 1 stock share split, this will double the total number of Shares Outstanding. Similarly, this total number will be reduced by half if they should engage in a reverse stock split of a 1 for 2 shares consolidation. The main reason a corporation would be interested in this mathematical trick with the share prices is because they want to reduce the company share price to an easier buying price range for smaller-pocketed individual investors. It will similarly boost the liquidity when they do so.

A company might also decide to consolidate their shares if their company share price has taken a severe hit. This will double the share price and restore it to what is often times an exchange-mandated minimum price range so that it meets the ongoing listing requirements. It might harm the stock's overall liquidity in the process, but it will likely discourage short sellers' targeting the issue since it makes it considerably harder for them to borrow shares for the physical short sales.

It always helps to consider a real-world example to demystify confusing concepts like this. In June of 2015, NFLX Netflix, Inc. revealed that they would engage in a seven for one stock split. The idea was to reduce the stock price drastically so as to make it more affordable. This would also increase the numbers of investors in the stock issue, they hoped. They did manage to increase the numbers of shares by a full seven-fold and cut the underlying price per share to one-seventh of its prior levels in the process.

With Blue Chip Stocks, increasing the number of Shares Outstanding generally boosts the value of the stock and the overall market capitalization of the issue as well. Because these larger and more successful companies tend to deliver success in the form of greater earnings and higher dividend payouts over the years, their prices which reduce in the wake of the stock split tend to float gradually back to where they were before the split.

Sharpe Ratio

Sharpe Ratio refers to a means of calculating returns which are risk-adjusted. This particular ratio has grown into the standard in the investment industry for these types of compilations. Nobel laureate William F. Sharpe originally created and popularized it. It represents the average return which investments earn above the risk free rate per unit of volatility.

It is also the total risk involved with the investment. When individuals subtract from the mean return the risk free rate, it allows for the performance based on risk taking to be determined. One of the facts that this calculation assumes is that those investors whose portfolios represent only investments with zero risk will reflect a zero Sharpe ratio. This type of portfolio would hold U.S. Treasury Bills as an example.

All else being equal, the higher a Sharpe ratio proves to be, the better the return on a risk-adjusted basis are. Over the years, this ratio has expanded to the point that it is now the most commonly utilized means for compiling risk-adjusted returns. There are limitations to it however. It fails when contemplating those portfolios that possess substantial risks which are not linear. This would include stock warrants or options. In the intervening years, there have been alternate risk-adjusted return means of calculating performance put forward. Among these are Return Over Maximum Drawdown RoMaD, the Sortino Ratio, and the Treynor Ratio.

There are many uses for the Sharpe Ratio. It finds common employment as a means of contrasting the risk to return ratio of a portfolio after a new asset class or individual asset becomes added. It always helps to look at a concrete example to better understand the concept. Godfrey the British portfolio manager wants to add a hedge fund in to his presently fifty percent and fifty percent composed portfolio of stocks and bonds. It currently possesses a .67 Sharpe ratio. Once he would add in the hedge fund component, his allocation would be 40 percent, 40 percent, and 20 percent, with stocks, bonds, and a diversified hedge fund holding (that invested in other hedge funds), respectively. This boosts the ratio to .87 in this particular case.

What it tells Godfrey is that while the hedge fund may be higher risk as a standalone investment, it does boost the Sharpe-displayed risk to return features of the newly reallocated portfolio. This improves the diversification factor for Godfrey. Had the additional prospective investment decreased the ratio, this would have indicated to Godfrey that he should not include the new investment in his portfolio.

Another helpful use of the Sharpe ratio lies in its practical ability to describe the excess returns of a portfolio. It helps to reveal whether such higher returns result from an over reliance on risk or intelligent investment and diversification choices. While a single fund or even portfolio might experience out-sized returns to its competitors, such an investment would only be a good recommendation if the greater returns are not a result of a larger amount of risk incurred. In general, the larger the Sharpe ratio for a portfolio, the higher its performance on a risk-adjusted basis has proven to be in the past. Negative ratios describe a portfolio that would have equal performance with a lower risk competitor.

Critics of the Sharpe ratio claim that its interpretations can result in misleading conclusions. Hedge funds also can misuse the ratio as they look to make their returns on a risk-adjusted basis look better than they actually are. They might do this by increasing the measurement intervals. It would reduce the volatility factor over time. They might also compound their monthly returns while not compounding the standard deviations. They could smooth out their returns by only occasionally updating the values of their illiquid assets. Another means at their disposal is to employ price models which underestimate their monthly losses or gains. They might also cut out their extreme returns by eliminating both the worst and best monthly returns for each year. This would lower the standard deviation.

Short Squeeze

A short squeeze relates to a scenario where a traded stock or commodity which has been heavily shorted suddenly moves aggressively higher without advance warning. This creates a self-fulfilling prophecy in which the short sellers feel so painful a loss that they are forced to close out their shorted positions. They actually increase the upward momentum and pressure on the stock by doing so. Such short squeezes give the impression that short sellers have no choice but to abandon their own short positions at a significant loss typically.

These are often triggered by sudden positive news announcements or company developments which give the idea that a stock may be beginning a turnaround in its fortunes. It could be this is only a temporary effect, yet not many short sellers are able to afford to hold losses which are running away limitlessly on them. In these cases, they stop the proverbial bleeding by closing them out, even though this means booking the so- far only paper losses.

When the stock begins to rise astronomically and quickly, the trend becomes self- reinforcing many times as the short sellers all trip over each other in their stampede towards the proverbial exit doors. When stocks go up 15 percent in only a single trading session, the short sale holders will often have not choice but to sell out and cover these loss-making positions via buying back the stock. When sufficient quantities of short sellers all do this at once, the stock price rises even more.

There are two practical means of determining which stocks are at greatest risk of falling victim to a short squeeze. The tools are short interest and short interest ratio. With short interest, this refers to the aggregate shares which are short sold as a percentage of all outstanding shares. Short interest ratio proves to be the actual numbers of shares that are sold short divided using the average daily trading volume of the stock in question.

Considering a hypothetical example helps to understand this concept better. A biotech company Britex possesses a drug which is a participant in advanced FDA clinical trials for treating skin cancer. Investors may be highly skeptical about whether or not such a drug will really work effectively and without dangerous and unacceptable side effects. Because of their doubts, 10 million shares of the Britex stock out of their total 50 million shares may have been short sold. This means that the short interest on Britex stock proves to be 20 percent. As the daily trading volume averages approximately a million shares, the SIR would be five. This SIR conveys that it would require five trading days for the short sellers to be capable of purchasing back all of their shares which they have sold short.

It could be that the enormous short interest has caused the price of the stock to drop from $15 to around $5 per share in advance of the clinical trial results. If the results were successful as the announcement came out that it treated skin cancer effectively, Britex stock would gap massively up on the news results. It could rise to more than $8 because speculators will simply pour into the stock. Short sellers would then be desperate to cover their short positions as soon as possible. The short squeeze in Britex shares would then be on in full force. This could press the stock to significantly higher levels because of the rapid unwinding of the short positions.

Those investors who are contrarians seek out stocks that are overly shorted exactly because a serious risk of short squeeze exists. They can build up massive long positions in such heavily shorted securities when they determine that the odds of success are much greater than what the short interest implies. They are taking on a calculated risk and hoping for a tremendous risk to reward potential payoff when the stock is only trading for a few dollars per share. They assume risk only limited to the price of the long positions, since the stock can not drop below zero. The potential for profit is in theory limitless.

Special Drawing Rights (SDR)

Special Drawing Rights are currency units of the International Monetary Fund. These units were originally worth .888671 grams of gold and $1 when they were initially created under the gold standard in 1969. In 1973 the pegged currency system set up at the Bretton Woods conference collapsed.

The IMF then re-defined these SDRs as a basket of the major world reserve currencies. Until October 1, 2016, SDR baskets are comprised of U.S. dollars, euros, British pounds, and Japanese yen. On October 1 this definition will be broadened to add in the Chinese renminibi. The IMF created these unique currency units in order to supplement the existing currency reserves of countries who are members.

Every day the IMF figures up the SDR value and puts it up on their website. The value is a composition of its various parts. They figure the value as measured in U.S. dollars by adding up the value of each currency in the basket in dollars. To do this, they utilize the noon time exchange rates from the London market fixing.

Every five years, the IMF has an Executive Board meeting to review the components of the Special Drawing Rights. They have the ability to hold this meeting earlier should financial circumstances call for it. The idea is to make certain that the basket continuously mirrors how important various currencies included are in the financial and trading systems of the world. The review that ended in November of 2015 decided that the Chinese renminbi currency had become freely usable enough to include as the basket's fifth currency alongside the dollar, euro, British pound, and Japanese yen.

They also adopted a new method for determining how much of each reserve currency will make up an SDR. Equal weighting is now being given to the exports of the currency issuing nation and a composite financial indicator. With the financial indicator, each of the components is being given an equal weighting. It is based on the reserves in the currency held by other countries, the amount of foreign exchange turnover for that currency, and the total of international debt securities and bank liabilities which are held in that currency.

Until October of 2016, the Special Drawing Rights components are U.S. dollars at 41.9%, euros at 37.4%, British pounds at 11.3%, and Japanese yen at 9.4%. As of October 1, 2016 the new SDRs are instead comprised of U.S. dollars at 41.73%, euros at 30.93%, Chinese renminbi at 10.92%, Japanese yen at 8.33%, and British pounds at 8.09%. This represents the new SDR value in a change more significant than any made in decades. The next scheduled review for the SDR is set to occur on September 30 of 2021.

Special Drawing Rights can be given out to member states of the IMF as a proportion of their IMF quotas. This gives every member an international reserve asset that will not cost them anything. Charges are made on allocations and then utilized to cover any interest owed on SDR holdings. Member countries that do not utilize their holdings which are allocated do not pay since any charges equate to the interest they receive. Members whose holdings become greater than what they are allocated receive interest on the extra ones.

SDRs today are only used in limited capacity as reserve assets. Their main purpose is to function as the account unit of the IMF and a few international organizations. The SDR is not actually a claim against the IMF or a true currency. Instead it represents a possible claim against the IMF members and their currencies.

Statistical Arbitrage

Statistical arbitrage turns out to be a scenario where a disparity in price exists between the natural price of an asset, or its inherent value, and the current market price. There are traders who specialize in arbitrage situations who will try to gain advantage from this fairly unusual situation of disparity hoping to profit from it as it naturally corrects. Some traders believe that statistical arbitrage will always yield a profit, at least on a paper trade basis. The reality is that in actual trading, unforeseen events and a limitation in investing resources could easily interfere with their capability of making money efficiently enough to be worth doing.

Statistical arbitrage is used in contrast to the generic form of arbitrage to distinguish its differences. The statistical variety relates to the actual techniques utilized in gaining advantage from the disparity that exists in two markets. With generic arbitrage, it could be that a stock price is higher in the stock market of one country than another where it is listed. In theory, traders could guarantee themselves profits simply by purchasing the stock on the cheaper exchange and simultaneously selling it on the dearer listed one. The guarantee depends on how high the transaction costs and currency conversion costs will be. There is also a considerable risk that the two divergent prices may correct themselves naturally before the traders are able to both buy and sell the security on the different exchanges.

This statistical arbitrage is a bit different from general arbitrage. In the statistical variant, such asset disparity is not simply between two or more markets. Instead it has to do with the price of an asset currently and the underlying value of the same asset. A company security proves to be a good example to contemplate. The market price will be decided by the interaction between traders in the form of supply and demand. The stock also possesses an intrinsic value which is derived from the dividends it declares to its investors and how this relates to competing investments. There may be variance in the market price because of temporary effects and external factors, as with relevant industry-specific bad or good news.

Those traders who engage in statistical arbitrage operate under the assumption that eventually the price of the asset will go back to its correct underlying value. Because of the disparity, they anticipate that the price in the future will change, and then they position accordingly to profit. In normal circumstances, these traders might consider and employ literally hundreds of different stocks at once so that they are able to effectively reduce their overall risks of an unforeseen event stopping the stock from going back up to its normal price in a fast enough time frame so that the trader makes money on the deal.

There is another meaning for statistical arbitrage. There might be a type of imbalance from the values that would typically be anticipated. Casino games like roulette are the classic example of this. Because half the spaces are red and the other half are black, players betting on red will win double their stakes should they be right. The wheel also contains a 0 that does not pay anything. This means that the chances of correctly ascertaining the color are actually just under one out of two. This house advantage is a disparity that could also be considered to be a statistical form of advantage. There is no way for the players to benefit from this, but casinos make a fortune off of it on a regular basis.

Stock Broker

Stock brokers are professionals who are both licensed and registered with the Financial Industry Regulatory Authority or FINRA. In general, stockbrokers work for a broker dealer or a stock brokerage firm. Stock brokers are not to be confused with financial advisors or financial planners, who perform many different services for their clients.

Stock brokers have a primary responsibility. Their job is to purchase and sell stocks, bonds, mutual funds, and other related investments on behalf of their clients. These clients can be retail investor individuals or institutional clients. Institutions as clients refer to not for profit companies, universities and colleges, foundations, and other similar groups.

Stock brokers trade stocks for their clients over a stock exchange or sometimes an over the counter market. Among the larger and better known stock exchanges are the New York Stock Exchange and NASDAQ. They are compensated for these trades with commissions or fees that the trader pays. These fees range widely from one type of stock broker to another. Online stock brokers offer the lowest commissions to their clients. These types of brokers usually charge under $15 per trade.

There are a variety of names for stock brokers in the industry. These various titles refer to different licenses the brokers may hold, the various services they deliver to their clients, and the kinds of securities which they trade. Stockbroker is an older designation for these individuals who are now more commonly referred to as brokers, reps, registered reps, or financial advisors.

Not all of these titles refer to exactly the same type of professional. The scope of a financial advisor or financial planner is generally much broader than that of a stock broker. A stock broker would primarily handle the trades in and out of given securities. Financial advisors and planners look at the entire picture of a person's investments and future goals to come up with a comprehensive investment and financial plan for the individual.

The requirements to become a stock broker vary. In the U.S., these professionals usually need to hold a bachelor's degree. The brokerage firms are preferably looking for applicants who have a business degree in a subject such as finance, economics, accounting, or a related field. Those applicants who possess master's degrees in business or finance receive preferential hiring treatment. Because they are in greater demand, they are able to command higher salaries than applicants who only hold bachelor's degrees.

Once a stockbroker candidate is selected, they must be sponsored by the brokerage that hired them. They can only take the exams required by the stock market industry if they have the sponsorship of such a brokerage firm. There are a variety of exams that are available to stock broker candidates. American stock brokers have to take and successfully pass the Series 7 exam, as well as the Series 63 exam or the Series 66 exam. Once they have completed such exams, they can be registered with the Financial Industry Regulatory Authority. At this point, the candidate is officially a registered representative, or stockbroker.

In the past, a stock broker was a professional that only wealthy investors and individuals could afford. They were able to access stocks and other investments through these brokers. Minimum account sizes kept out smaller investors generally.

Thanks to the Internet, access to the markets broadened considerably. Discount brokerage firms and discount stock brokers proliferated. These allow for individual investors to trade stocks and other investments for low and reasonable fees with much smaller minimum account sizes. They do not offer personal advice to their clients. Thanks to these changes that technology empowered, most any individual is able to invest in the markets today.

Stock Buybacks

Stock buybacks occur when companies repurchase their own company shares from the markets. They are sometimes called share repurchases. A buyback is like a company choosing to invest in itself, since it is actually employing its own cash reserve to purchase its own stock.

Companies may not be shareholders in themselves, which means that their shares are absorbed back into the company. This has a net effect of decreasing the quantities of stock share which are outstanding. This also increases the size of each owner's stake in the company as there are not as many shares and claims on the company's earnings.

There are two means in which stock buybacks occur. They can be done via tender offers or open market purchases. In a tender offer, all shareholders receive such a tender offer from the company to submit some or all of their shares by a specific deadline. Such an offer divulges the quantities of shares which the company wishes to buy back as well as the price range they are agreeable to offer.

These tenders are nearly always at premium prices versus the current market level. Investors who are interested in participating will let the company know how many shares they wish to sell them at the price they will take. The company involved in the share repurchase would then put together the right combinations so that it could purchase the shares it wants for the lowest price.

Companies can also enter the open markets to engage in stock buybacks. They do this precisely as individual investors by buying shares at the going market price. The difference between the company and an individual investor doing this is that the market sees a company repurchasing its own shares as a significantly positive action. This generally leads to the stock prices rising quickly.

A company management will state that the share repurchase is their best option for deploying the firm's excess capital at that given point in time. The management of a firm is supposed to be interested in maximizing the returns for their stake holders. These stock buybacks do usually boost the value of shareholders. There are other motives for company managements buying back shares. They may believe that the stock market has overly discounted the prices of its stock shares.

Stock prices can decline from many different causes. These might be that earnings were less than anticipated, the economy is poor, or there are negative rumors surrounding the company. Firms that pay out millions of dollars to invest in their own shares show that the company management feels the market has punished their share prices unfairly with the discount. This is always seen positively.

Stock buybacks can also create better fundamentals for a company's balance sheet. Since the repurchased shares become either cancelled or treasury stock, this lowers the number of outstanding shares as a result. This decreases the balance sheet assets as the cash is spent. With fewer assets on the balance sheet, the return on assets ROA goes up in the process. Return on equity ROE also grows as the outstanding equity is reduced. The markets generally prefer higher ROAs and ROEs. Managements that do share buybacks just to boost their balance sheet fundamentals are looked at negatively and as problematic.

Stock Market Index

A stock market index refers to a collection of stocks which are combined together to create a bellwether for a group of similar companies in the market. The idea is to present an index which tracks a certain sector, market, currency, commodity, bond, or other type of financial asset.

Stocks which are collected in such an index are put into a so-called basket. An example of this is easy to understand. A person who wished to invest in the DJIA Dow Jones Industrial Average index would buy into the shares of the index basket that represented the 30 component companies. This means that the investor would then own 30 different companies' stock shares.

The idea behind indices is that they track the underlying assets or market. The XAU Gold and Precious Metals Index is comprised of those companies which mine precious metals including gold. Purchasing shares in this index means that an investor has the benefit of exposure to the entire gold mining sector. They achieve this without having to acquire shares in all of the gold mining firms of the globe. It is accomplished because shares in XAU represent all of the gold mining shares in the form of the entire industry.

These indices were fashioned to imitate particular markets. This does not mean they will ever be accurate all of the time nor even 100 percent at any given point. This is because there are a wide range of factors that can change the market course which indices will not always capture with perfection immediately.

Not every stock market index is liquid. This means that it could be hard to get in and out of some index-based positions. It is also the case for some stock company securities too. Because of these problems, there are alternatives to a stock market index. These are called ETF Exchange Traded Funds. Such ETFs have the advantage of being constructed in order to imitate an index. This is done in the same way that indices imitate stock markets and various other assets. The ETF has the advantages of being immediately ready for trade and a pre-arranged package. This makes an ETF a true mini portfolio available for an affordable price with reasonable fees (especially as compared to mutual funds).

There are many stock market indices that are well-known throughout the world. The most famous of these is surely the DJIA Dow Jones Industrial Average. This 30 stock company index trades every day on the NASDAQ and NYSE New York Stock Exchange. The component companies of this most famous of indices on the planet include such internationally respected giants as the Walt Disney Company, General Electric Company, Microsoft Corporation, McDonald's, and Exxon Mobile Corporation.

Another internationally followed index is the S&P 500. It measures the values of 500 of the large cap stocks of the United States. The NASDAQ Composite index follows the fortunes of fully 4,000 different company stocks as they trade daily. Yet another stock market index often called the total market index is the Wilshire 5000. While somewhat less famous than the other three, this index of indices follows the performance of every publicly traded corporation which is headquartered within the U.S. The four indices mentioned here address the daily progress of the large American companies. A competing index the Russell 2000 follows the performance of an impressive 2,000 smaller corporations of the U.S. markets.

The market index values are called points. This means that if the London FTSE 100 rose 150 points in a single day that the value increased versus the prior day's close to that point. It means that the total net gains of all the composite companies collectively increased by a net of 150 points.

Indices such as these assist investors by helping them to keep tabs on the health of various industries in which they may have interests or capital invested. If the DJIA continues to drop repeatedly for a period of many weeks or a month, investors could reasonably conclude at least some of the companies within the underlying index have run into serious trouble. This would be a prescient warning to evaluate the portfolio and perhaps liquidate some of the holdings in favor of other ones which were performing better.

Stock Split

Stock splits occur when corporations decide to expand the number of underlying shares in the company. They do this by setting out a ratio for the stock split. They might say that for every one share of stock, there will now be two, which would double your existing shares. This would be called a two to one stock split.

If you had one hundred shares of the stock before the split that were trading at twenty dollars per share, then you would possess fifty shares of the stock trading at ten dollars each share after the split occurred. The value of the total shares owned does not change as a result of a stock split, only the amounts of shares that you possess and the per share price of the stock in question. In either case, they would still be worth two thousand dollars.

Companies mostly engage in stock splits because of a liquidity motivation. There are many companies that feel that more expensive stocks keep investors from buying them. By splitting the shares, the price of the shares declines proportionally. They hope that this will result in a scenario where greater quantities of shares of the stock are then purchased and sold. The downside to this argument is that the higher volume of the shares traded could cause larger drops and increases in the price of the stock, which leads to greater volatility in the share prices.

While numerous investors believe that stock splits are beneficial, there is no real evidence to support this feeling. Stocks do not automatically rise back to the price that they maintained in advance of the split. The extra shares do not result in greater amounts of dividends being realized by the investors either, since each share then represents proportionally smaller earnings, assets, and dividends of the company involved in the split.

While most companies go through stock splits as the price rises, a select few have steadfastly refused to do so. Berkshire Hathaway proves to be the most famous case of this. In the 1960's, it traded at only $8 each share. In recent decades, you have seen its value jump up to $150,000 per share. The Washington Post has also seen its non splitting shares trade upwards of six hundred dollars each. The shareholder base of both companies has remained consistent and stable as a result of not splitting the stock shares.

Stocks

Stocks are financial instruments that are issued by publicly traded corporations. These shares of stocks prove to be the tiniest portion of ownership that you can acquire in a company. Even by owning a single share of a company's stock you are a small part owner of the firm.

Owning shares of stock gives you the privilege of voting for the underlying company's board of directors, along with other critical issues that the company is considering. Should a company decide to distribute earnings to share holders as dividends, then you will get a portion of them.

With the ownership of stock, your liability in the company is only limited to the value of your shares. This means that should a company lose a lawsuit and be forced to pay an enormous fine or judgment, then you can not be made to contribute to it. The company's creditors also can not pursue you if the company runs into financial trouble and goes bankrupt.

Two different types of stock shares exist. These are common shares and preferred shares. The vast majority of shares that are issued are common stock shares. These are the shares that members of the public hold most of the time. They come with full voting rights and also the possibility of receiving dividends that the company pays out.

Preferred stocks come with fewer voting rights but give preferential treatment for dividend payment. Preferred stock issues are paid out before common share dividends. Companies that offer preferred stock typically pay dividends on both classes of shares anyway. Preferred stocks also have a higher claim on the assets of a company if it fails.

Liquidity is a feature of stocks that should always be considered. Common stock shares are almost always more liquid than are preferred shares. Large companies offer the greatest amount of liquidity in the trading of their stocks. Because of the depth of the stock markets, you are able to purchase and sell the shares of practically all companies that are publicly traded at any time that the exchanges are working.

When you purchase a stock, you are looking for two different kinds of gains.

Cash flow or passive income with stocks comes from the dividends that they declare and pay out. Capital gains appreciation is realized when you buy a stock at a lower price than the price that you get when you later sell it. While cash flow dividends are smaller payments that are realized on a generally quarterly basis, capital gains turn out to be larger one time returns made when you sell the underlying stock shares investment. At this point, you would no longer own the stock and you would have to purchase another stock in order to work towards cash flow gains from dividends, as well as other possible capital gains.

Straddle

A straddle is a a type of option strategy which is designed to assist traders in succeeding in markets that are either neutral or aggressively breaking out to one side or the other. While there are other similar result strategies that are both sophisticated and extremely complex like iron butterflies and iron condors, straddles are among the least difficult to grasp such strategies that accomplish the same results without the difficulty and confusion. Executing such a strategy only needs the person to buy or sell a single call and put at the same time.

In the universe of these straddle options, there are two types. These are long and short straddles. To put either one on, the option trader must obtain or sell an equivalent number of put and call contracts that both have the exact same expiration dates and identical strike prices.

A long straddle involves buying a put and call at this identical expiration date and strike price. It increases in value by gaining from a change in market price that drives the contracts' volatilities higher. So long as the market price moves solidly in one direction or another, this type of long straddle position will allow the holder to profit.

Conversely a short straddle needs a trader selling both a call and a put simultaneously at the identical expiration date and strike price in order for it to be activated. When the individual sells these option contracts, he or she collects a premium for profit. Traders will thrive in a market that has very little market change or volatility. Profit opportunity is solely based upon the market not moving convincingly in either the upward or downward direction. When the market begins to thrust either up or down, then the received premium becomes in danger.

When markets begin to move sideways, traders may be unclear which direction they will break out towards. This is where the long straddle comes in handy. It allows for traders to profit if the market moves convincingly in either direction. In purchasing both a call and a put, they are able to cash in on the moves of the market whichever direction it takes. The call captures the upside when the market goes up, while the put gains significantly when the market falls.

There are some drawbacks to this long strategy of straddles. The strategy is expensive to put on, there is a risk of total loss of premiums paid, and there can be a lack of volatility. The cost can be reduced by purchasing out of the money options instead of at the money options. Risk of loss is a serious factor in this trade. All of the money paid out on the straddle is at risk if the market does not move convincingly in one direction or the other.

The goal is to attempt to exit faster from the losing side of the straddle while taking as high a gain as possible from the winning side of it in order to maximize returns and turn a profit. Should the losses on the option grow faster than the gains on it, or if the market does not move sufficiently to one side or the other, then the trader will lose on the strategy potentially all of the money they paid for the it. Finally, if the market does not gain in volatility or move in one convincing direction, then both the call and put options contracts will decline in value each day until eventually the options expire worthless and all premiums paid become a total loss.

Conversely the short straddle has a characteristic that is both its greatest strength and weakness at once. The traders sell the puts and calls equivalently instead of paying for them. It is the premiums received which generate any and all income and profits from the strategy. The downside to this upfront income and potential profit is that traders assume an unlimited risk to obtain this premium at the beginning of the trade. So long as the market remains basically level, the short straddle position is safe and the premiums they obtained the traders will eventually capture. Every day the market stays steady, the options contracts lose more of their time and volatility value, gradually accruing the received premiums to the benefit of the option seller.

Should the market choose a single direction though, the traders must pay not only for the losses which build up, but they must return the received premium which they gained upfront. The only way to bail out of this strategy and cut the potentially limitless losses lies in repurchasing back the very options they sold for a loss. They can do this in a profitable point as well to lock in a portion of the profits. Eventually, the options will expire and whatever premium value they obtained is the maximum profit, if the market did not move against them in one direction or the other.

Strangle

A strangle is a strategy in which traders buy or sell calls and puts which are very slightly out of the money at the same time. They must have the same expiration dates but typically have different strike prices. The long version of this strategy provides a limited amount of risk and unlimited profit potential.

It makes money if the traders are convinced that the stock or index which underlies the options contracts will move aggressively to one side or the other and experience substantial volatility in the short term. A long strangle is also known as a debit spread, since the traders pay out a net debit in order to establish the trade.

It is possible to realize huge gains using this type of long strangle option strategy. For this to happen, the underlying security has to experience a powerful move either upward or downward by the date of expiration. The formula for determining profit on such a trade is as follows: Profit is gained when the underlying instrument's price is greater than the strike price for the long call plus the net premium paid or the price of the underlying security is less than the strike price of the long put minus the net premium they paid. The profit amount actually equals the price of the underlying instrument minus the long call strike price (and minus the net premium paid), or the strike price for the long put minus the underlying price (and minus the net premium they paid).

The risk is also limited in this strategy to the total premiums the traders pay. The highest possible loss on a long strangle option is realized if the underlying issue trades between the strike prices of the options which were purchased on final expiration day. On that date, the two options will be worthless and expire as such. The options traders at this point suffer total loss on all premiums paid to open the trade at the beginning. Another way to say this is that the maximum loss equals the total premiums paid plus commissions paid.

The breakeven points are two. The upper side breakeven point equals the long call strike price plus the net premium paid. The lower side breakeven point equals the long put strike price minus the net premium they paid.

The opposite strategy to this long strangle is known as a short strangle. Short strangles such as these are employed by traders when they do not believe there will be much movement associated with the given underlying security, stock, or index. The traders receive a premium, which represents the ultimately maximum potential profit, when they open this trade. They also receive a net credit when they enter into the sales of the two call and put option contracts. This is why these are referred to as net credit spreads.

While maximum gains for a short strangle are limited to the total net premiums received, the potential losses are unlimited. This is because the traders are on the hook for a limitless amount of decline or increase in the underlying security price. In the end, the only such protection traders of short strangles have is the amount of premium which they receive in the form of a net credit upfront at the beginning of the trade. It is possible to cut potential losses ahead of the option contracts' expiration date by buying back the call and put at the then going market rate. Similarly, they can realize their paper gains earlier than expiration date by simply closing out the trade through a purchase back of both calls and puts for the fair market prices.

Swap

A Swap refers to a particular derivative contract. They allow for two opposite parties to exchange certain types of financial instruments as the name quite literally implies. While in theory the instruments involved in such an exchange could be practically anything, in reality the majority of them prove to deal with cash flows on a principal amount with which the two entities concur.

In general, the underlying principal will not be exchanged in the arrangement. The two cash flows each instead make up a single leg of the swap contract. The one will usually be variable while the other one is fixed. The variable one is generally based on an agreed upon benchmark interest rate, index price, or alternatively free-floating currency exchange rate.

These swaps never trade over exchanges. This prevents retail investors from becoming involved in them. Instead, these instruments prove to be specially traded over the counter contracts between financial institutions or firms. The most typical form of swaps is the interest rate swap. Other forms include currency, commodity, debt equity, and total return.

Interest rate swaps involve the participants changing out cash flows for the underlying rates based upon the idea of a principal amount. They do this to speculate or to hedge against the possibility of interest rates rising or falling. It is always illuminating to consider a real world example to better understand a difficult concept like this one. International British based banking giant HSBC may have recently issued out $5 million in five year maturity bonds that come with a yearly interest rate based upon the LIBOR London Interbank Offered Rate plus 1.5 percent. While the LIBOR rate remains at 1.8 percent, this would be low for the historical average range. HSBC would be nervous about the possibilities of the rates climbing.

To offset said risk, HSBC engages with Deutsche Bank in order to receive the annual LIBOR plus 1.5 percent on the principal. So Deutsche Bank will pay the interest payments on the HSBC most recent bond issue. In consideration for this, HSBC pays to Deutsche Bank a fixed yearly six percent interest rate on the same $5 million over the next five years. HSBC gains if the rates increase substantially during the next five years. Deutsche

Bank gains advantage if the rates should rise just slightly, remain flat, or decline instead over the five years period. It is important to realize that in the majority of cases, HSBC and Deutsche Bank would work through an intermediary company or other financial institution which would also participate in getting a piece of the swap deal for their trouble. Determining if such swaps make sense for two different companies comes down to the relative comparative advantage in the floating rate or fixed exchange lending markets which each enjoys.

Currency swaps involve the two participants changing principal payments and interest on debt which was originally denominated in other currencies. With these forms of swaps, the principal is not only notional. It is actually changed back and forth along with the interest payments. Entire nations can engage in these currency swaps. As a clear example, China has opened a currency swap with Argentina. This assists Argentina with stabilizing its own foreign reserves as a result. China gains the advantage of their currency being a little bit stronger and more desirable reserve currency as a result.

With commodity swaps, the pair is exchanging a predetermined floating commodity price. This could be the price of Brent Crude spot. They do this for a mutually decided on time frame. The most typically involved commodity swaps actually are for crude oil.

Debt equity swaps revolve around exchanging debt for equity. With publically traded firms, this literally means bonds in exchange for stocks. It helps corporations to effectively refinance their own debt in a far easier and less hassled way than getting approved for financing.

Finally, total return swaps are those which involve changing out a fixed interest rate in return for the total returns off of an asset. The group which will furnish the fixed rate will thus not have to spend its precious capital in order to hold the index or stock which it gets in exchange.

Swing Trading

Swing trading refers to a wide range of shorter time frame trading strategies used in the stock market. Once a purview of only wealthy or professional full time traders this form of trading has become far more broad-based and accessible to regular investors. This is thanks to the vast proliferation over the past few years of the Internet revolution, an explosion in information and charting capabilities, and a range of affordable, efficient and fast online trading platforms.

Those who practice swing trading try to realize gains in a financial instrument such as stocks by holding them for from only overnight to even several weeks. The majority of swing traders will employ a technical analysis to consider various stocks that might offer shorter term momentum in price. It is possible that such traders will also use intrinsic fundamental analysis of the stocks alongside their analysis of patterns and trends in the price.

Because swing trading requires speed and availability to execute these types of trades, the majority of those traders or investors who utilize it are day traders or those who work from home. The institutional traders work with enormous sizes which prohibit them from quietly entering and exiting stock trades. It is the individual lone-wolf trader who can take advantage of these shorter-term movements in the prices of stocks. They have the advantage of not having to go head to head against the large investors of the trading business.

The ultimate hope for swing trading (which differentiates it from pure day trading) is that the trader will be able to realize a more substantial move in the price than the intraday trader can manage. This is because the swing trader takes for granted bigger ranges in the price and movement. With this in mind the traders who practice it must use careful cash management and stop loss orders in an effort to reduce their loss potential. Swing traders are utilizing charts with longer time frames ranging from 15 minutes through hourly to even daily and weekly charts.

Many swing traders confine their efforts to an ETF exchange traded fund or a particular stock when they engage in these relatively shorter-timeframe trading periods. It is rare for them to hold on to their stocks for more than three to four weeks. It separates these traders from the buy and hold or longer-term timeframe investors. Such investors could conceivably maintain a given investment for several years and into decades when the company is performing well.

Swing traders are not all using the identical trading strategies either. A great number of them will employ mean-reversion techniques. This is simply a complicated way of saying that they wish to purchase their stocks at lower prices and hope for a move in the direction to sell them later at higher prices. There are also traders who seek out momentum play stocks which are already moving ahead sharply. They ascribe to the concept that a winning stock will continue to act like a winning stock. This is the reason that they buy at high price points hoping to sell the stocks for even greater price levels.

Other swing trading strategies revolve around earnings release plays. They might place a short term trading bet that they company will outperform Wall Street's expectations. They could similarly sell the ones that they believe will under-perform the consensus view with their earnings.

Some swing traders employ still more sophisticated and complex strategies using macroeconomic concepts as part of their formulating ideas. They may hold that a given economic data release will come out higher or lower than the general consensus forecast. They could make a market position in an effort to benefit from such a result. When they do this, traders must be correct not only regarding the economic data release, but also concerning the impacts such news will have on their chosen asset in question.

Systemic Risk

Systemic Risk refers to those dangers that threaten the entire financial sector, another segment of the market, or the entire market. Analysts and economists also call this volatility, "undiversifiable" risk, and market risk. Such risk is especially dangerous because it can not be entirely avoided nor accurately predicted or forecast. There is no practical way to mitigate such risks to the entire system by diversifying assets. Instead, it can only be managed (though never perfectly) via effective hedging strategies or through the optimal allocation of assets.

Another way of considering such Systemic Risk is that it entails the very real possibility that a company-level or bank-level failure could set off serious volatility and instability. It might begin a chain reaction that leads to collapse in a whole industry, market segment, or even entire national or multinational economy. This risk to the system caused much of the Global Financial Crisis of 2008. At this tumultuous time in American and Western economic and geopolitical history, there were a number of financial companies in particular that were labeled too big to fail simply because they posed a real risk to the entire system.

This is the case because institutions like these are extremely large and systemically important in their own market industries. In extreme cases they might represent a dangerously large portion of the entire economy of a nation. Firms that are highly entangled with a number of other ones also prove to be systemically risky.

The federal government of the United States engages in the study of systemic risk so that it can justify becoming involved in the national economy from time to time. They do this with the idealism that they can lessen the impacts of company-centered events that cause sometimes severe ripples. The Feds feel with surgically- and precisely-targeted actions or regulations that they can reduce the severity of the consequences of these failures on a macroeconomic level. One example of this was the Dodd-Frank Act of 2010. This massive package of additional rules, regulations, and laws was intended to stop another Global Financial Crisis and Great Recession from happening. The heavy-handed regulation of important banks and other financial companies is supposed to reduce risk to the system.

It is instructive to look at the historical real-world examples of which companies posed such Systemic Risk in the middle of this greatest financial crisis since the Great Depression of the 1930s. It was the so-called "Lehman Brothers moment" that nearly brought down the entire Western-based financial and banking system in 2009. The size and scope of Lehman Brothers and its connectedness to the entire American economy caused it to be a massive source of risk to the system.

As the company collapsed the effect of this spread far and wide through the entire national and even international financial system. In the United States first, the capital markets froze. This meant that companies and individuals were no longer able to access loans. In some cases, they still could obtain them, but only if they had the highest standard of creditworthiness so they would not entail any risk of default for the embattled banks and other lenders.

At the same time, AIG the American International Group insurance company experienced intense and insurmountable financial problems. As the world's largest insurance company, they were overly connected to the other banks and financial companies of the globe. This made them a serious Systemic Risk not only to the American financial system, but also to the British, European, and Asian financial systems.

Their own portfolio of highly toxic assets connected with subprime mortgages and residential MBS mortgage backed securities meant it suffered from repeated calls for collateral, a downgrade of its credit rating, and an evaporation of liquidity. This only worsened and became a vicious downward spiral as the values of these poisonous assets declined further every month.

For some unknown reason, the same U.S. government that would not prop up Lehman Brothers intervened dramatically to save the AIG by loaning them over $180 billion. It may have been because various regulators, analysts, and economists, were convinced that the failure of AIG would have led to many additional banks, insurance companies, and financial firms collapsing.

Trader

Trader describes any person who participates in selling and buying financial assets on any of the global financial markets. These individuals might do this on their own behalf or instead on that of an institution or another individual. Some people have the tendency to confuse the titles trader and investor. The primary difference between the two pertains to the amount of time that each type of individual holds on to the asset in question. Traders generally keep assets for much shorter time frames in an effort to take advantage of rapidly developing trends. Investors on the other hand usually possess a longer time frame horizon for investing.

Such a trader might work on behalf of a financial institution. When this is the case, he or she will trade utilizing the firm's credit and money. The person is then typically a salaried employee who has the opportunity to earn bonuses which are based on performance and returns garnered for the employing firm. Many other traders are self-employed. In these scenarios, they use their own money and credit to trade and also get to keep any and all of the profits personally.

There are definite disadvantages to trading shorter term. Among these are the spread between bids and ask that must be paid each time both in and out of the instrument and also the commission fees. This is how traders are able to run up substantial commission costs, as they often pursue such short term trading strategies in and out of financial instruments in an effort to realize profits. Thanks to the growing quantities of extremely competitive discount brokerage firms (like TD Ameritrade, E*TRADE, and Interactive Brokers), commission fees have become less of a disadvantage. With the advent of the all-electronic trading platforms offered (such as Meta Trader 4), foreign exchange market spreads have tightened considerably.

Still, the tax situation in the United States disadvantages traders and short term speculators on purpose. The Internal Revenue Service in America assesses steeply higher capital gains taxes on what they consider to be short term capital gains. Traders pay taxes on this money as if the gains were ordinary income, while longer term capital gains assess at a flat 20 percent rate.

With the institutions, they often fit out and maintain dedicated trading rooms to provide a work space for their proprietary traders to purchase and sell huge varieties of financial products for their companies. In these interesting scenarios, every trader receives a specified and pre-determined limit for how big their positions can be, how great a loss they are allowed to accrue before the positions will be force closed out, and the maximum amount of maturity time on the given positions. Because these institutional trading firms run all of the associated trading risk, they have the privilege of keeping the majority of any and all of the profits. The traders are engaging in this activity as employees who work for a salary and potential bonuses for a job well done.

The vast majority of individuals instead trading for their own personal accounts do this either from a small office or from the convenience of their own home. They will choose to work with electronic trading platforms (whenever possible) provided through a competitive discount broker in order to keep trading costs as low and reasonable as possible.

The advantage to the discount brokers is that they assess far lower commission fees per transaction. The disadvantage which is the flip side of this coin is that they do not offer financial advice, or they instead provide a bare minimum amount of it. A great number of the discount brokers do provide margin trading accounts to their members. This helps the traders to quickly and effectively borrow money off of the broker (without having to provide advance notice of a trade) in order to engage in a larger purchase. While this boosts the position sizes they can afford, it also multiplies the potential for losses at the same time.

Trading Blocks

Trading Blocks are pacts between various countries typically having a common geographical area. They form them for protections against non-member nations' imports. These trading agreements are also a type of economic integration that has more and more impacted the global trade patterns and trends. A few different kinds of trading groups like these exist today.

Preferential Trade Areas are the first and probably most common form. These PTA's occur when countries of a common geographical area decide to eliminate or at least reduce the tariff barriers that exist on certain goods which they import from other nations in the PTA. This represents the first small but critical step in the development of full scale trading blocks.

The next logical progression in the trading agreements development is to form a Free Trade Area. If two or still more nations within the region concur on eliminating or at least reducing the barriers to all trade on every good imported from the other members, they establish this second step in the chain.

The third step forward is to establish a Customs Union. This means that all trade barriers and tariffs between the group members are canceled, and a unified external tariff policy against non members is placed. It allows the member states to negotiate trading deals with third parties as a single more powerful trading block. They can enter agreements this way with other trading blocks or even the World Trade Organization if they wish.

Full economic integration begins to occur if the members of the trading block continue down the path towards its eventual logical conclusion. This leads them to a common market, the first major leap into economic integration. Member nations are now trading freely in every area of economics and resources, not only physical goods. It entails all services, labor, capital, and goods barriers being eliminated.

They also work to reduce and finally eliminate any non-tariff barriers. The common markets are only truly successful when all micro economic policies and other rules are brought into harmony as well. These include anti-competition laws and anti-monopoly regulations. Some trading blocks at this stage also begin to implement key industry common policies, like the EU's Common Fisheries Policy and Common Agricultural Policy.

There are numerous advantages to members of a trading block once they are fully formulate and established in practice. Free trade within the block allows member states to specialize in areas of production in which they have the greatest comparative or absolute advantages. Trade increases between key members as they have improved access to one another's national markets. Trade creation is the inevitable result. It refers to the phenomenon that free trade creates as more expensive domestic producers are outcompeted by more economically efficient and less expensive imports from other trading blocks members.

Lower priced imports also mean a greater consumption effect and higher demand. Economies of scale allow the producers in these nations to benefit and apply the savings to lower pricing for their customers. More jobs are often created because of the higher and growing trade between the block members. Finally, companies within the block may have to be more efficient against their own block rivals, yet they do gain effective economic protection against less expensive imports out of non-block member based corporations. The EU shoe industry is a good example of this. They are economically protected by tariffs on cheaper shoe imports from Vietnam and China.

There are some significant disadvantages of these trading blocks too. Trading blocks usually distort global trade by reducing the benefits of global specialization and comparative advantages of the world as a whole. Those producers which are less efficient than global competitors will be shielded from the outside of block more efficient ones. Trade is diverted away from the most efficient producing companies which are only guilty of being based outside of the trading block area.

Treasury Bills

Treasury Bills prove to be among the largest category of United States issued Treasuries. They are also called T-Bills for short. Treasury Bills have maturities of a year or less. They never pay investors interest before they mature, making them somewhat like zero coupon bonds. The government instead sells Treasury Bills at a face value discount, which causes there to be a positive yield to maturity. Numerous economists and ratings agency consider Treasury bills to be the lowest risk investments that American and foreign investors can purchase.

T-bills come issued with varying maturity dates. These typical forms of weekly Treasuries can have four week maturity dates, thirteen week maturity dates, twenty-six week maturity dates, and fifty-two week maturity dates. Every week, the government runs single price auctions for its Treasury bills. The quantity of thirteen week and twenty-six week Treasury bills available for purchase at auction are actually announced every Thursday. They are then offered on Monday and issued on the next Thursday.

Four week T-bill quantities get announced Mondays for next day auctions. The bills become issued on Thursday. Fifty-two week bills become announced only on the fourth Thursday, to be auctioned the following Tuesday and issued that Thursday. Associated purchase orders have to be received before 11 AM on Monday auctions at Treasury Direct. Minimum purchases for these T-bills are a reasonable $100, marked down from the former $1,000 minimum. The Treasury redeems T-bills that mature every Thursday. The biggest buyers of T-bills prove to be financial institutions such as banks, and primary dealers in particular. These Treasuries in their individual issue all get one of a kind CUSIP numbers.

Sometimes the Treasury cash balances are lower than usual. At these times, the Treasury often opts to sell CMB's, or cash management bills. They sell these in much the same way as T-bills, at auction with a discount. Their main difference lies in their irregular amounts and shorter terms of fewer than twenty-one days. They also possess different week days for auction, issue, and maturity. As these CMB's mature on the identical week day as typical T-bills, commonly Thursdays, they are termed on cycle.

When they instead reach maturity on another day, they are known as off cycle.

Treasury bills are regularly sold on the secondary market too. Here, they are both quoted and sold via annual discount percentages, known as a basis. The secondary market trades these T-bills heavily.

The Treasury has modernized its means of offering T-bills to investors recently. Treasury Direct is their means of selling T-bills over the Internet, so that funds can be taken out and then deposited straight to the individuals' bank accounts. This permits investors to make better rates of interest on their savings than with simple bank account interest.

Treasury Bonds

Treasury Bonds are also called T-Bonds. These financial instruments prove to be government debt issued by the United States federal government at a fixed rate of interest. Such debt securities come with maturity dates of longer than 10 years. The T-bonds offer interest payments twice per year. Because they are federal debt instruments, their earned income may only be taxed by the federal level authorities of the Internal Revenue Service. Though nothing is really risk free in the investing world, investors generally consider these bonds to be virtually without risk, since they are issued by the United States federal government. Investors perceive them to have a minimal amount of default risk.

Such Treasury Bonds turn out to be among the four kinds of Department of Treasury issued debt. They employ all of these to finance the runaway spending activities of the Federal Government. In these four debt types are the T-bills, Treasury notes, T-bonds, and TIPS Treasury Inflation Protected Securities. Each of these different debt securities is different according to both their coupon payments and their varying maturities.

Despite this, every one of them are the benchmarks for their particular fixed income categories. This is because they are American government backed, almost free of risk, and guaranteed by the revenues and tax base of the United States Treasury. In theory the Treasury can always levy higher taxes to make sure the interest and principles are repaid on these financial instruments. As they are all the lowest returns in their investment category, they are also deemed to be benchmarks for the various fixed income types of investments.

Such Treasury Bonds come standard issued with maturities which vary from 10 years to as long as 30 years. Their denominations start at $1,000 minimums. Each coupon interest payment pays out on a semi-annual basis. The bonds themselves sell via an auction system. The most of them that investors can purchase is $5 million when the bid proves to be non-competitive or as much as a full 35 percent of the entire issues when the bids turn out to be competitive.

It is important to understand what a competitive bid actually is. These types of bids declare that the bidder will accept a certain minimum interest rate bid. These become accepted according to the comparison versus the bond's set rate. With noncompetitive bids, bidders are guaranteed to receive the bonds so long as they will take them at the pre-set interest rate. Once the bonds have been auctioned off, the buyers may sell them off via the secondary market.

Investors call the active market for Treasury bonds re-sales the secondary market. Thanks to this enormous market, T-bonds and T-bills are extremely liquid. It means they can be easily resold on a constant continuous basis. It is this secondary market that causes the T-bonds' prices to gyrate considerably in the markets. This is why both yield rates and current auction rates for the T-bonds determine their prices via the secondary market.

As with all other kinds of standard bonds, these Treasury bonds will experience declining prices as the rates at auction increase. Conversely, the bonds will experience rising prices when the auction rates decrease. The reason for this inverse relationship is that the future cash flows of such bonds becomes discounted according to the higher rate.

T-bonds are also important because they are part of the yield curve for the fixed income markets. As one of the four principal investments which the American federal government offers, they make up this yield curve. The curve is critical because it pictorially displays the range of maturity yields. It is typically sloping upward since lower maturities provide lower rates than do the farther out maturity varieties. There are cases though when the farther out maturities experience peak demand. This causes the yield curve to become inverted. In such a scenario, the farther out maturities will have lower rates than the closer dated maturities.

Turtle Trading System

The Turtle Trading System proved to be a classic system that followed trends. It works by trading on breakouts much like those used in the Donchian Dual Channel System. In this particular method of trading, two breakout figures are important.

The first is a longer 55 day channel breakout point to enter the trade. The second one is a shorter 20 day channel breakout point to exit the position. If the prior trade turned out to be a losing one, then the system employs a dual length method of entering the trade using the shorter 20 day chancel breakout entry point. Stop losses in the Turtle system are set based upon the ATR Average True Range.

This system at first proved to be a secret. In the late 1970s and early 1980s, bits and pieces of classical successful trading systems pioneered by legendary traders Richard Donchian, Jesse Livermore, and Darvas were taken and cleverly combined into what became known as the Secret Turtles Trading System and Rules.

It was Richard Dennis who actually took the new system and created a challenge and test. He wanted to prove that regular individual people could become successful traders if only they had a successful system to follow in trading stocks. He created a class of 14 individuals in 1983 to put this to the test.

Richard Dennis gathered together these 14 regular people who had no stocks or commodities trading experience before joining his mentorship program. He taught them and trained them in the rules of the highly secretive system and program. The class of new traders was then given individual actual dollar accounts so they could trade.

For the next year they traded according to the Turtles Trading Breakout System to prove the point that any people could make money trading if they had the right instructions and a proven system to devotedly follow. At the end of that first year, the experiment demonstrated that the 14 traders had returns which averaged 80%.

Years later after the experiment and program had ended, one of the first Turtles revealed the secrets of the system. Curtis Faith proved to be an original 1983 class Turtle Trader and he unveiled the now not so secret Turtle Trading Rules to Wall Street and general investors on his site www.OriginalTurtles.org. This is how it came out that the system utilized trend following in its proven approach.

It was this website that at last shared the rules of the Turtles Trading System with the world. The rules fell under four main sections of theories for highly profitable trading. The first one was position sizing. This taught would be traders how to know the right amount to buy and sell in a particular trade.

The second set of rules pertained to entry points. They showed traders the best way to know how to time trades. They taught the method for knowing when and at what price level to get into the trade in the first place.

The third group of instructions gave details on how to set stop loss levels. No mater how many successful trades the system provides, it must manage its losses. No system is right all of the time. This is why it is critical to have price levels at which to takes losses and exit out of a losing position.

Finally the system had a section of rules on profitable exit points. Winning positions could not be left to run forever. A point came when it was the optimal time for traders to take their profits. These rules set out the right price levels to cash out of winning positions. Both stop loss and profitable exit points were based on formulas that worked off of the Average True Range.

Underlying Assets

Underlying assets refer to any asset or valuable commodity which determines the value of a derivative based upon the asset. This term is frequently and importantly utilized to discuss derivatives trading. Options are a good example of this. Derivatives themselves prove to be financial instruments that investors trade. Their price is derived from the asset that underlies them. This underlying asset will be the investible instrument like an individual stock, a stock market index, a currency or currency pair, a commodity, or futures. The price of the derivatives will be based upon these.

Options for a given stock provides the holder of the option with the right (but not the obligation) to purchase or sell the stock at a certain strike price (a given price point) on a particular date at some expiration point (a future date that is predetermined). In the case of an option, the underlying assets will always amount to the stock of the company in question.

This underlying asset helps to identify the financial instrument in the agreement that gives the contract its value. Investors in such a contract will always have the right, or option, to purchase the underlying assets for a pre-arranged price on the expiration date. The asset that underlies the contract provides the security of the agreement itself. The two trading parties consent to exchange the underlying asset if necessary as a contract clause in the derivative agreement.

Famed and legendary investor Warren Buffet has notoriously and correctly declared such derivatives to be "financial weapons of mass destruction." This proved to be the case in the Global Financial Crisis of 2008-2009. A wide range of derivatives based on shaky underlying assets literally blew up the world economy and banking system in financial carnage that is still reverberating throughout the economies of the world nearly ten years later.

Take some real world examples that will help to clarify the complex ideas. Berkshire Hathaway sells stock market index put options on worldwide stock market indices that range from the FTSE 100 in London to the American-based S&P 500. These options are unusual because the do not have an expiration date until the years ranging from January of 2018 to

January of 2026. On those particular dates of the varying contracts, it will be the underlying assets of the relevant stock market indices which will decide the amount of money that Berkshire pays out to the option holders.

In theory, the indices could approach zero, though this is highly unlikely. Yet Berkshire Hathaway would be forced to come out of pocket to the amount of up to $27.6 billion to these put holders if they did. When Berkshire sold these puts, they received $4.2 billion as premiums for their risk when they sold these during the years from 2004 to 2008. Guarantor of the options and Berkshire Hathaway founder Warren Buffet has cheerfully invested these billions in premiums and made considerable returns on them since those years in which they sold them.

Another classic example surrounds PepsiCo. The California-based company always reports its earnings in U.S. dollars. Yet it has operations all over the world because of its diversified soft drinks, bottled water, chips and snacks, alternative energy drinks like PowerAde, and juices divisions. This means that it must borrow, invest, and earn money in a range of currencies on every continent. The company has utilized currency swap agreements to help reduce the volatility of changing currency exchange rates on its costs to borrow and earn money in other currencies. The underlying assets would be Euros, British pounds sterling, Canadian dollars, Australian dollars, Japanese yen, Swiss francs, and other major world currencies.

In the end, there are literally trillions worth of derivatives which derive their actual value from an underlying asset of one type or another. This might be interest rates determined in London (the now-infamous LIBOR), stock market index values, or oil and gold hard commodities. Such derivatives make it possible for investors to engage with another party in a zero sum game where the stakes depend on the rises and fails of most any asset or market in the world. Neither party has to be directly involved in the underlying market or asset, thanks to these financial weapons of mass destruction called derivatives.

Unit Trust Fund

A Unit Trust Fund is effectively a vehicle in which individuals can invest their money. Investors can sink their funds into these investments using a range of financial service providers. These include an investment management company, a stock broker, and even sometimes a local or larger bank. These Unit Trust Funds are essentially a large pooled reserve of capital. They permit assortments of investors to combine their liquid assets to invest them. All of the investments together amount to the aggregate assets of a fund.

It is generally the case that such a Unit Trust Fund will have the legal structure like a mutual fund but which is unincorporated. They permit the funds to contain these shared assets and ensure that all profits become dispersed directly back to the individual unit share owners rather than reinvesting them. Such an investment fund becomes established under the auspices of a trust deed. Each investor is literally a member of the trust fund beneficiaries.

A Unit Trust Fund's success comes down to how experienced and professional a management company which runs it actually proves to be. The managers are allowed to invest in a wide range of investments. Some of the most typical of these include mortgages, securities such as stocks and bonds, real estate property, and cash equivalents such as CDs and money market funds.

The Unit Trust concept is widely utilized in Great Britain and a number of former British colonies and current day British territories. Among these are Jersey and Guernsey of the British Channel Islands, the Isle of Man, Ireland, Fiji, Australia, New Zealand, Singapore, Malaysia, South Africa, Kenya, and Namibia. Within the United Kingdom at least, unit trusts are interchangeable with the phrase mutual fund, though they are quite different from the American versions of mutual funds.

With regards to the assets of a Unit Trust Fund and their value, this can be expressed by taking the price per unit and multiplying it times the amount of units. Naturally there will be expenses taken off of this figure before it is considered final. Some of these expenses include management fees, trading transaction fees, and other relevant costs.

It is the unit trust fund managers who manage the trust in order to realize the greatest potential returns and profits. Trustees will be assigned in order to make certain the manager of the fund is properly pursuing the various objectives and goals of the Unit Trust Fund. Ultimately these managers work for the unit holders who have all rights to the assets of the trust in question. In between the stakeholders in the trust and the manager of the fund in question are the registrars. These middlemen are merely a type of liaison standing in between the two parties. They carry out a number of administrative duties.

These unit trust funds turn out to be open-ended in nature. This means that as new or existing investors add additional money to the trust, then more units will be created at the unit buying price that is current. Similarly, as holders sell their units for cash, an equivalent amount of the fund assets will be sold off at the present selling price per unit.

The income of the fund managers is realized by the bid and offer spread. This represents the difference between the price of buying the units and the price of selling them. This spread will vary from one moment to another and be based on the types of assets the fund manages. It might be merely a couple of basis points for those assets which can be liquidated expeditiously and simply, as with government sovereign bonds. The spread could be even five percent or still higher for assets which are more difficult to buy or sell. Real estate properties are examples of less liquid assets that take longer to transact.

Value Investing

Value investing is the strategy that Benjamin Graham developed for investing in stocks. Warren Buffet later made it famous after he left Graham's company and went on to found Berkshire Hathaway. Buying stocks this way involved a level of discipline practiced by insurance underwriters. The method focuses on several key ideas. Investors have to consider risks involved carefully, avoid stocks which show a high amount of uncertainty, and allow a margin of safety.

Graham developed his different investing techniques while managing money as President of his Graham-Newman Corporation. He focused on net working capital investments, arbitrage, diversification, and tangible assets. Investors continue to use all of these but the first one over seventy years later.

Net working capital originally functioned as a cornerstone of value investing until changes in transparency rules and market technology made it obsolete. Net working capital investments were those where the stock's shares traded at a large 30% or higher discount to their amount of working capital.

The idea was that a value investor could buy dollar investments for effectively 70 cents or less. Some of these companies failed. This was mitigated by diversifying into many different stocks. On a combined basis, these companies brought Graham and his investors good returns. Warren Buffet utilized this category of investments heavily in his early years running the Buffet Partnership that eventually became Berkshire Hathaway.

Arbitrage proved to be the value investors' secret weapon. Graham passionately believed arbitrage would routinely provide 20% annual returns. This boosted the total return on the overall value investing portfolio. Arbitrage seeks to make money on discrepancies in price with little or even no risk.

If a company makes an offer for a rival at $60 per share, but the shares trade at $57, there is a $3 price discrepancy between that point and when the deal closes. This amounts to possibly 5% that investors can acquire in a matter of a few months. Assuming the deal closes, there is no risk in this trade. Value investors simply use arbitrage as a way to profit from a security and the money time value that is literally undervalued.

Diversification remains a critical component of Graham's investing strategy. He believed in diversifying into as many individual investments as made sense. He also practiced diversification into different kinds of asset classes. Value investing puts a certain percentage into common stocks, preferred stocks, mutual funds (which did not yet exist when Graham created the strategy), and bonds. This went along with the main premise that first investors must avoid losing their money. Receiving a good return on investment money is secondary to this idea.

Tangible assets is another value investing principle that still holds today. Graham was interested in the actual physical assets that lay behind his common or preferred stocks and bonds. This might include factories, office buildings, equipment, real estate, or rail cars. He would only buy into companies whose assets were great enough to fully back up the principle and dividend or interest payments. They would have to liquidate these assets to get back their investment money. Graham told those who valued invested to constantly look at the bonds they held and be prepared to change to other bonds if they had stronger assets.

Benjamin Graham and value investing also proved to be among the earliest groups to practice tactical asset allocation. If investors studied and determined stocks were overvalued, they should sell stocks and move money into bonds. When stocks were undervalued, he counseled investors to sell bonds and go heavier into stocks. This is still a cornerstone idea of investing today.

Virtual Digital Currency

A Virtual Digital Currency is a form of money which is completely separate from physical cash, like coins or banknotes. What makes it a currency is that it does bear certain similar characteristics to the physical currencies. Its advantage is in the fact that borderless transfer and instant transactions become possible through it. Crypto currencies and virtual currencies are both considered to be forms of digital currencies.

Such forms of money can be utilized to purchase literal goods and services, though the purely virtual ones are often limited to specific economic systems such as social networks or online gaming communities. Another definition for Virtual Digital Currency is an Internet-based medium of exchange which permits instant and borderless transfers of ownership of real world goods and services.

As a going concern, these Virtual Digital Currency units are relatively new. Their origins lie in the heady dot come bubble heyday of the 1990s. Among the very first of these digital currencies proved to be E-gold. This currency was actually a technologically revolutionized version of a gold standard that arose in 1996. It had the backing of tangible real gold underlying it.

Liberty Reserve was another relatively early comer to the world of virtual currencies in 2006. It allowed participants to convert dollars and Euros into Liberty Reserve Dollar and Euros. Both could be exchanged back and forth without restrictions, hassles, or government regulation for a reasonable one percent charge. The two services had centralization and were heavily utilized by money laundering operations. It was inevitable that the United States Federal government would shut them down in time.

Another form of Virtual Digital Currency known as Q coins or QQ coins was so effective in China after it arose in 2005 that it created a destabilizing impact on the official Chinese exchange of the Yuan currency, thanks to speculators. These digital coins came from the Tencent QQ messaging platform.

Attention given to crypto currencies renewed the global interest in such Virtual Digital Currencies. Bitcoin the gold standard and best-loved and most traded of them came about in 2009. It has since evolved into the most heavily accepted and best-respected of the various crypto currencies.

Several of the respected international central banks and settlement bodies of the world have waded into the murky waters of these digital virtual currencies in recent years. The European Central Bank issued a report in February of 2015 entitled "Virtual currency schemes – a further analysis." This claimed that such virtual currencies were actually digital representations of value which are not issued or guaranteed by any central bank, institution of credit, or e-money authority. The report claimed that in some instances, these virtual currencies may be employed as an alternative choice to traditional money. The prior ECB report from October of 2012 stated that such virtual currencies were unregulated digital monies that developers issued and oversaw. At the time, the ECB said these were accepted and traded among the various members of specific virtual communities.

The Swiss-based Bank for International Settlements (BIS) also issued its own "Digital Currencies" type of report in November of 2015. They defined digital currencies as assets which are represented in a digital form and which possess at least some characteristics of money. They said that these can be expressed in the denomination of a sovereign currency and overseen by an issuer who is responsible for both issuing and converting the digital money into traditionally accepted cash currencies. This means that digital currency is a representation of electronic money, or e-money, per the BIS report. They determined that any currency which is decentralized or automatically issued and which has its own units of value is a virtual currency.

Volatility

Volatility in investments has to do with the possibility of stocks or other investments undergoing a dramatic gain or loss in price and value in a certain amount of time. Investors consider the volatility of stocks and other investments when they decide to buy more shares of the asset, sell their current holdings, or to buy shares of a new offering. Whatever an investment's volatility proves to be, investors' goal should always be to make the highest return that they possibly can for the lowest chances of experiencing losses.

With stocks, a great concern is how stable the assets of a company are that underlie the stock itself. A sudden loss of confidence in a public company would also likely cause a sharp decline in the price. The stock price drop and accompanying volatility is actually created by the public's perception of something within the company, like changing leadership or a coming acquisition.

In fact the stock might come back in a relatively short time frame as the public decides that the company is stable after all. But such factors might be more troubling and enduring, causing the volatility of the stock to become too high. When such volatility persists, many investors will decide not to buy additional shares or even to sell off the ones that they hold.

The overall conditions of a market can also influence investment volatility. As the stock market all around shows higher signs of volatility, individual investments will likely suffer the same fate. This occurs as consumers become worried about the whole economy, or if political situations force investors to take more conservative trading positions. Should such impacts grow sufficiently significant, then even stable stocks can become lightly traded while investors sit on the sidelines to watch for the troubling issues to get resolved. In the meanwhile, the stocks and their underlying options might make dramatic rises and drops in price from higher volatility.

Volatility is a fact of life that investors have to be capable of handling. Still, some stocks and investments demonstrate higher degrees of volatility than do others. Investors can gain an insight into this amount of individual volatility that an investment might have thorough looking into its historical levels of price and accompanying volatility.

Using this data with projected trends in the economy and markets, investors can get a good picture of the amount of an individual investment's volatility to determine if they are comfortable with it before they invest in the offering.

Wall Street

Wall Street is a physical street that is seven blocks long and runs from Broadway to the New York East River. It lies to the south of the Manhattan borough of New York City. The street is incredibly significant because it has played host to a number of the most important financial entities in the United States.

The city originally got its name because of an earthen built wall that Dutch Settlers of the city erected in 1653 to ward off an anticipated invasion of the English. The street's importance grew so rapidly that before the Civil War in America this was already known as the nation's sole financial capital. In the district of Wall Street there are many important buildings and headquarters.

The street contains the Federal Reserve Bank, the New York Stock Exchange, the International Commodity, Cocoa, Sugar, Coffee, and Cotton Exchanges, and the NYSE Amex Equities. There are also numerous municipal and government bond dealers, investment banks, trust companies, and insurance and utilities' headquarters located here. A great number of the major American brokerage firms have their headquarters in this financial district.

Because of Wall Street, New York City is sometimes called the most important financial center in the world as well as the greatest and most powerful city economically. Investors find the two biggest stock exchanges in the world as measured by market capitalization here in the NASDAQ and the New York Stock Exchange. A few other significant exchanges also make or made their headquarters here. These are the New York Board of Trade, The New York Mercantile Exchange, and the one time American Stock Exchange.

In the 2000's there were seven major Wall Street firms here. These included Lehman Brothers, Merrill Lunch, Morgan Stanley, Goldman Sachs, Citigroup Inc, JP Morgan Chase, and Bear Stearns. Several of these companies failed outright or had to be sold at urgently distressed prices to rival financial companies in the Great Recession that ran from 2008-2010. Lehman Brothers had to file for bankruptcy in 2008. The U.S. government made JP Morgan Chase buy Bear Stearns. The Treasury and the Federal Reserve then forced Bank of America to purchase Merrill Lynch.

The catastrophic collapse of this many major financial firms dramatically downsized Wall Street with massive re-structuring. It proved to be especially severe for the economies of New York City and the surrounding states. This was because the financial industry in New York produced nearly a quarter of all income in the city. It also amounted to about 10% of all tax revenue for the city and 20% of taxes for the state of New York. City and state government revenues and budgets suffered dramatically from this loss of revenue for years. The Boston Consulting Group estimated in 2009 that as many as 65,000 jobs were permanently gone as a result of the financial crisis.

This city and financial center has grown to become a global symbol for investment and high finance. Movies have been made about it including two with the same title Wall Street and its sequel Wall Street: Money Never Sleeps. The financial district has become a part of modern mythology in many ways starting back in the 1800s.

The street emerged as a hated symbol of the greedy robber barons who took advantage of workers and farmers to the populists of the 19th century. When times were good it represented the way to get rich quick. Following such terrible stock market crashes as 1929 and 2008 the street looked like the home of financial manipulators who could crush major international companies and even derail the economies of entire nations.

Warren Buffett

The man affectionately referred to as the "Oracle of Omaha" is Warren Buffett. Buffet has distinguished himself for decades as among the greatest of investment gurus in modern history. He has an earned reputation as one of the most respected businessmen and is consistently ranked as one of the richest people. Besides turning everything he touches into gold, Buffett is an incredibly generous philanthropist intent on giving away his vast fortune before he dies.

Warren Buffett was born in 1930 in Omaha, Nebraska. His father Howard served as a successful stockbroker and eventually as a U.S. congressman. The boy began to prove his abilities for business and finance in his early years. His friends have revealed that as a boy the math prodigy could figure the sums of large columns of numbers in his head. He demonstrated this uncanny ability for others as he grew older. By only 16 years old, Buffett had entered the University of Pennsylvania business school. He graduated from the University of Nebraska at 20 having amassed a small fortune of around $10,000 earned from childhood businesses.

The budding youth read a life changing work The Intelligent Investor, Benjamin Graham's 1949 book. This led him to work on his master's degree under the guidance of this author and investor at Columbia Business School. In 1951 once he earned this degree, he worked as a securities salesman at Buffett-Falk & Company for three years before serving as an analyst for his mentor Graham at the Graham-Newman Corp for another two years.

In 1956 Warren Buffett established his own company the Buffett Partnership Limited back in hometown Omaha. He employed Benjamin Graham's investing techniques to identify companies which were undervalued and earned millions of dollars. By 1965 he had gained control of textile company Berkshire Hathaway. He dissolved his partnership operation in order to focus exclusively on Berkshire Hathaway in 1969.

Within a few years Buffet had phased out the company's main textile making division and turned this outfit into an investment holding company. He began to acquire shares and assets in companies involved in media like

The Washington Post, in energy such as Exxon, and in insurance like GEICO. The Oracle of Omaha could even take failing companies and turn them into thriving successes, as he did in 1987 with Salomon Brothers, a scandal ridden investment firm.

His holdings later included Coca-Cola, Citigroup Global Markets Holdings, the Gillette Company, and Graham Holdings Company. He served as a director of these companies at various points, including from 1989 to 2006 at Coca-Cola. In more recent years, Warren Buffett's Berkshire Hathaway has bought H. J. Heinz, merged it with third biggest food and beverage business in North America Kraft Foods Group, and acquired battery giant Duracell.

Warren Buffett has also been among the most generous and celebrated of philanthropists in history. Since June of 2006, he has been working towards giving all of his fortune to charity. His donation to the Bill and Melinda Gates Foundation represented 85 percent of all of his wealth. This proved to be the single biggest charitable donation in all of American history. He and Bill gates have been working on the Giving Pledge campaign from 2010 to encourage other wealthy donors to contribute to these philanthropic endeavors. Despite this generosity with his massive wealth, Buffett still ranks near the head of the world Forbes billionaire list each year.

Wilshire 5000 Index

The Wilshire 5000 Index is also called the Total Stock Market Index. The reason for this impressive sounding name is that its ultimate goal is to track the aggregate returns of most ever publicly traded stock that is based in the United States and trades over one of the major American stock market exchanges. This index is not necessarily the most famous one in the investing universe though. The truth is that despite this fact, it remains the biggest market index on earth, when it is measured by actual market value.

The Wilshire 5000 Index is actually a misnomer. There are not only 5,000 firms within the index as many incorrectly suppose. Instead, there are over 6,700 individual companies' stocks within it. The number of firms actually changes all the time. When the Index was first created, it actually had only 5,000 composite companies. As more business have been created and traded publically on the major three U.S. exchanges since the Wilshire's inception, this has necessarily required that they add more net numbers of companies in order to keep up with their objective of representing all major American corporations.

In order to be a candidate for inclusion in the Wilshire 5000 Index, there are three criteria which the firms must meet. They have to be headquartered domestically within the United States. They must also trade actively over one of the significant stocks exchanges in America. Finally, their pricing data has to be easily accessible to both members of the general public and the American investing community.

The Wilshire index actually does not evenly weight all of its constituent members, as is typical with other market cap weighted indices as well. In fact, they provide a greater weighting to firms that are more highly valued and an underweighting to those companies which possess a lesser firm value. The ticker symbol for The Wilshire 5000 Index proves to be TMWX. The index is famous for its efforts to track the all around American stock markets' performance.

Some publically traded United States' based corporations are routinely excluded from any inclusion in The Wilshire 5000 Index. Among these are the stocks which trade over the OTC BB Over the Counter Bulletin Board platform and system. This includes the stocks from micro cap companies and those which are valued as penny stocks. All companies which trade on the NASDAQ, American Stock Exchanges, and NYSE New York Stock Exchanges are typically included. It is what makes the Wilshire index the most truly diverse of all American indices anywhere.

Those larger companies which are a part of the Wilshire index have a greater weighting and will thus have greater impact on the movements of the underlying index.

With the Wilshire 5000 Index, the 500 biggest firms command over 70 percent of the total value of the index. This actually means that it is an economic performance measurement of only American companies, the largest 500 of which dominate the up and down movement of the index.

It is important for investors to realize that the ETFs, index funds, and other mutual funds based on the Wilshire 5000 have a unique expense characteristic. The costs of maintaining a passive portfolio of over 6,700 different stocks which are constantly changing naturally will be higher than for a index fund that has only 30 or even 500 composite constituent corporations within it, as in the Dow Jones 30 companies' index or the S&P 500 composite index. Despite this fact, the fees do not amount to a much higher percentage wise difference for investments in the Wilshire 5000 Index.

Other Financial Books by Thomas Herold

The Money Deception - What Banks & Governments Don't Want You to Know

High Credit Score Secrets - The Smart Raise And Repair Guide to Excellent Credit

Other Books in the Herold Financial IQ Series

99 Financial Terms Every Beginner, Entrepreneur & Business Should Know

Personal Finance Terms

Real Estate Terms

Bank & Banking Terms

Corporate Finance Terms

Investment Terms

Economics Terms

Retirement Terms

Stock Trading Terms

Accounting Terms

Debt & Bankruptcy Terms

Mortgage Terms

Small Business Terms

Wall Street Terms

Laws & Regulations

Financial Acronyms

9 781087 868776